Advance Praise for
College Success Strategies,
Second Edition

by Sherrie L. Nist and Jodi Patrick Holschuh

"I am impressed with the nice balance between instruction and reading, and exercises—this text works along the lines of a 'work-text' in which students read and try on the concepts or strategies as they go."

> —*Karen Becker*, Youngstown State University

"[The Self Assessment feature] is an excellent way for students to find out what skills and strategies they currently know and use. The writing style of this text is very appealing. It presents information without making judgments about the ability or skills of the student. The writing acknowledges that the student wants to be successful and presents information with that positive frame of mind."

> —*Bonnie M. Smith*, St. Mary's University of Minnesota

"This book helps students identify their strengths and weaknesses as students and provides examples and activities that will enhance their understanding of how they learn and how to learn."

> —*Kathleen Speed*, Texas A&M, College Station

About the Authors

Sherrie L. Nist is currently the director of the Division of Academic Enhancement at the University of Georgia, where she also holds the rank of professor. Before becoming the director, she taught reading and studying courses to college students in the same division. Sherrie received both her master's and doctoral degrees from the University of Florida. It was as a graduate student that she first became interested in how students learn, particularly in the factors that seem to influence a smooth transition from high school to college and the academic struggles that first-year students seem to face. She has published more than eighty articles, textbooks, textbook chapters, and other professional pieces that relate to how college students learn and study. She has presented the results of her research at more than 100 national and international professional meetings. She also has received honors and awards for her contributions to both teaching and research. When not working, Sherrie loves traveling, cooking, and, of course, reading and learning new things.

Jodi Patrick Holschuh is currently an assistant professor in the Division of Academic Enhancement at the University of Georgia. She completed her doctoral degree in 1998 at the University of Georgia. (Sherrie Nist was her major professor.) An award-winning teacher, Jodi teaches courses to help students learn effective and efficient study habits. She has presented many conference papers and has written several articles, book chapters, and books on the topic of helping students learn in college. She became interested in learning more about strategies for academic success while working as a tutorial coordinator at the Philadelphia College of Textiles and Science. It was there that she realized students could be studying hard yet still struggling to pass their courses. Her research interests include students' beliefs about learning, making the transition from high school to college learning, strategies for academic success, and motivation. When she is not writing, teaching, or researching, Jodi loves rediscovering the world as her son and daughter learn new things. She also loves to read good books and travel to new places.

College Success Strategies

Second Edition

Sherrie L. Nist
University of Georgia

Jodi Patrick Holschuh
University of Georgia

PENGUIN ACADEMICS

PEARSON
Longman

New York   San Francisco   Boston
London   Toronto   Sydney   Tokyo   Singapore   Madrid
Mexico City   Munich   Paris   Cape Town   Hong Kong   Montreal

Senior Acquisitions Editor: Susan Kunchandy
Senior Marketing Manager: Melanie Craig
Senior Supplements Editor: Donna Campion
Production Manager: Donna DeBenedictis
Project Coordination, Text Design, and Electronic Page Makeup: Elm Street Publishing
    Services, Inc.
Senior Cover Design Manager: Nancy Danahy
Cover Illustration/Photo: © Image 100 Ltd./Punchstock
Senior Manufacturing Buyer: Dennis J. Para
Printer and Binder: RR Donnelley & Sons Company/Crawfordsville
Cover Printer: Phoenix Color Corporation

For permission to use copyrighted material, grateful acknowledgment is made to the
copyright holders on p. 295, which is hereby made part of this copyright page.

Library of Congress Cataloging-in-Publication Data

Nist, Sherrie L. (Sherrie Lee), [date]–
College success strategies / Sherrie L. Nist, Jodi Patrick Holschuh.—2nd ed.
        p. cm.
Includes index.
  ISBN 0-321-33218-0
  1. Study skills. 2. Learning, Psychology of. 3. Academic achievement. 4. College student
orientation. I. Holschuh, Jodi. II. Title.
  LB2395 .N545 2006
  371.3'028'1—dc22

                                                                  2005043148

Copyright © 2006 by Pearson Education, Inc.

Please visit us at http://www.ablongman.com/studyskills

For more information about the Penguin Academics series, please contact us by mail at
Longman Publishers, attn. Marketing Department, 1185 Avenue of the Americas, 25th Floor,
New York, NY 10036, or by email at **www.ablongman.com**

ISBN 0-321-33218-0

1 2 3 4 5 6 7 8 9 10—DOC—08 07 06 05

In memory of the family members my husband, Steve Olejnik, and I lost in 2004—Mollie Doone Olejnik, Tony Olejnik, Ann Olejnik, and Harry Olejnik.

—S.L.N.

To my family—my husband, Douglas, my daughter, Maia, and my son, Samuel.

—J.P.H.

Contents

PART THREE   STRATEGIES FOR COLLEGE LEARNING   121

Preface

We decided to write a second edition of *College Success Strategies* largely because of ideas that came to us from teaching both graduate and undergraduate classes using the first edition. We realized that students needed to know more about the underlying principles of becoming an effective college learner. They wanted more information about time management and overcoming procrastination, and they needed guidance on using technology for learning. Although the first edition covered these topics, we believed we could do more. We also noticed that students applied the learning and study strategies presented in the text more effectively with longer, more representative college texts than with brief excerpts. Thus, we decided that we could strengthen the material in the book by including these new elements. We think that this new edition is even more effective at helping students become the college students they hope to be.

What's New in the Second Edition?

In the second edition of *College Success Strategies*, we have given the book a facelift so to speak, focusing on five key changes: (1) reorganizing the book to make it more reader-friendly; (2) adding new chapters; (3) adding additional features; (4) providing more emphasis in each chapter on using technology to learn; and (5) including complete text chapters rather than the brief excerpts that were in the first edition. The second edition is divided into four rather than six parts, shifting chapters around to better streamline the text. Part One introduces students to active learning in college; Part Two helps students determine their own learning characteristics; Part Three introduces strategies for effective learning; Part Four helps students prepare for college-level exams.

The second edition also adds **two new chapters** on strategies for college learning. **Chapter 10 discusses strategies for getting ready for studying.** It includes a discussion of creating effective learning environments, gearing up for class, and previewing text chapters. **Chapter 13 presents strategies for reviewing before exams.** It includes making specific study plans, working in study groups, and ways to improve memory.

This edition also contains several additional features to help students maximize learning:

- **Add to Your Portfolio** allows students to apply each strategy presented in the book. By creating a portfolio over an entire term, students will have tangible evidence of the progress they have made in their thinking, learning, and studying.

- **Get Going** focuses on tips and strategies for gaining motivation and overcoming procrastination.

- **Timely Tips** centers on strategies for time management. It will also discuss how many of the strategies have practical application beyond the classroom.

We have made every attempt in the second edition to help students understand how to use technology as a learning tool. On most campuses today, understanding how to use technology is a necessity, not a luxury. Many professors will expect students to submit work and communicate with them via email, make PowerPoint presentations in class, use Web-based supplements such as WebCT, and even take computerized exams. And while *College Success Strategies* does not necessarily teach how to do these things, it does remind students of the importance of learning how and it also provides additional suggestions in each chapter (some you may never have thought of) for becoming an active learner by using technology.

Finally, rather than providing brief text excerpts, we have included **two full text chapters,** one from psychology and one from history. These chapters are located in the appendixes. *College Success Strategies* is designed to apply the strategies learned to each chapter. We believe that in order to truly understand the full benefit of the strategies presented it is important to apply them to full pieces of text rather than to shorter excerpts.

Continuing Features from the First Edition

Although *College Success Strategies* is new and improved, the major premise behind the book remains rooted in the importance of academics. As such, the majority of the text continues to focus on the four key academic factors that must interact if learning is to be maximized: (1) characteristics of the learner; (2) the tasks learners must complete in each class; (3) the strategies that help learners read, understand, and remember what the professor expects them to learn; and finally (4) the texts with which learners interact.

We have retained the best features from the first edition of *College Success Strategies.* Each chapter still concludes with the **"Real College"** scenarios. Each scenario features a college student who has a problem related in some way to that chapter. By helping these college students solve their problems, students will be able to further apply the ideas and strategies discussed in the chapters. We believe that students may see part of themselves in many of the scenarios. These scenarios, by the way, are based on real issues that our students consistently face as they work toward becoming active learners.

We have also retained the **self-evaluations** at the beginning of each chapter. These assessments help students to assess and reflect on their own learning before reading the chapter.

The end of each chapter still contains a **"Thinking Critically"** section. These activities ask students to reflect and evaluate their experiences using the strategies.

In addition, *College Success Strategies* continues to feature these informative boxes:

- **Studying Smarter** provides quick and easy tips or inspirational quotations to help students get a jump on their learning and studying.

- **Networking** focuses on using technology for learning actively. Some are activities students can try and others are suggestions for incorporating technology to enhance learning.

- **Success at a Glance** depicts key information in a visual way to help students remember it better.

Using *College Success Strategies*

College Success Strategies was designed not only to get students reading about what it takes to learn actively but also to start them thinking and talking about it. The self-assessment activities at the beginning of each chapter provide students with a snapshot of their strengths and weaknesses related to the topics discussed. The activities at the end of each chapter ask students to discuss important questions with classmates, to think critically, and to reflect on academic issues. We believe that active learners use numerous senses as they go about learning in college. They read, they write, they discuss, and they visualize. Interacting with information in a variety of ways encourages active processing, and active processing leads to academic success.

As students read and discuss the chapters in the four parts of *College Success Strategies*, they can apply the strategies learned to two text chapters in the appendixes. One chapter, titled "Cognition and Intelligence," is from a psychology text; the second, titled "The Nation Divides: The Vietnam War and Social Conflict, 1964–1971" is from a history text. Applying the strategies to longer pieces of text will give students practice that simulates regular college classes. As students preview, annotate, rehearse, and review the material, they learn how to monitor their learning to know their level of understanding. *College Success Strategies* teaches students to be active learners in charge of their own understanding.

The text boxes in *College Success Strategies* provide students with important information and should not be overlooked. From these boxes students can pick up quick and easy studying tips, learn more about using technology, improve their motivation and time management skills, and overcome procrastination. All of this information focuses on helping students become more self-confident and successful.

Finally, as students work through *College Success Strategies*, they will build a portfolio showcasing their new-found skills. At the end of each chapter, students can apply the strategies to a content area course (e.g., psychology, biology, history, geography, etc.) as a way of seeing if they can transfer strategy use to college learning. Ultimately, this should be the goal. Once students use the strategies as part of their daily academic life, they are well on their way to being active learners.

Visit Our Web Site

College Success Strategies is supported by the Longman Study Skills Web site. For additional resources, exercises, activities, and Web links to help make your college experience a successful and rewarding one, be sure to visit the Web site at www.ablongman.com/studyskills.

For additional instructor and student support materials—such as the Longman Student Planner, the Longman Instructor's Planner, and our various reading and writing software—please contact your Longman sales representative or visit us on the Web at www.ablongman.com.

ACKNOWLEDGMENTS

There are many individuals who contributed directly or indirectly to the second edition of *College Success Strategies*. Certainly it is important for us to acknowledge the students whom we continue to have the privilege to teach. As is always the case, our students help to ground our writing in reality—the reality of the many pressures currently faced by today's college students and the reality of just how important life-long learning has become. We were especially struck as we wrote the second edition by the major impact that technology has on students' learning. Today's students are truly the first generation of college students who are expected to know and keep abreast of new technological advances that can enhance learning.

In addition to our students, our thanks go out to the numerous professors and graduate students on the University of Georgia campus and beyond who have willingly shared their concerns and their expertise about learning and what it takes to be successful in their particular disciplines. This text would have not been nearly as effective without their valuable insights. A special thanks to Denise Pinette Domizi, Eleanor Pardini, Daniel Forbes, and Gretchen Pettis for their suggestions and willingness to share the parallel note-taking strategy in *College Success Strategies*, and thanks also to Audrey Haynes for the use of Web notes from her political science class.

Certainly, we acknowledge our respective families—our spouses, parents, siblings, and children—who always offered their continuous support, and sometimes even additional insights, as we sometimes turned our attention from them to work on this book. As always, we appreciate their understanding, support, and advice.

We acknowledge the major support we have received from Susan Kunchandy, our editor at Longman. Susan's enthusiasm about creating the second edition of *College Success Strategies* as part of the Penguin Academics Series was contagious. We greatly appreciated all her wonderful suggestions, and her encouragement contributed to the excellent additions and improvements of this book.

Finally, we would be remiss if we failed to acknowledge all of the assistance we received from those we have worked with at Longman: Erika Lo, Melanie Craig, Donna DeBenedictis, and Nancy Danahy, and at Elm Street Publishing Services: Karin Vonesh, Jonathan Lyzun, Angela Gelsomino, Zak Semens, and Leah Strauss. Everyone's patience, attention to detail, and helpful suggestions made working on this book an enjoyable experience.

SHERRIE L. NIST
JODI PATRICK HOLSCHUH

PART ONE

WELCOME TO COLLEGE SUCCESS STRATEGIES

College learning is very different from high school learning. If this is your first term in college, you may already have noticed many of those differences. In Chapter 1, we discuss the differences between college and high school as well as several special situations you will eventually encounter in college.

Chapter 2 introduces the concept of active learning. You learn about what active learning is and why becoming an active learner can help you succeed in college. You also learn about the four factors that influence learning: (1) characteristics of the learner, (2) the tasks, (3) the texts, and (4) the strategies. We talk about how the factors work together to influence student learning. These four factors guide the organization of the remainder of this book.

Chapter 3 presents several theories on how people learn. You will also learn about the role of learning styles and some strategies to help you stretch your memory.

Chapter 4 discusses the importance of interacting with your professors. You will learn about what professors' jobs consist of and some general tips for working with your professors.

Chapter 5 begins our discussion about college tasks. In this chapter, you will learn how to identify and gather information about the tasks for each of your college courses.

CHAPTER 1

NOW THAT YOU'RE HERE

Read this chapter to answer the following questions:

- How does studying in college differ from studying in high school?

- What special situations can you expect to encounter in college, sooner or later?

SELF-ASSESSMENT

DIRECTIONS: On a scale of 1 to 5, with 1 being "strongly disagree," 3 being "somewhat agree," and 5 being "strongly agree," respond to each of the statements below. This should give you a good idea about how much your college experience differs from what you experienced in high school.

	Strongly disagree ←→ Strongly agree
1. My college professors seem to expect much more of me.	1 2 3 4 5
2. My college classes move at a faster pace.	1 2 3 4 5
3. My college classes require more than just memorization.	1 2 3 4 5
4. My college classes give me few chances to earn extra credit.	1 2 3 4 5
5. My college classes require me to spend more time studying.	1 2 3 4 5
6. My college professors give less frequent exams.	1 2 3 4 5
7. I have more freedom in college.	1 2 3 4 5
8. I often feel anonymous in college.	1 2 3 4 5
9. I have experienced motivation problems in college.	1 2 3 4 5
10. Managing my time effectively is more challenging in college.	1 2 3 4 5

Now add up your score. The higher your score, the more differences you are experiencing in making the transition from high school to college. The more differences you experience, the more time it may take you to make the adjustment. But don't despair! The skills you will learn in *College Success Strategies* will help you make this transition.

Starting college! You may feel as if you have been preparing for this day forever. You've taken a college preparatory curriculum in high school, you've talked with friends or siblings who are already in college, and you may have visited several campuses before deciding which school to attend. Or you may be returning to college after several years of working, having already gone through careful life assessment and financial budgeting. Regardless of your situation, you are probably excited about what the next few years have in store for you. And some of you may even be a little wary and unsure of yourself as you begin down the college path.

Studying Smarter

Avoid the need to cram! Pay some attention to every class every day.

In this chapter, we will discuss some of the ways in which college differs from high school. In addition, we will present eight situations that you are sure to encounter in college sooner or later and will offer suggestions about how you might deal with them. Keep in mind as you read this chapter that campuses differ in size and in the expectations they have of students. For these reasons, some of the generalizations and solutions offered here might not apply exactly to your particular situation.

How Does College Differ from High School?

How many times since high school graduation have you heard one of your relatives say something like this: "Oh _____ (insert your name)! Enjoy these college years. They will be the best of your life." Although this statement is probably true—college is enjoyable and memorable—it is also demanding and, in many instances, just plain different from high school. It's a time in your life when you will go through many changes as you prepare for the world of work that follows. In this section we will discuss some of the reasons why high school and college differ.

- **Reason 1: College Requires Greater Independent Learning.** Your high school teachers may have been willing to give you lots of test preparation help. They may have prepared study guides or even provided the exact questions that would be asked. Although college instructors also want you to be successful—we have never met a professor who wants students to fail—they don't give students as much study help. Sure, most professors will answer questions about course content and things you don't understand, but they will not provide you with a variety of supplementary learning materials and they certainly will not give you test questions. They expect that you know effective and efficient study strategies and if you don't know how to study for their courses, they expect you to learn how.

TIMELY TIPS

Learning How to Learn

Did you know that learning how to learn on your own may be one of the most important benefits of going to college? As you move into the world of work, most employers will expect you to do a considerable amount of learning on your own. Employees who need lots of guidance in learning new things aren't nearly as valuable as those who are self-starters. So one of the most important skills you want to foster early in your college career is the ability to learn on your own. In fact, you should make mastering this skill one of your top priorities in college.

- **Reason 2: College Courses Move at a Faster Pace.** If you ask first-year college students about the differences between high school and college, one of their most common responses would be that college courses move much faster than high school classes. What might have taken a full year to cover in high school will probably be covered in a semester in college. It's not uncommon for college professors to move through three, four, or more chapters in a week, expecting you to keep up. In addition, more topics are generally covered in greater detail. However, college professors may go into detail on just a few points and expect you to fill in the rest of the details on your own.

- **Reason 3: College Courses Require You to Think Critically.** In your high school classes, perhaps you were required to memorize lots of facts for exams. You may even have been discouraged from questioning either your high school textbooks or your high school teacher. But as you proceed through college, you will find yourself in classes where your professor wants you to do more than memorize. You might have to critique an essay on gun control, read and respond to a historian's view of the Vietnamese conflict, or compare and contrast conflicting scientific theories. All of these tasks require you to think critically because you need to go beyond memorization to applying or synthesizing the information.

- **Reason 4: College Classes Have Few Safety Nets.** Usually on the first day of a college class your professor will give you a syllabus. The syllabus outlines the course requirements and also generally tells you how your grade will be determined. Something that will become clear as you read your syllabus is that many of the safety nets that you had in high school, such as extra credit assignments or other bonuses to improve your grade, have all but disappeared. This means your course grade will be determined by the grade you earn on a limited number of tests or papers. So you'll need to give every assignment your best efforts.

- **Reason 5: College Requires You to Study Longer and More Effectively.** You will probably find out pretty quickly that both the amount of time you put into studying and the way you study in college will have to change if you want to earn high grades. Many of our students tell us that they really didn't have to study in high school. "Studying" was reading over a study guide or reading over class notes for about a half-hour. Many students begin college without ever having to read their texts and some have never taken essay exams. It is important to realize that studying in college requires not only more time, but also a variety of study strategies to have at your disposal.

- **Reason 6: College Provides Fewer Chances for Evaluation.** In high school, it may have seemed as though you were always taking tests or writing papers. Chances are, you were tested over small amounts of material (only one or two chapters) and you had numerous chances for evaluation.

GET GOING

Keeping Up with Assignments

Many students enter college thinking that if there is no test coming up that week that they have nothing pressing to do. But, because you may have four or five chapters on each exam (or even more), you will need to stay on top of your reading each week. Don't procrastinate on your reading because you will need time to process all of the material.

If you did poorly on one test, you could usually make it up on the next one. In college, on the other hand, you will probably have fewer chances to be evaluated. At first, the idea of taking fewer tests per course in a term may seem appealing. But think about the big picture. If you have only three exams, you are going to be held responsible for much more information at one time than you were in high school. What at first seems to be an advantage—fewer tests, homework that goes unchecked, a longer period of time between exams—may actually work against you, unless you know how to stay on top of things.

- **Reason 7: College Gives You Greater Freedom and Greater Responsibility.** Legally, you become an adult at age 18, which just happens to be about the same time you graduate from high school. In college, no one makes you stay on top of your schoolwork or keeps track of your comings and goings or checks to see that you have done all of your reading and studying before heading out for a night on the town. This freedom comes with a tremendous amount of responsibility. It is your responsibility to prioritize the tasks you *have* to do against the things you *want* to do.

- **Reason 8: College Provides Greater Anonymity.** If you attend a moderate to large college or university, you will be faced with being somewhat anonymous, and in some cases, very anonymous. By anonymous we mean that you *can* become just another face in the crowd. Most of you probably attended high schools where you got to know your teachers and your classmates fairly well. Your teachers not only knew your name, but also were concerned about whether or not you were learning and understanding the information presented in their classes. For the most part, in college, your professors have few opportunities to get to know you well. All is not lost, however. Most of the time, students are anonymous only if they want to be, regardless of how large or small their campus may be. You can become more than a "face" to your professors by making appointments to talk with them. You can join clubs that have faculty sponsors. You can take part in a variety of campus activities with other students who share your interests.

- **Reason 9: College Requires You to Be Proactive.** Being proactive means that it's your responsibility to take the initiative in a variety of situations. In high school, either your teachers or your parents may have insisted that you get help if you were having problems with a particular course. And you may have followed their advice reluctantly. In college, however, it becomes your responsibility to know the resources that are available on your campus, so that if you do run into difficulties, or need the services of some office, you'll know how to find the information you need or where to go to get assistance. If you are proactive and find out a little about them before you need their services, it will save you time in the long run. However, you don't want to wait until you are in dire need of these resources before seeking them out. Some of these services may include:

  - **The Library.** In addition to providing resources, the library is a great place to study, to do research online, or to meet your study group. Most campuses have library orientations that help students learn to navigate large and complex systems.
  - **The Learning Center.** The campus learning center can be an excellent source of assistance because most offer a variety of services, from academic counseling to assistance with writing, studying, and mathematics.
  - **Tutorial Services.** Like learning centers, most campuses offer tutorial services for a broad range of courses. Generally, tutoring is provided by undergraduate students who earn top grades in the areas that they tutor. This tutoring is usually free, but appointments are often necessary.
  - **Health Services.** Because getting sick enough to need the services of a doctor is inevitable, know where your campus health facility is and what the rules are to be able to see a medical professional. Don't wait until you feel as if you're on your deathbed. Find out where to go and what to do early on.
  - **Counseling Center.** More and more students are enlisting the help of a trained professional from their campus counseling center. If you find that you have problems that are getting in the way of your academic success, you should seek out help. Sometimes talking with a friend works. If it doesn't, find out more about the services offered through the counseling center.
  - **Student Center or Student Union.** On most campuses, the student center is the hub of campus where you can meet friends, but most also offer a wealth of resources. Sometimes campus organizations and clubs have offices in the student center. Social event and concert tickets can be purchased there. General information about campus such as bus schedules, campus maps, and event schedules can be obtained. Often, the campus

NETWORKING

Your School's Web Site

Access the Web site of the college or university you are currently attending. Search the Web site for information about some of the services discussed in this chapter such as the learning center, health center, or counseling center. What did you find out about these services that you didn't know before? What other services did you find?

Check your syllabi to see if any of your professors listed their e-mail address. If they did, write a brief e-mail to introduce yourself or to ask a question. Also, if any of your professors have personal Web pages, check them out.

bookstore is located in or near the student center. When you don't know where else to turn, the student center is a good place to start if you need information about your campus.

So, college is different from high school in many ways. You must think differently about the expectations, learning conditions, level of responsibility, and studying methods than you did in high school. This is not bad. It simply means you will have to make some transitions in the way you learn and study in order to be successful.

SUCCESS AT A GLANCE

How High School Differs from College

	High School	College
Independence	Less independence	Greater independence
Pacing	Slow	Fast
Level of Critical Thinking	Less critical thinking	Greater critical thinking
Safety Nets	Teachers provide many	Professors provide few

(continued)

	High School	**College**
Study Effort	Limited and sporadic	Greater and effective
Evaluation	Many opportunities	Limited opportunities
Responsibility	Rests on others	Rests on you
Anonymity	Little	Lots
Importance of Being Proactive	Low	High

What Special Situations Can You Expect to Encounter Sooner or Later?

Now that you have seen some of the ways in which high school and college differ, let's examine this transition from another perspective. We'll present eight situations that most college students will encounter sooner or later, and we'll also examine how you might cope with or handle each situation. All of these situations will be addressed again throughout this text, so you will be able to explore these ideas in greater detail.

In a perfect world, none of the following situations would occur. All students would go to class every day, distribute their study time over several days, stay on top of their reading, and make the dean's list every term. However, the world of college is an imperfect place. So, let's discuss some of the situations that you might encounter in college, some for which you might not be prepared. As you read each section, think about how you might handle the situation and what additional information might help you cope better.

- **Professors Who Take Roll.** Someone may have told you that the only time you really *have* to show up for classes in college is on test days, or that if you can get the information on your own, professors don't really care whether you are in class. Although many professors don't take attendance, eventually you will run across one who does, and, in reality, most actually do want you present in class. Many professors truly believe that attending class will help you learn. We believe this as well, so even if your professor does not take roll, it's still a good idea to attend class.

- **An Early Morning Class.** Most college students are not morning people. In fact, there's even scientific evidence to indicate that the biological clocks of college-aged people are preset to stay up late at night and to sleep late in the morning. However, the college officials who determine the times of class periods evidently are unaware of this research. Unfortunately (for most college students), a time will come when you will have to take an early morning class.

If you do have that early class, try to juggle the rest of your schedule so that you can go to bed earlier than usual. Additionally, try to take one that meets only two or three days a week, thus allowing you a little more flexibility on other days.

- **A Course or Professor You Don't Particularly Like.** It's perhaps sad but true—there will be courses you don't like, and professors with whom you fail to connect. Even if you have a wide range of interests and you can get along well with almost everyone, at some point you'll probably have to make it through a rough class. You can take one of two routes when this happens.

    Route A: You can think of every excuse imaginable not to do the work or go to class. You can blame your attitude on the professor or the boring material that you are expected to learn.

    Consequences of Route A: A poor course grade, feeling bad about yourself, and having to work doubly hard in another course to bring up your overall grade point average.

    Route B: Acknowledge that you really don't care much for the course or the professor. It's one course, however, and you can make it through. Study with someone who seems to like the course. Try to motivate yourself with small rewards. Tell yourself that this is temporary and the course will soon be over.

    Consequences of Route B: Perhaps you will not earn an A in the class but you will emerge with your ego and your grade point average intact.

- **Cramming for a Test.** Imagine you have a big test in a couple of days (or worse yet, tomorrow) and you've done very little preparing. Now it's *cram time*! Personally, we've never met a student who didn't have to cram at some time. And cramming occasionally probably isn't a horrible thing, but it shouldn't become the way you live your academic life. If you have to cram occasionally, try to use the strategies you'll learn in this book to study to your advantage. And, as soon as possible, regroup so that you don't have to go cram again.

- **Difficulty Maintaining Motivation for Academics.** Most college students experience motivation problems at some time or another. It usually doesn't last long, but for some students the decline in motivation is long enough and severe enough to interfere with their schoolwork. Other students experience a lull in motivation in just one class, generally a class with which they may be experiencing difficulty. Still others begin the term with good intentions, yet quickly develop general motivation problems in every class. If you are having motivation problems, try setting some specific, reachable goals. Whether your lack of motivation is concentrated in one particular course, occurs at a specific period of time (such as around midpoint), or is generalized across all your academic courses, goal setting can help you stay focused and improve your motivation to learn.

- **Personal Problems and/or Illness.** No one plans on getting sick or having serious personal problems, but at some point you will likely experience both predicaments. However, there are some things you can do to salvage even a bad situation. First, as you plan your schedule for the term, build in some flexibility, just in case. If everything goes according to plan, the worst thing that can happen is you'll have some extra time to study, work, or play. Second, as mentioned earlier, use the services that are available on your campus. Third, develop a set of reliable peers who can be there for you in times of illness or other problems. Often knowing that some other person can help you out makes all the difference in the world.

- **Frustration.** It's a given that you will experience frustrations and stressful situations, but it's how you deal with them that makes the difference. Try not to let things build up to the point where you can't cope. As much as possible, deal with frustrations as they arise. Evaluate all the alternatives. And try not to become stressed by things you have no control over. So . . . take a walk. Go work out. Spend a few minutes venting to a friend. In time it will work out.

- **Juggling Too Many Responsibilities.** College students tend to be busy people—going to class, studying, attending meetings, working, exercising, taking part in campus organizations, and the list goes on. Add to all of this family responsibilities, social interactions, and some good old time to play, and you can easily become overcommitted. Although you certainly want to get the most out of your college experience, try to think about how new responsibilities will affect you. Remember that your primary job in college is to be a student. Then you can ask yourself: "What other kinds of responsibilities can I take on?" Will you have so much to do a month from now that you will constantly feel stressed out and frustrated? If you can think about this in advance and learn to say "No" when you find yourself maxing out, you will be able to keep all those balls in the air and be a much happier student.

Studying Smarter
I will study and get ready, and perhaps my chance will come.
— **Abraham Lincoln**

REAL COLLEGE
Wanda's Woes

DIRECTIONS: Read the following "Real College" scenario and respond to the questions based on the information you learned in this chapter.

Wanda was a pretty good student in high school. She earned good grades and "studied as much as she needed" to make As and Bs. She just naturally assumed that she would earn similar grades in college. But here it is, only three weeks into the fall semester, and things aren't going as planned. She didn't do well on her first chemistry test because she had to cram and asked the professor for an extra credit assignment. Her professor chuckled and shook his head no. Then there's the pace. Things seem to be moving so fast. She's having a difficult time keeping up. From her perspective, she's studying about the same amount of time as she did in high school, but her efforts don't seem to be paying off. In addition to these academic problems, she feels alone and isolated. She likes her roommate, and would like to get to know her better, but her roommate knows a lot of people already so she's not around much. It seems so hard to make new friends.

1. What advice do you have for Wanda?
2. What could she do to help herself academically? Socially?

☐ THINKING CRITICALLY
Something to Think About and Discuss

DIRECTIONS: Now that you have read about some of the differences between high school and college, analyze your own experiences and respond to the following questions.

- What do you think is the biggest difference between high school and college?
- What do you wish you had learned in high school that would better prepare you for a positive college experience?
- Have you been in the situation yet where you were enrolled in a course or had a professor that you did not like? How have you dealt with this situation? How would you deal with it if you haven't already experienced it? What suggestions do you have for others who might be in the same predicament?
- Think about a time when your motivation to learn was low. What caused you to lose motivation? What did you do to restore it?

☐ ADD TO YOUR PORTFOLIO

1. Sometimes professors can seem intimidating, especially when you first begin college, but most college teachers are personable people who enjoy interacting with students. In order to get to know one of your professors a little better, make an appointment to talk with her. You might discuss course expectations, ask for studying pointers, or discuss your past successes or problems with similar courses. Write up a one-page summary of your conversation.

2. Find out where you can get help with academic problems. Is there a learning center on your campus? If so, what services does it offer? How do you go about making an appointment in the learning center? Jot down this information for future reference.

3. Find out where you can get counseling assistance. Is there a counseling center that can help you make the adjustment to college? What if you just need someone to talk with? How do you go about making an appointment to see someone? Jot down this information for future reference.

CHAPTER 2

ACTIVE LEARNING: WHAT'S IN IT FOR YOU?

Read this chapter to answer the following questions:
- How do active learners differ from passive learners?
- What are the benefits of active learning?
- What are the four factors that influence learning?
- What is the holistic nature of active learning?

DIRECTIONS: On a scale of 1 to 5, with 1 being "rarely," 3 being "sometimes," and 5 being "most of the time," evaluate how active you are as a learner.

Rarely ←——→ Most of the time

1. When I read my texts, I can make connections with what I have read earlier in the course.   1 2 3 4 5

2. After I read my texts, I can restate the key ideas in my own words.   1 2 3 4 5

3. After lectures and when I am finished reading my texts, I can clearly state what I don't understand.   1 2 3 4 5

4. I can take meaningful and organized notes for a full class period without losing concentration.   1 2 3 4 5

5. When I prepare for tests, I use my time wisely.   1 2 3 4 5

6. I seek out help when I am having problems understanding the material presented in a course.   1 2 3 4 5

7. I use different strategies for learning, depending on the course and the type of exams.   1 2 3 4 5

8. If information I hear or read fails to fit with what I already know, I try to examine the issue from a variety of viewpoints.   1 2 3 4 5

9. When I enter a testing situation, I have a good idea of how I will do.   1 2 3 4 5

10. I am motivated to learn in most of my classes.   1 2 3 4 5

11. I feel confident about myself as a learner.   1 2 3 4 5

Now, add up your score. The higher your score, the more active you are as a learner. The lowest score you can receive is eleven; the highest score is fifty-five. Your score gives you an overall picture of how much work you have to do and also lets you know which areas of active learning you need to work on.

What Do Active Learners Do?

You hear it all the time, read about it in magazines and newspapers, and even watch television programs dedicated to one theme: ACTIVITY! Be active, exercise. It's good for your health. It seems as though everywhere you turn there's another piece of research or another claim about the importance of being active. Let's take the premise that you are tired of being out of shape. You take the big step and join a fitness club or gym, so that you can work yourself back into shape. Such good intentions! But

Studying Smarter
When trying to change your study habits, be open-minded and try new approaches.

what if you went to the gym and merely watched other people exercise? Would you become fit? Of course not, because you would not be an **active** participant. Learning works in the same way. If you are not an active participant in learning, you won't become mentally fit, nor will you maximize your performance in the classroom.

To define active learning, we'll discuss the differences between active and passive learning by examining seven characteristics of active learners and contrasting them with the characteristics of passive learners. Active learners:

- **Read with the Purpose of Understanding and Remembering.** We'd bet that no one deliberately sits down to read with the purpose of *not* understanding the text. However, we're certain that you have been in situations where you "read" an assignment, closed the text, and thought, "What in the world was that about?" When you respond to a text in that manner you are reading passively. Active readers, on the other hand, set goals before they read and check their understanding as they read. When they finish, they can explain the main points and know that they have understood what they have read.

- **Reflect on Information and Think Critically.** Being reflective is an important part of active learning because it means that you are thinking about the information. In other words, you are processing the information. You may make connections between the new information and what you already know, identify concepts that you may not understand very well, or evaluate the importance of what you are reading. An active learner reflects constantly. In contrast, passive learners may read the text and listen to lectures, and even understand most of what is read and heard, but they do not take that crucial next step of actually thinking about it.

- **Listen Actively by Taking Comprehensive Notes in an Organized Fashion.** We are always amazed at the number of students who engage in activities other than listening and note taking in their lecture classes. We've seen students reading the campus newspaper, doing an assignment for another class, working crossword puzzles, or chatting with a classmate. Perhaps the all-time winner for passive learning, however, was a student who regularly came to class with a pillow and blanket and fell asleep on his girlfriend's shoulder. Unlike these students, active learners are engaged learners. They listen actively to the professor for the entire class period and they write down as much information as possible. To be an active note taker, you must be more than simply present. You have to think about the information before you write.

- **Know that Learning Involves More Than Simply Putting in Time.** Most students know about the importance of having good time-management skills and expect to invest time in studying in order to be successful. But just putting time into studying is not enough. It is the quality of that time—what you actually do with it—that makes the difference. In college, effort does not count—performance does.

NETWORKING

Going Online

There is so much information and misinformation available to you on the Internet that it takes an active learner to be able to sift through it. To practice your skills as a critical thinker, go online to your local newspaper or to a news magazine and use the search function to find a current article that interests you. Try to actively engage in the article to find out the author's intent. Question the author as you read. Does any of the information seem suspect or unsupported? Does it agree or disagree with what you already know about the topic? Use the answers to these questions to help you reflect on the information you find.

- **Get Assistance When They are Experiencing Problems.** Because active learners are constantly monitoring their understanding, they know when their comprehension breaks down, and they ask for help before they become lost. In addition, active learners can often predict the courses (or even particular concepts within courses) that may give them trouble. They have a plan in mind for getting assistance should they need it. Active learners may hire individual tutors, take advantage of free peer tutoring, or seek assistance from their professors. Although passive learners may seek help at some point, it is often too little, too late. In addition, because passive learners do not reflect and think critically, they often don't even realize that they need help.

- **Accept Much of the Responsibility for Learning.** Active learners understand that the responsibility for learning must come from within, while passive learners often want to blame others for their lack of motivation, poor performance, time-management problems, and other difficulties that they might experience. When active learners don't perform as well as they'd hoped, they evaluate why they didn't do well, and change those studying behaviors the next time. Passive learners, on the other hand, often approach every course in the same manner and then get angry with professors when their performance is poor. It is only when students accept the responsibility for their own learning that they can truly be called active learners.

• **Question Information.** Active learners question information that they read and hear, while passive learners accept both the printed page and the words of their professors as "truth." Active learners don't question *everything*, but they do evaluate what they read and hear. When new information fails to fit with what they already know, they may differ in the conclusions they draw or in the inferences they make.

SUCCESS AT A GLANCE

Differences Between Active and Passive Learners

	Active Learners	**Passive Learners**
Reading	Read to understand and remember.	Read but may not understand or remember.
Reflecting and Thinking Critically	Make connections between what they already know and new information in texts, lectures, and from studying with peers.	Don't think about and process information that they read and hear.
Listening	Are engaged during lectures and take organized notes.	Pay little attention during lecture and take unorganized or incomplete notes.
Managing Time	Put in quality study time.	May put in a lot of study time, but it isn't quality time.
Getting Assistance	Realize when they need help and seek it early.	Seek too little help too late.
Accepting Responsibility	Understand they are responsible for their own learning, analyze weak performance if it occurs, and change the way they study accordingly.	Blame others for poor performance, approach every course in the same way, and fail to learn from their mistakes.

(continued)

	Active Learners	**Passive Learners**
Questioning Information	Question new information that doesn't fit with what they already know.	Accept what they read and hear in lectures as true and don't question.

Benefits of Active Learning

As you can tell by reading the last section, being an active learner involves both *skill* and *will*.

- By **skill,** we mean that you have the tools to handle the studying and learning demands placed on you. You have a variety of study strategies that you consciously employ, and these strategies change depending on the text, the task, and your own personal characteristics as a learner, as we will discuss further in the next section. In addition, you know how to mange your time, when and where to get assistance if you are having difficulty, and you can monitor and evaluate your learning.

- By **will,** we mean that you have the desire and motivation to follow through. Skill is nothing without will. For example, you may have a friend, relative, or peer who is knowledgeable but not motivated in the classroom. Even though he reads widely and can intelligently discuss a variety of issues, he does little work associated with school and rarely studies. Teachers may say that this person is "bright but lazy," or ". . . isn't working up to his potential." In other words, students such as these may have the skills to do well; for some reason they simply do not have the will. And because skill and will go hand in hand, unmotivated students—those who do not have the will—may experience difficulty in college and end up dropping out or being "asked" to leave.

It's much easier to teach someone the skills needed to be an active learner than it is to give them the will. Skill is something that can be developed only if one has the will to do so. Think about the example used earlier in the chapter pertaining to exercise: If you go to the gym to develop skill, and you have the will to put in the effort to persist in developing your athletic skill, you'll be successful. But if you work out for two weeks, then only sporadically, then not at all, you might lack the will to be successful, even though you might have the skills to do so. No one can force you to go to the gym, just as no one can force you to study effectively, to plan your time, or to go to class. That all is a matter of will, no matter how much skill you have.

> ## GET GOING
>
> ### Developing Will
>
> One way to develop the will to learn is by setting your own purpose for learning. Many students seem unaware of what they hope to get out of their courses, so it is no wonder they are not motivated to learn. For one of your courses this semester, figure out what you hope to accomplish by the end of the class. If you make your plan for a course you don't particularly enjoy, it just may help you find your will.

Active learning, then, has numerous benefits, both in terms of academic and psychological payoffs.

- In terms of **academic payoffs,** active learning leads to higher grades, increased time to pursue extracurricular and social activities, and most importantly, gained knowledge. Active learners tend to earn higher grade point averages, seek more involvement with their professors, and like to learn new things. And while all active learners certainly don't believe that they are studying simply for the "love of learning," they are more apt to find learning new things more of a challenge than a chore or a bore.

- The **psychological payoffs** to active learning may even outweigh the academic benefits. Have you ever heard the saying, "Success begets success"? This saying means that being successful motivates you to do what it takes to have greater success. In other words, once active learners experience academic success, they want to continue along that path. Being successful will make you feel good about yourself, create greater self-confidence about learning, generate positive feedback from family, and often will influence your future goals. Everyone knows that it's much easier to continue to use the skills you have acquired if you get positive feedback about how you have applied those skills.

Studying Smarter
The difference between a successful person and others is not a lack of strength, not a lack of knowledge, but rather in a lack of will.
—Vince Lombardi

Four Factors That Influence Active Learning

As you can see, active learning is a complex process. Part of the complexity of learning is caused by the many factors that you have to consider. Cognitive psychologists, those who study how people learn, suggest that there are four key factors that influence learning:

1. Your own characteristics as a learner;
2. The tasks your professors ask you to do;
3. The texts with which you interact; and
4. The strategies you select.

We briefly cover each of these factors here, but will discuss each factor in greater detail in later chapters.

Factor 1: Characteristics of the Learner

As a student, you bring a variety of unique characteristics to each learning situation. These characteristics play a key role in how well you will perform, your interest in the material, and the strategies you will select to learn the course content.

- **Motivation** is one of the most important characteristics you can bring to a learning situation. Without motivation, you would find it hard to get out of bed each morning. And you will probably experience frustration and failure as a student. General interest in the topic being studied helps, but if you are open to learning new things and expanding your interests, you will be more successful. Motivation is discussed in Chapter 7.

- **Background knowledge** plays a role because the more you already know about a topic, the easier it is to learn. This means that it might be a good idea to select at least some courses during your first semester or two that you know a lot about. Using the knowledge you already possess is discussed in Chapter 3.

- Your **ability to concentrate** on what you are reading or studying also affects your learning. Everyone has times when his mind wanders and concentration is difficult. But if you frequently leave class or finish reading a chapter feeling that you got little or nothing out of it, learning may be difficult. There are things you can do to improve your concentration, however. Attention and concentration are discussed in Chapter 11.

- Your **beliefs about knowledge and learning** is a characteristic that is rarely discussed, but is very important. What do you believe knowledge is? Do you believe that knowledge consists of information that is transmitted from your professor to you? Or do you believe that you can be a part of creating knowledge? How you answer questions such as these influences the way you learn. Beliefs about learning are discussed in Chapter 8.

These characteristics and others not only help determine what you will learn, but also how you will study course material. Active learners understand the importance of being aware of these characteristics as they approach learning tasks, whether the tasks are easy or difficult.

TIMELY TIPS

Getting to Know You

Figuring out your own characteristics as a learner can help you with more than succeeding in your classes. Once you know yourself, you can begin to make changes regarding relationships with others, how you manage your time, how you keep track of your obligations, and even how to meet your goals for your future. This is because you are learning all the time—not just in your classes—and your learning characteristics will impact your existence outside of the classroom and into your life. As you read *College Success Strategies*, think about how you can apply these concepts to your life.

Factor 2: The Tasks

Simply put, tasks are what your professors ask you to do. You can think of them as daily tasks, such as reading your text before you attend lectures; or larger tasks, such as preparing for various kinds of tests or writing papers. Most professors are pretty clear about what the tasks are. They will let you know the number of tests you will have and the kind of tests they will be (e.g., essay, multiple choice, etc.), as well as their expectations about papers, lab participation, or library work. Some will even let you examine copies of old tests or student papers so that you can see the kinds of questions they will ask or what their writing expectations are. Others will give you example test questions so that you can get an idea of how the questions will be asked.

But some professors aren't so clear in defining course tasks. Some may even give you conflicting messages. Therefore, it is important to try to get your professor to be as clear as possible about the tasks you must undertake. If you don't know what is expected of you, then you can't select the proper learning strategies or the most effective way to approach your texts. We discuss issues relating to tasks in many of the chapters in this book, but most directly in Chapters 4 and 5.

Factor 3: The Texts

Texts are crucial to learning in college. In fact, it has been estimated that 85 percent of all college learning involves reading. Students often think of texts as simply **textbooks.** Certainly textbooks are a major source of information in many of your college classes, but texts also come in other forms. **Periodicals, newspapers, novels,** and **essays** are printed texts. Another type of text that is being used more often on university campuses is **computer text,** sometimes called nonlinear or hypertext. You may even be required to view films or documentaries, which are **visual texts.**

In addition to textbooks, **lecture notes** are the other most frequent type of "text" with which college students must interact. Strategies for note taking are discussed in Chapter 14.

Whatever types of text you are expected to use, you should know how the particular text is organized. In most textbooks, each chapter is usually organized in the same fashion. In addition, your professor's lectures probably follow the same pattern each day. Even visual texts have organizational patterns. Once you have determined how your text is organized, learning the material becomes a much easier task. Like learner characteristics and tasks, texts are an important part of the learning puzzle. Texts are discussed in more detail in Chapters 10 and 11.

Factor 4: The Learning Strategies

The final, and perhaps the most complex, factor that influences learning is the strategies that you choose. It is important to realize that strategies should be chosen based on your characteristics as a learner, the tasks you have to do, and the texts used. Thus, a large portion of this text, Chapters 12, 13, 15, and 16, is devoted to learning strategies.

Strategies for active learning have several features in common.

1. Once you learn them, you can use all of these strategies on your own. Because studying is mostly a solitary activity, it is important to be able to use strategies without guidance from someone else—a professor or a friend, for example.

2. These strategies have specific underlying processes that research has consistently shown to lead to better performance. For example, all of the strategies you will learn have a self-testing component, which immediately tells you whether or not you understand the information.

3. The strategies require participation on your part in the form of critical thinking and reasoning. They will help you to think beyond the text and to analyze, synthesize, and apply the information.

4. The strategies are flexible. You can modify them according to your own learning preferences, the tasks, and the texts.

The Holistic Nature of Active Learning

Active learners possess three different kinds of knowledge about the strategies they use during learning. It's not enough just to know how to use a particular strategy; in order to be an efficient and effective learner, you need to have declarative, procedural, and conditional knowledge (Paris, Lipson, and Wixson 1983).

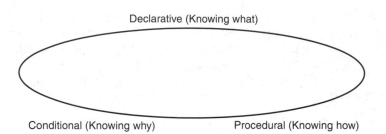

1. **Declarative Knowledge.** Declarative knowledge is *knowing what*—what you need to do and what strategy you need to use. For example, if you were in a history class and the task was to get ready for an essay exam in which you would need to synthesize information, declarative knowledge enables you to select the proper study strategy that matched the task. You might say to yourself, "I need to begin by predicting some questions, and then I need to practice answering those questions."

2. **Procedural Knowledge.** Procedural knowledge involves more than knowing what you should do. It is *knowing how* to do it. Returning to our history example, you would have to know how to go about predicting questions that are likely to be on your test. You might search your lecture notes for hints your professor gave about important ideas, look to see what she spent a lot of time on in class, think about the larger themes that were discussed, or look for overlap between your lecture notes and your text. Once you have predicted your questions, then comes the practice. You need to have a plan—sketch out an outline of the key points you want to include in your answer, say those points to yourself, and practice writing out the answers to one of the questions you predicted. You might even show it to your professor if she is willing to give you feedback. As the term procedural knowledge suggests, you have "procedures" to follow once you have identified the appropriate strategies.

3. **Conditional Knowledge.** Conditional knowledge means knowing under what conditions to use certain strategies—*knowing when and why*. Using our history example again, you would know that you would have to use test preparation approaches that would lead to synthesis since that is what the task requires. Therefore, you would not want to use strategies that encouraged only memorization. When you achieve conditional knowledge, you will know how to apply the most appropriate learning strategies for all of your courses.

Becoming an active learner, especially if you have been a passive learner, takes some time and effort. It doesn't happen overnight. Most students, especially first-year students, are located somewhere in the middle of the active–passive continuum. That is, rarely are students totally passive or completely active learners when they begin college. Becoming an active learner is a sort of work in progress.

Look back at your score on the self-assessment at the beginning of this chapter. Your score probably was not eleven, the lowest possible score, nor fifty-five, the highest. You probably fell somewhere in between. But by thinking about the factors that influence learning, and about the three types of knowledge, you are already on your way to becoming a better learner.

☐ REAL COLLEGE
Malcolm's Malingering

DIRECTIONS: Read the following "Real College" scenario and respond to the questions based on what you learned in this chapter.

Meet Malcolm. Malcolm has a good attitude about being in college, but he's having a little trouble academically. Perhaps Malcolm does not understand that numerous factors must interact in order for him to be an active learner.

Malcolm decided after the first week on campus that he was made to be a college student. He has signed up for volunteer work, joined two campus clubs, and found several local hangouts where he can socialize with friends. He has discovered that he loves his freedom—the fact that he can come and go as he pleases. He never knew that a day could go by so quickly. Because he is often up late trying to study while lying on his bed or just hanging out with his roommate, he has trouble getting up for his 8:00 A.M. math class. Some days he is late; on other days, he never even hears his alarm. His other classes also present problems. He hates his history class because there is so much to read, and English, well . . . who cares about iambic pentameter?

Malcolm is stressed out because he wants to do well, but he has already missed two math quizzes because of oversleeping and made a D on the first test. He thought he should have done much better because he did most of the homework, which is about as much as he had in high school math classes and he made As and Bs then. In English, he made a C on his first writing assignment, which he felt was good for him. In history, he has no grades yet because there is only a midterm and a final, but he is far behind on the reading assignments. Right now, things don't look promising for Malcolm!

Based on what you read in this and other chapters in this book, what advice do you have for Malcolm? As you are thinking about this advice, remember what we said earlier about the four factors of active learning: (1) your characteristics as a learner; (2) the tasks you must complete; (3) the texts you use; and (4) the strategies you select. How might Malcolm consider each of these factors in order to become a more active and effective learner?

☐ THINKING CRITICALLY
Something to Think About and Discuss

Consider the four factors involved in active learning to respond to the following questions.

- How do you think motivation, interests, and attitudes influence your own college performance?

- Have you ever been in a class where you were confused about the task? How did you handle your confusion? How might you handle it now?

- Think about how each of your professors lectures. How do their lecturing styles influence your note taking?

- Currently, what kinds of study strategies are you using to learn new information? Do you use the same strategies for every class?

☐ ADD TO YOUR PORTFOLIO

Write down at least two things you can do right now to move toward becoming a more active learner. They can be small things, such as sitting closer to the front of the classroom to help you focus better and take better notes. Or you might try reading a section of one of your text assignments and then stopping to reflect on what you remember. Both are little changes, but if you make two small changes this week and two small changes the next, and so on, you will be well on your way to becoming an active learner. As you go through the semester continue to add to this list of activities; by the end of the term you will be pleasantly surprised at how far you have come.

CHAPTER 3

HOW YOU LEARN

Read this chapter to answer the following questions:

- What role does memory play in learning?
- How do the two major theories of learning differ?
- How can you stretch your memory?
- How can you use your senses to be a more effective learner?

SELF-ASSESSMENT

DIRECTIONS: Respond to these questions to determine your knowledge about how memory works.

1. T F Researchers know how human memory works.

2. T F Most people attend to all the sensory information around them.

3. T F If you want to remember something forever, you should store it in short-term memory.

4. T F Short-term memory holds only five to nine pieces of information at one time.

5. T F Usually, to move information from short-term to long-term memory you must rehearse the information.

6. T F Information processed at deep levels will be remembered for a long time.

7. T F Using mnemonics can hinder memory processing.

8. T F Creating acronyms can improve memory processing.

9. T F A person with a visual learning style can learn only by seeing things.

10. T F To remember more you should learn using all of your senses.

Answers: 1 F, 2 F, 3 F, 4 T, 5 T, 6 T, 7 F, 8 T, 9 F, 10 T. Read the rest of this chapter for a detailed explanation of why these statements are true or false.

Have you ever heard a student comment that he doesn't do well on tests simply because he has a bad memory? Does it seem to you that the older the person, the poorer the memory? And why can you remember some things very easily, while other information needs to be pounded into your head? The answers to all of these questions have something to do with the way memory operates. Because researchers can't actually "see" memory, no one knows for sure exactly how memory operates. But scientists do know that certain sections of the brain are responsible for certain types of memories. Although there are different theories about how information gets into and is retrieved from memory, the theories do have commonalities. As you read about the two most common theories, keep in mind that they are just that: plausible explanations about how memory works.

Studying Smarter
Rehearsing class information daily increases your memory of it by at least threefold.

The Role of Memory: Two Theories

The Parts Theory

According to what we will call the parts theory, there are three different types of memories, or what we refer to as parts. It is easiest to think of memory as sort of a flowchart that might look something like this:

Sensory Store   →   Short-Term Memory   →   Long-Term Memory
                                        (STM)   (LTM)

The first part, the **sensory store,** serves as a kind of filter. That is, your senses are often bombarded with information, much of which you can't remember. For example, if you are looking up a number in the telephone book, you don't look at every number. You run your finger down a specific page until you find the number you are looking for and then you use that piece of information in some way. For the most part, you probably have no recollection of the other names, addresses, or telephone numbers that were in that column. Your sensory store has filtered that information for you. Likewise, it is very likely that as you walked to class this morning you saw many other students, but can't recollect the faces of the ones that you passed. That's your sensory store at work as well.

Although your sensory store can never be filled up, it can overload. Think about a situation in which your senses have been overwhelmed. It may have been at a place like Disney World where there are so many sights and sounds that it is difficult for your sensory store to take them all in. It may have been when you were trying to study for a history exam but your roommate had the TV on, your next door neighbor was listening to loud music, a fire truck was blaring its siren, and dogs were barking in the distance. When too much vies for your attention, it's difficult for the filter to function in your best interest.

Under normal circumstances, however, when you identify a piece of information that you need to remember, your sensory store filters out what you don't need and you actually are not even aware of the process. What happens to the information that you need to remember? According to the parts theory, your **short-term memory (STM)** takes over. STM holds the information for a brief period of time—less than thirty seconds—unless you do something to retain it. In addition, short-term memory can hold only a small number of items, from five to nine pieces of information; this limit is sometimes referred to as 7 ± 2 pieces of information. Let's return to the phone number example. You have just looked up the number of the campus health center. Phone numbers are seven digits so it is within the capacity of STM. You pick up your phone to make the call just as your roommate walks in with a brief question. You answer her question, and begin to dial the health center. But you can't remember it. Only about a minute has passed, but the number didn't stay in short-term memory long enough for you to use it.

You can do two things to increase the amount of time that information stays in STM. You can rehearse the information by saying it several times or writing it down, or you can "chunk" the information to reduce the number of pieces you have to remember. When you **chunk** information, you group it together so that you are learning fewer pieces of information. For example, grouping the numbers in a phone number into two groups—531-2958 rather than thinking of it as seven separate numbers—5-3-1-2-9-5-8 makes it easier to remember and helps hold the information in STM. Likewise, it is easier to remember your Social Security number in three chunks—000-00-0000—rather than as nine separate pieces of information.

TIMELY TIPS

The Importance of STM

Although most students rarely think about how memory influences their learning, it is a crucial part of being able to retain information over time, something that you must be able to do if you are going to be an effective learner. It is interesting to think about the different parts of memory and what would happen if one of the parts failed to function properly, or not at all. That was just the premise of the movie *Memento*. In this film, the main character loses his short-term memory as a result of a head wound. In order to remember things and to track down the individual who raped and killed his wife, he tattooed himself and took photographs as ways of recording what he had learned. Had he not done this, every minute of his life and all information that he "knew" would have been forgotten. Although this is certainly an extreme case, it drives home just how crucial STM is to learning and remembering.

But what if you need to remember the information longer than a minute? Then your **long-term memory (LTM)** takes over. LTM has an unlimited capacity; it never gets full, which is why you can remember things that happened when you were a small child. In fact, older people can often remember things that happened decades ago but have difficulty remembering things that happened last week because the older the memory, the more firmly it is fixed in LTM. In order to get information into LTM (like information that you study for an exam) you have to rehearse. Just as rehearsal will help you hold information in STM, it also helps you put information into LTM so you can remember it for an indefinite period of time. Therefore, if you write it, repeat it several times, listen to it over and over again, and/or talk it through with someone, you will be able to remember it later. (You'll learn more about rehearsal in Chapter 12.) According to the parts theory, the more and different ways you rehearse influence how much information you can remember and for how long.

Some things seem to get into LTM without rehearsal. For example, years from now when you are sitting around with friends, the September 11, 2001, date might come up. We can guarantee you that you will remember where you were and what you were doing when you heard that two airplanes had crashed into the World Trade Center in New York City. Tragic or personally traumatic events somehow are easily etched into our long-term memories without effort.

Think for a minute about how this theory of memory applies when you are taking a test. For example, throughout a multiple-choice exam, your sensory store must filter out distractions, such as the hum of the air conditioner, the noise from the hallway, or the person behind you with a persistent cough. Your STM must hold each question while you think about the correct answer. Finally, you must retrieve the information you need from your LTM in order to answer the question.

The Levels of Processing Theory

Not all psychologists agree that the parts theory explains how memory works because they do not believe that there are separate systems in the brain. Another plausible explanation is what is called the *levels of processing theory*. Scientists who purport this theory believe that the degree to which you can remember and retrieve information depends on the level or depth to which you have processed the information: Material that is processed at a shallow level cannot be remembered very well or for very long, but information that is processed at a deep level is remembered considerably better.

According to the levels of processing theory, it's not important to process everything at a deep level. In fact, if we did that we often would be wasting our time. For example, if you simply want to remember the phone number long enough to call the health center to get an appointment, repeating the number several times or writing it down in an attempt to process it deeply would be a waste of time. You would still need to rehearse the information, but for just long enough to make the call. This type of rehearsal is called **maintenance rehearsal**—engaging in just enough rehearsal to process the information shallowly so that you can use it for a brief period of time and then forget it. This is not the kind of rehearsal you would want to use when studying for an exam.

On the other hand, if it was important for you to remember that telephone number for a long period of time so that you could retrieve it quickly a few days later, you would need to engage in **elaborative rehearsal**—making the information meaningful and rehearsing to the point where the information is at your fingertips. For example, you might note that the last four digits are the same as your grandmother's address. Usually, when you use elaborative rehearsal, you are engaging in deep processing because you want to use or retrieve the information easily at some time in the future. If you were studying for an essay exam in history, for example, it would be important for you to use elaborative rehearsal in order to have access to the information at test time. Elaborative rehearsal includes writing the information in an organized way, repeating the material, or personalizing it in some way to make it easier to remember.

Stretching Your Memory

Although you will have to do more than memorize in most of your college classes, we are not suggesting that the role memorization plays is trivial. In just about every course you take, you will have to do some memorization of information. When you are trying to memorize, there are ways to stretch your memory to make it easier to learn and retrieve material. **Mnemonic devices** help you stretch your memory, and you most likely already use them, but may not be aware of their name.

In general, mnemonics encourage the personalization of information so that you have easy access to it at some future date. Mnemonics are good for learning lists of items or for learning sequences of events or processes. They can be visual to help you create images or they can be a string of letters or a nonsense sentence—anything that enables you to remember information better. Even if you were unfamiliar with the term mnemonics, you have probably used them without knowing it. For example, you may have learned the rhyme "use i before e except after c, or in words sounding like a, as in neighbor and weigh." This mnemonic is known by almost every elementary school child.

GET GOING

Who's Who?

In the past few weeks you have probably met quite a few new people. Have you found that you just can't remember all of their names? To remember names, it is important to engage in memory techniques. At the very least, you must be motivated and make a concerted effort to remember by saying the person's names several times to yourself. But you can also use mnemonics to help. When you meet someone, repeat the name and form a mental image (Amy—Amy has red hair—I picture a fire on Amy's head), or use an association (Holly—just like the holly at Christmas time). It might also help to use the method of loci by recalling an object in the place where you have met this new person and associating the name with the object (Mark—dartboard). Try it yourself. As odd as it may sound, it really works.

Try out the following techniques to stretch your memory.

- **Acronyms.** You can use mnemonics to learn a list by creating an acronym. This means taking the first letter of each item you are trying to memorize and making them spell something. Your mnemonic device doesn't have to make sense to anyone but you. In fact, the more outrageous the memory device, the easier it generally is to remember. For example, if you needed to remember the parts of the forebrain, you might use this mnemonic: 4brain=TLC. This mnemonic works since you are probably already familiar with the letters TLC being used together, as in *tender loving care*. In this case, TLC stands for *Thalamus, Limbic* (system), and *Cerebral* (cortex). You could then create other mnemonics that would help you remember the parts of the midbrain and the hindbrain or the functions each of these portions serves.

- **Imagery.** Forming images is another powerful way to help you remember when you review. Like other mnemonics, images can be very personal and don't have to make sense to anyone except the person forming the images. Images work best when the information you are trying to learn is concrete rather than abstract. In other words, it is difficult to make images for concepts such as courage, democracy, or freedom, and it is much easier to make images for ideas such as cell division, presidential elections, or chamber music. Images work well because they give you both verbal and visual labels for things. A simple example may help you understand this idea. The three letters *d-o-g* together form a very familiar word—dog. Few people would have trouble understanding this word when they saw it in print. But what would happen if you asked each person who read that word to tell you his or her image of a dog? Would everyone describe *dog* in the same way? Of course not. Your image of a dog would be based on some experience you have, whether it's a dog you currently own or one that bit you when you were a child.

- **Method of Loci.** In the method of loci technique, you image a place that is familiar to you such as your living room, the street where you live, or your residence hall. Then you walk down this path through your memory. As you proceed, you attach a piece of information you have to learn to different places and objects to help you remember it. Remember the path markers can be as strange as you want (and the stranger the better) because that will make it easier for you to visualize. One of the authors uses a simplified version of the method of loci to remember who attended certain meetings. She visualizes the room and the table where the meeting was held, starts at one end and mentally walks a path around the table, visualizing where each person was seated.

We realize that some of these techniques may sound strange, but we guarantee that they help stretch your memory under the right circumstances. And they can be fun to create, which also helps you remember information.

The Role of Learning Styles

When students talk to us about their difficulty remembering information, they often mention learning styles as a reason why memory sometimes breaks down. However, when we use the term learning styles, we are referring to how students learn best. Researchers who study this issue suggest that there are three main kinds of learners:

- **Visual learners,** or those who learn best by watching or seeing. Visual learners like to be shown how to do things and often learn best through diagrams or by using imagery. If you are a visual learner, if someone asks you how to spell a word, you probably have to write it down yourself first, rather that simply trying to spell the word in your head or out loud.

- **Auditory learners,** or those who learn best by listening or speaking. Auditory learners can learn easily through listening to lectures or by talking information over with a peer. If you are an auditory learner, you probably rarely miss a class lecture and you may participate in study groups for many of your courses. You may rehearse information by saying it over, either to yourself or out loud.

- **Kinesthetic learners (also called tactile learners),** or those who learn best by touching or movement. Kinesthetic learners generally learn best through writing or even typing things out. If you are a kinesthetic learner, you may rehearse information by writing it several times. You also may enjoy lab courses where there is a hands-on approach to learning.

Sometimes in study skills classes, instructors will have students take a learning styles inventory to find out how they learn "best." We believe these tests oversimplify

NETWORKING

Learning Styles Inventories on the Web

The Internet is loaded with learning styles assessments. You can find questionnaires that assess learning styles the way we have mentioned above (visual, auditory, kinesthetic), you can find out about multiple intelligences, and you can take personality inventories designed to help you figure out how you learn best. You can even find out about the learning style of your dog. If you have never taken a learning styles assessment, you might want to. But remember to take the results with a grain of salt—don't try to base your entire approach to studying in college on your score.

the complex task of college learning. These tests also often pigeonhole students into one of the three categories and then give them suggestions for learning and studying based only on that particular style. Students can feel trapped when their preferred mode cannot be used in a particular course. For example, it is hard to be kinesthetic in a philosophy course. Additionally, even in this day of technology, the fact remains that most colleges use the traditional classroom structure where students must read texts, listen to lectures, take notes, and take exams. Therefore, you need to tap as many of these learning styles as possible if you are to be successful in college. That is why we suggest that rather than relying on one particular learning style, which may actually impede your learning, you use strategies that incorporate them all. We call this learning through your senses.

Using Your Senses to Learn

Many first-year students are "one-trick ponies." That is, they prepare the same way for all of their classes, regardless of the type of test they'll have. They study biology the same way they study history. However, in college, it is important to use a variety of strategies and all of your senses to learn. In history, for example, you would want to read your text, listen actively to the lectures, and take a good set of notes. In that way, you would be using your senses to begin to get the information into your memory. You have a record of the important information to study from and you are actively engaged. As test time approaches, you might study with a group of other students, make time lines as a way of outlining major historical events, and predict and answer essay questions. You would be listening, reading, discussing, and writing as a way of engaging all of your senses. Contrast that approach with simply attending all the lectures. Which student do you think would remember more at test time?

Although we encourage you to use all of your senses to learn, we also realize that many students prefer one mode of learning over another. That's fine. We always encourage students to go with their strengths at the same time realizing that they can use strategies and approaches that are related to their weaker mode. In fact, most students have to approach learning in college by

Studying Smarter

Computers have become a necessity on college campuses, a "luxury" that no student can do without. In fact, many colleges now require freshmen to purchase or lease a computer before they begin their first semester. Although many students come to campus computer savvy, few actually use their computers as part of the learning and studying process. Try to think about ways the computer can make you a more efficient learner. Learn how to use the online library. Take your laptop to class to take and then reorganize your notes. Create diagrams and flowcharts for scientific material and summarize key points. These are just a few ways to use your computer to help you learn.

using a multiple sense approach. For example, in the sciences, there are generally diagrams to learn and understand. You can't ignore that task just because you aren't a visual leaner. Likewise, just because you learn best visually, you still must attend and listen actively to lectures.

In Chapter 12, we will present a variety of strategies that will assist you in learning and remembering information. We have divided these strategies according to the three major types of learners:

- **Visual learners** learn best by seeing information. When they read their texts, they often visualize what the page looks like. They like to create diagrams, flowcharts, concept maps, or concept cards. They also tend to use imagery to remember information.

- **Auditory learners** learn best from listening or hearing information. They may be able to actively listen to lectures, but they may take horrible notes. They like to study with others so they can hear what others say. They also like to say information out loud.

- **Kinesthetic learners** learn best by doing. They learn best through writing and may write information in an organized way as a method of rehearsal. They like to be shown how to do things rather than having to figure it out through reading or listening.

☐ REAL COLLEGE
Leo's Learning (Style)

DIRECTIONS: Read the following "Real College" scenario and respond to the question based on what you learned in this chapter.

Leo knows he is a kinesthetic learner. He loves to work on cars and learned everything he knows by having hands-on experience at his uncle's body shop. Now that he is in college, he finds that he is having a lot of trouble remembering the material in his classes. The professors talk so fast, and he has never been a good note taker. Although he is not sure how this would work in some of his classes, he wishes there were more opportunities to try out some of the things his professors were presenting—to use his kinesthetic abilities.

To try to remember what was discussed in class, Leo tries to memorize all of the key terms. He writes the information on cards and repeats it over and over again until he thinks he has it down cold. However, sometimes he finds that he can't remember even the simplest definitions on exams. Although Leo finds this really disturbing, he chalks it up to a bad memory.

Using what you have learned about how memory works, how to stretch your memory, and using your senses to learn, how would you suggest Leo modify his approach to maximize his learning?

☐ THINKING CRITICALLY
Something to Think About and Discuss

- Which one of the theories of memory makes more sense to you, the parts theory or the levels of processing theory? Why does one make more sense than the other?

- Think about an event that became part of your long-term memory with little or no effort. Why do you think this happened? Why are some events more memorable than others?

- Why do you think it is often difficult to get course information into long-term memory? What are some steps you could take to help the process along?

☐ ADD TO YOUR PORTFOLIO

1. Think about yourself as a learner and assess the learning style that seems most like you. You can either take one of the online assessments, or better yet, assess your own learning style by writing down how you think you learn. Summarize what you learn about yourself.

2. Try some of the mnemonic methods for stretching your memory the next time you prepare for an exam. Write down at least one mnemonic per method. Evaluate the effectiveness of each method. What worked and what did not work for you?

CHAPTER 4

INTERACTING WITH YOUR PROFESSORS

Read this chapter to answer the following questions:

- How are professors ranked?
- How can you make a positive impression on your professors?
- How can you approach a professor to ask for help?

SELF-ASSESSMENT

DIRECTIONS: On a scale of 1 to 5, with 1 being "extremely uncomfortable" and 5 being "extremely comfortable," respond to each of the statements below. This should give you a good idea of how comfortable you will be interacting with your professors.

	Extremely uncomfortable ←→ Extremely comfortable				
How comfortable do you feel:					
1. Asking a question during class about something you don't understand?	1	2	3	4	5
2. Approaching your professor to make an appointment to see her?	1	2	3	4	5
3. Meeting with your professor to discuss a grade you made on an assignment?	1	2	3	4	5
4. Questioning an answer to an item on a multiple choice test?	1	2	3	4	5
5. Participating in class discussions?	1	2	3	4	5
6. Interacting with your professor in a social situation?	1	2	3	4	5

Chances are you stated that you would feel uncomfortable in some of these situations. Read on to learn new strategies for interacting with your professors.

Studying Smarter
See your professors during their office hours. Making personal contact is especially important for courses in which you are having problems or in courses that require writing.

College can be intimidating at times. Sometimes it's easy to find yourself in situations where you want to initiate conversations with classmates or professors but you simply can't muster the nerve to follow through. This uncomfortable feeling can be especially painful if you are very shy or feel like the new kid on the block. One situation that seems to make many college students uneasy, particularly first-year students, is approaching professors. Whether it's to ask for assistance, to clarify a reading assignment, or to discuss a grade on a paper or an exam, talking with your professor doesn't have to be so threatening. Just try to keep in mind that professors are people, too.

What Is a Professor?

Take a minute to consider the characteristics that you believe define a professor. Did you think about words or phrases such as smart, well educated, reads a lot,

well informed? When college students are asked to complete this task, they generally write down descriptors that have to do more with the education a professor has
rather than terms that focus on other traits. For example, when we carry out this
activity with our students at the beginning of the term, we rarely get comments
such as fair-minded, cares about students, helpful, or energetic, nor do we get comments such as mean, unapproachable, distant, or unfair. The point that we want
to make here is that most students seem to lump all professors in the same bag:
professors are smart, they have a considerable amount of education, and they are
the source of knowledge in the classroom.

Some research suggests that students enter college at various stages of knowing
and reasoning. These students interact with and respond to their professors in very
different ways (Baxter-Magolda 1991).* Professor Baxter-Magolda suggests that
there are four different "ways of knowing": absolute, transitional, independent, and
contextual.

- **Absolute knowers** tend not to question what their professor says and believe
  that the professor is the authority. They believe that it is the job of professors
  to communicate knowledge to students.

- **Transitional knowers** realize that there can be several different sides to a
  story and that the role of the professor is to guide students. Professors are still
  seen as authority figures whose opinions supercede those of classmates. They
  may argue with their classmates, but rarely with their professors.

- **Independent knowers** believe that knowledge is open to a variety of inter-
  pretations and believe that the professor should promote the sharing of
  opinions and should allow students to define learning goals. Independent
  knowers like to discuss issues with their professors, not just look to them
  for answers.

- **Contextual knowers** believe professors should promote the application of
  knowledge in a specific context and that students and professors should critique each other. Contextual knowers believe that knowledge is a shared experience and that they are more or less on equal footing with the professor.

This research is important because it indicates that the way students view the
professor's role in the classroom is based on their own stage on the knowing continuum. Interesting, and perhaps not very surprising, is that most first-year students are primarily absolute knowers; as students progress through college they
move more toward being independent and contextual knowers. It is also important because absolute knowers interact differently with their professors than contextual learners.

*Baxter-Magolda, M. B. (1992). *Knowing and reasoning in college*. San Francisco, CA: Jossey-Bass.

SUCCESS AT A GLANCE

Rankings of College Professors

	Degree Held	Years in Rank
Assistant Professor	Masters or doctorate	4–7
Associate Professor	Masters or doctorate	5–7
Full Professor	Masters or doctorate	Until retirement

For example, some students are unsettled by talking with professors because they believe that the professor is the one who determines their grade. These students fail to acknowledge that grades are earned, not given, and therefore they see the professor as the power person in the classroom. Because they view the professor as having all of the control, they see little value in talking to professors. What they don't realize is that knowing how to interact in a positive way with their professor can go a long way in helping students *earn* a better grade. Notice that we didn't say that just because the professor knows who you are and gets the impression you are trying he will *give* you a better grade. We know of no professor who awards a grade just because a student has gotten to know him. But knowing how to talk with your professor can go a long way in making a positive impression and in helping you feel more relaxed with that professor and other professors in the future.

Most professors have what are called advanced degrees. The degree required generally depends on the type of post-secondary institution in which an individual teaches. For example, a community college may require teachers to have a minimum of a master's degree, while a four-year college or university would expect a doctoral degree. It is becoming more and more common for colleges to prefer or require the professors they hire to have a terminal degree—a doctor of philosophy, or Ph.D. for short. A person can have a doctor of philosophy in botany, English literature, history, education, or just about any other discipline you can think of. Usually, it takes an individual three or more years after he or she has completed a master's degree to earn a doctorate.

TIMELY TIPS

What's in a Name?

Many students have problems knowing just what to call their professors. Do you call her Professor Jones, Dr. Jones, or Ms. Jones? We think you are always safe in referring to your professor as Professor Whomever until she makes it clear what she wants to be called. It's interesting to note, however, that students are more apt to refer to their male professors as Professor or Dr. and their female professors as Ms. or Mrs. A word to the wise: Be particularly careful about using the proper title.

A professor who has a brand-new Ph.D. under her belt usually will be hired at the **assistant professor** level. Each new assistant professor receives guidelines from her institution that outline what she must do in order to get promoted to the next level, which is **associate professor.** Depending on the type of post-secondary institution, the criteria for promotion may be weighted heavily on the professor's ability to teach, but it might also be on the research she publishes, the committees she serves on, and the service projects in which she participates. Often, faculty must be evaluated as having superior accomplishments in two of these areas—teaching, research, and service—in order to get promoted. It takes between four to seven years to reach the associate professor level.

The next rank, **full professor,** is reserved for those who are able to sustain exemplary teaching, research, and/or service records for another several years, since college teachers usually must hold the rank of associate professor at least five years before being promoted to full professor. Full professors generally have high status because they have outstanding track records.

The ranking system of professors is quite complex and unlike that of any other profession. One of the more interesting aspects of the promotion system that college faculty go through is that at every level they are judged by their peers. That is, a committee of faculty who already have been promoted to the associate professor level examine the credentials of those who are trying to advance to that level. Those of us who are part of this unique system often wonder how and why it has become so complicated.

We believe that students should be somewhat familiar with this ranking system so that they can better appreciate how much work their college professors must invest in order to be promoted. Some college students believe that all professors have to do is to teach for a few hours and then sit in their offices and wait for students to come and ask them questions. Nothing could be further from the truth. Certainly, most professors enjoy interacting with students and teaching, but the majority have other expectations and responsibilities that extend beyond the classroom. Even when professors are at colleges where they are not expected to conduct research, publish in professional journals, or write books, they usually have a heavy teaching load, serve on numerous committees, and are expected to stay abreast of developments in their discipline. College professors tend to be busy people.

Some General Tips About Interacting with Professors

The saying "the first impression is a lasting one" holds true when interacting with professors. Recall the first time you met someone with whom you eventually became friends. What was your first impression? Chances are that you liked that person right from the beginning. You didn't become best friends overnight, but there was something about the person that made a good impression on you and made you want to get to know him better. Because you only get one chance at a first impression, it's important to make a good one right from day one. How can you do that? Here are some general tips to help you out.

- **Sit Up Front in Class.** When you are up front, you are more likely to stay alert and focused on the lecture, especially if you are in a class with many other students. If you can't get a seat in the front, at least try to sit in the professor's line of vision. Professors notice who is out there and who is paying attention—even in large lecture classes.

- **Ask Questions.** Some professors begin or end each class with a question and answer period. Others will tell students to raise their hands at any time during the lecture if they have a question. And more and more professors are encouraging students to ask questions over e-mail. When you ask *well thought-out questions*, you make a good impression because professors sense that you are interested and that you are keeping up with the course material.

- **Ask for Help Sooner Rather than Later.** Waiting until the day before the test, or worse yet, five minutes before the test, to ask a question about course material that was presented a week earlier makes a terrible impression. As soon as you realize that you are having trouble, make an appointment to see your professor, a tutor, or some other person designated to provide assistance.

- **Read the Syllabus.** The syllabus contains a wealth of information and should always be your first source when you have questions about grading, due dates, course topics, or expectations. If, for example, your professor hasn't discussed how your course grade is determined, before you ask him to explain it, check your syllabus first. If the information is not on there and he hasn't explained it in class, then by all means ask.

- **Know and Follow the Class Rules.** Most professors have pet peeves about something. For us, it is students who continually come to class late. Even though we have our attendance policy in the syllabus and clearly state that we dislike it when students are tardy, we always have someone who just can't seem to get to class on time. It's important for students to know the rules that are in place (i.e., what happens if you miss a test) and to follow them. Don't be the student in the class who the professor uses as an example of inappropriate behavior.

- **Talk with Your Professors Via E-mail.** As we briefly mentioned above, most professors encourage students to communicate with them through e-mail. In fact, some professors require students to interact with them using e-mail at several points over the term as part of their course grade. In addition, many professors have Web pages where you can view the syllabus, download class notes, and obtain additional information about both the course and the professor.

NETWORKING

Locating Your Professor's Web Page

As a way of learning a little more about one of your professors, check to see if he or she has a Web page. You can begin by looking at the professor's departmental Web page. For example, if you want to see if your botany professor has a Web page, first find the Web page for the botany department. Department Web pages generally list each faculty member with links to their individual Web pages. At smaller colleges, which may not be large enough to have a botany department, look for the science department or perhaps the life sciences department instead. Once you find the Web page for your professor, you may find out about her research interests, where her degree is from, and even about her hobbies or family life. After you have checked it out, consider sending your professor an e-mail if you have any questions about the syllabus or course.

Talking with Your Professors

Like it or not, at some time in your college career, you will probably have to interact with one of your professors. Of course, not all professors are easy to talk with and some can make you more ill at ease than others, but if you can answer a few questions and use some common sense, you should be able to get through the situation. It can even be a positive experience if you follow a few simple guidelines.

Question 1: Why Are You Going to See Your Professor?

This question should be an easy one to answer. Do you need clarification about a project that is due? Are you having trouble understanding how to do the assigned chemistry problems? Do you want to explain a specific learning disability that you have? Are you trying to get clarification on why you received a low grade on your essay test? Did your professor request a conference with you? Are you going to see your professor just to get to know him a little better as did the student we mentioned in Chapter 1? Whatever your reason for seeing your professor, the answer to this question should be very evident. Begin your conversation with something such as, "Good morning Professor Carter. I am here to see you this morning because . . ." Beginning on this note lets your professor know why you are coming to see him. We realize that this advice is basic and that you might be asking yourself, "Why would anyone go to see a professor without having a clear purpose in mind?" but you would be surprised at the number of students who have sat in our offices without a clear notion of why they were there.

Question 2: What Are the Logistics of This Meeting?

Before you go to see your professor, it is a good idea to approach her either before or after class to set up a convenient meeting time. Some professors list office hours on their syllabi and announce that you can drop by during those hours without an appointment. In our opinion, however, it never hurts to check out a time with your professor in any case. When professors post office hours at the beginning of the term, they often don't realize that there will be days and times when conflicting meetings, conferences, or personal obligations make them unavailable during their stated office hours. We know that there is nothing more frustrating than actually going to see a professor during office hours only to find no one there. Thus, it is always appropriate to ask the professor something such as, "I noticed on the syllabus that your office hours on Friday are from 9:00 to 10:30. I just wanted to check with you to be sure that you would be in around 9:30 so that I could ask you a couple of questions."

TIMELY TIPS

Meeting with Your Professor

After making an appointment with your professor, find out where the meeting will take place. We have often assumed that students would know to meet us in our offices, but many mistakenly go to the classroom instead. If you have any questions about where you are supposed to meet your professor, be sure to get clarification. Once you know the building and room number, make certain you know

(continued)

the location. This is especially important on larger campuses where getting across campus for an appointment can take fifteen or twenty minutes, and it might take another ten minutes to find the office once you have found the building. Whatever you do, don't show up late. Showing up late indicates that you don't think your professor's time is worth much, and that's not the impression you want to make.

Question 3: How Do I Talk with My Professor?

Before you go see your professor for the first time, think about the approach you will take and what you will say. Depending on why you are going to see your professor, this can be an easy task or one that is a bit more difficult. In the two examples that follow, John goes to see Professor Thomas knowing full well that writing has always been a problem for him. Harry, however, usually did well in high school English, but he did poorly on his first college composition paper and goes to see Professor Thomas with somewhat of an attitude.

John's Approach   John has made an appointment to see his composition professor, Professor Thomas, because he did not do well on his first paper. Writing has always been difficult for John, but with the help of his past teachers he has managed to do fairly well. Professor Thomas seems like a fair-minded person and he said he was willing to talk with students about their writing problems. During his appointment with Professor Thomas, John acknowledges that he has weaknesses in writing and states that although he feels disappointed about his low evaluation on the first paper, it was pretty accurate. He takes out his paper and begins to ask the professor questions about the comments written on his paper. He takes notes on the suggestions that Professor Thomas gives and asks for clarification if necessary. At the end of the appointment, he thanks Professor Thomas, and tells him that those suggestions should help him do better on the next assignment. John leaves feeling positive about the conference. Professor Thomas has similar feelings and enjoys having students like John in his class. Although John isn't the best writer, he's working hard and taking advantage of the available assistance. Professor Thomas is sure John will improve on the next paper if he follows the suggestions they discussed.

Harry's Approach   Harry also is in Professor Thomas's composition class. Harry made good grades in English in high school but somehow he has forgotten that he actually did very little writing in those English classes. He really doesn't like to write that much, but he always thought he was pretty good at it. So, he was quite surprised and, in fact, downright upset when he got his first paper back with such a low score. "Doesn't Professor Thomas know that I made excellent grades in high school English and that my teachers rarely commented on any problems I might have had writing?

What's up with this guy?" thought Harry. Harry talked with the professor after class and made an appointment to find out if Professor Thomas made a mistake in grading his paper. Harry arrives about ten minutes late for his appointment with the excuse that he had trouble finding the office. He sits down, puts his paper down on Professor Thomas's desk, and says, "So, can you fill me in here? I have never got a grade like this on an English paper! My high school teachers never gave me less than a B and I even worked on the school newspaper for a while." Professor Thomas reads through Harry's paper, pointing out some of the more apparent problems. Harry only tries to justify his writing and seems not to be paying attention to Professor Thomas's suggestions for improvement. Professor Thomas asks Harry if he has any questions. "Not really," mutters Harry as he picks up his paper and leaves.

It's pretty obvious which of these students used the better approach. Even if you feel the same as Harry did–that there must be some mistake because you've received a low grade—Harry didn't get much out of his meeting because of his approach. Although students may have been rewarded for trying hard ever since kindergarten, college professors rarely award students higher grades simply because they are giving it all they've got. Telling the professor that you put in tons of effort does not count in college. It's only the results from that effort that count.

In addition, all things being equal—let's say that John and Harry had similar grades on all of their papers and John's average was a 79.2 and Harry's a 79.3— Dr. Thomas stated on his syllabus that his grading scale was the traditional 90–100 = A, 80–89 = B, and so forth. He also stated that he had the right to raise someone's grade but that a student would never receive a lower grade than he had earned. Therefore, although some might view grading such as this as subjective, because he believed John was open to making changes to his writing, Dr. Thomas ethically could award John a B and Harry a C.

Perhaps the biggest problem students have when they go to talk to their professors about concerns they are having with a course is that they don't go in with specific questions. For example, if you are in a mathematics or chemistry course and you find yourself totally lost, it's often difficult to know the questions to ask. You may sit in class and have no idea what the professor has been talking about. But going in and stating, "I don't understand the material," is only going to get you the response "Okay. So what concepts are unclear?" In order to articulate your questions as clearly as possible and to get the best advice possible, use the following suggestions:

- Go back to your notes or your homework problems and see where your understanding broke down.
- Show the notes or homework to your professor so that she can try to get an idea of the information you have been examining.
- Talk through how you have been thinking about the information. Saying something such as, "I understood everything up to this point, but then when we had to add this step, I became lost. Now I don't even have the slightest idea of how to solve these types of problems. This is what I know . . ."

GET GOING

Faculty Mentors

Research has suggested that students are more motivated in college when they feel connected to their institution. Campuses of all sizes have created a way for faculty members to socialize with their students by forming mentorships. Some campuses even provide small amounts of money for faculty to invite students into their homes for meals or other types of social functions. Students who are mentored by faculty outside the classroom persist at higher rates and tend to develop long-term bonds with their institutions. So, connect with some faculty members. It just might help you find the motivation you need for college success.

If you open your conversation with your professor with a general statement such as, "I don't understand any of this," you're probably going to get a response such as, "Are you reading the text? Are you coming to class? Are you doing all the homework problems? Well, you'll just have to work harder (or more)." None of these suggestions will be very helpful to you. When you can specifically state your problems, your professor will be able to offer more concrete advice.

Interacting with your professor is often not the easiest thing to do, especially if you are frustrated about your performance in the course, if the professor is distant and seems not to want to have to deal with students, or if you believe that you are being treated unfairly. On the other hand, most students find it enjoyable to talk with their professors and find that getting to know them better helps when they need recommendations for jobs, scholarships, or even admission to graduate or professional schools.

☐ REAL COLLEGE
Marsha's Mistake

DIRECTIONS: Read the following "Real College" scenario and respond to the questions based on what you learned in this chapter.

Marsha rolled over, opened her eyes, and saw the bright sun streaming in her window. She jolted straight up like a bolt of lightning. "What time is it? What time is it?" she yelled, jumping out of bed. She looked at her digital clock only to see

12:00 flashing over and over. She knew she was in trouble. She was supposed to be in class for a midterm exam at 8:00 and she knew that it wasn't anywhere near this light when she usually got up. She grabbed her wristwatch off the dresser—it was 9:30. The test was already over. "What am I going to do?" she thought. She liked her professor, Dr. Luther, but she also knew that he was a stickler for rules and that if you missed a test without some sort of major documentation as to why, you couldn't make up the exam.

Marsha's intentions were good. She had been studying for the test for several days, but she still felt that she wasn't ready. So she made the mistake lots of students make—she studied until 3:30 A.M. and set her clock for 5:30 thinking that would give her time to have one more hour to review. She was really tired when she finally went to sleep, but thought her alarm would wake her up. She didn't count on a power failure at 4:30! Now she was in real hot water. Dr. Luther would never let her make up the test with a lame excuse such as "My alarm didn't go off."

She knew she would have to make an appointment to talk with Dr. Luther. But how should she handle this situation?

1. Think about what you would do if you were in Marsha's shoes. Explain how you would handle the problem and why you would handle it that way.

2. Discuss solutions with your classmates. Are some solutions better than others? What are some factors you think Marsha should consider before she goes in to talk with Dr. Luther?

☐ THINKING CRITICALLY
Something to Think About and Discuss

From the information we have presented in this chapter and from your own interactions so far with professors, which of the following do you think are positive ways to interact with a professor and which are negative? Discuss your responses with your classmates.

1. You call two weeks in advance for an appointment to see your professor so you can be sure you have an appointment with him the day after the second exam.

2. You go ask the professor if you missed anything important during the three days in a row you were out sick.

3. You are having a hard time taking notes from your professor so you raise your hand during a lecture and ask her to slow down.

4. You send an e-mail to your professor to try to set up an appointment time.

5. You made an appointment to talk to your professor about a couple of concepts that were giving you trouble. You ask him "Is this important to know for the test?"

☐ ADD TO YOUR PORTFOLIO

Interview a professor. Set up an appointment with one of your current professors and interview him or her. Write up a one- to two-page summary of your discussion for your portfolio. The purpose of this assignment is to help you become more comfortable talking to faculty members. Here are some suggestions to get you started:

1. How did he choose his academic discipline?

2. What motivated her to teach at a college?

3. What other professional experience has he had besides teaching college?

4. How would she describe the ideal student and the ideal professor?

5. What is his philosophy of teaching or preferred teaching style?

6. What does she think all college students should learn about the field in which she teaches?

7. How would he describe the relationship between student and professor?

8. What does his job as a professor entail in addition to teaching?

9. How would she suggest studying for the course?

10. Any other questions you would like to ask (for instance, his hobbies, where he went to school, etc.).

CHAPTER 5

WHAT IS IT I'M SUPPOSED TO DO, ANYHOW?

Read this chapter to answer the following questions:

- What do we mean by task?
- How can you figure out what your professor expects?

SELF-ASSESSMENT

DIRECTIONS: Rate the following tasks. Place an *E* beside the tasks you consider the easiest, an *M* beside the tasks you consider of middle level difficulty, and a *D* beside the tasks you consider the most difficult.

1. _____ Taking a matching exam in history

2. _____ Analyzing a chemical process for a chemistry lab

3. _____ Writing a persuasive essay for English class

4. _____ Evaluating and drawing a conclusion about several articles presenting conflicting accounts of an event for political science

5. _____ Taking a multiple-choice exam over two psychology chapters

6. _____ Taking an exam over the bold-faced terms for biology class

7. _____ Debating a controversial issue in sociology class

8. _____ Giving an informational speech for speech communications class

9. _____ Solving calculus problems on a mathematics exam

How you rated these tasks probably had something to do with your own personal background and interests. For example, if you love mathematics you might have thought solving calculus problems was easy. However, there are some overarching ideas that you will learn about in this chapter that make numbers 1 and 6 the easiest, put numbers 2, 5, 8, and 9 somewhere in the middle, and make numbers 3, 4, and 7 the most difficult tasks.

In Chapter 2, when we introduced the idea that there are four factors that impact learning, we briefly discussed the role that task understanding plays in being an active learner. Because much of your success as a college student rests on your ability to interpret the task, we talk about it here in greater detail.

Studying Smarter
Be sure you understand what your professor expects from you. Ask questions. Knowing the task right from the start enables you to select the appropriate strategies.

There's more to studying and being a successful student than meets the eye and studying hard is not always studying smart. Your ability to understand what your professor wants you to do and the way you are supposed to do it goes a long way in making you a more efficient and effective student. Why? To answer this question, we'll explore two important aspects of task: What do we mean by "task," and how can you figure out what the task is?

What Is a Task?

The task for any course consists of two parts:

1. The type of activity in which you engage.
2. The level of thinking required as you engage in the activity.

NETWORKING

Using the Web to Understand Task

Find the Web page of one of your professors and look for information concerning task. For example, if you have multiple-choice exams, look to see whether your professor has put any example test items on the site. Also check out online information about the course. Sometimes rather than putting material concerning tests and other course requirements on their own personal Web page, professors will have a separate page for each course they teach. These pages can provide a wealth of information to help you better understand the task.

Part One: The Type of Activity

The activity you will be asked to engage in is usually a test, a paper, or a project which your instructor will use to evaluate you. But knowing that you have to take a test is not enough information to be able to carefully select an appropriate approach to studying. You need to know the *type* of test you will take.

- Is it an objective exam, which includes multiple-choice, true/false, or matching items?

- Is it a more subjective exam that requires answering essay, short answer, or identification questions?

- Is it a combination of both types?

Because you should not approach studying for multiple-choice tests in the same way you approach studying for essay tests, it's very important to know right from the beginning the basic type of test you will have. As we will discuss in greater detail later, the kind of reading you do, the way you think about the material, and the strategies you select all have a bearing on the kinds of tasks you are asked to complete in a course.

It is important to reiterate and alert you to the importance of precisely knowing the task by describing a situation that occurred to students enrolled in a large lecture history course. For each test, students were told that they would have "objective items" and two essay questions. On the first four exams, the objective items were always multiple-choice. When it came time for the final exam and the professor told students that they would have a test that was part objective and part essay, they assumed that they would once again have multiple-choice questions. Imagine their surprise when the tests were distributed and the objective items were fill-in-the-blanks. Many students were outraged and went to see the professor when they discovered that they had done poorly on the test. But the professor wouldn't budge. His definition of task for objective items included fill-in-the-blank as well as multiple-choice. The point here is clear: Get as much specific information as possible about the test. Ask the right questions. Just knowing that you will have an objective test is likely to be insufficient information.

If the task in a course consists of papers or projects rather than exams, the same advice holds true. Talk with your professor about specific aspects of the paper, especially if they seem unclear. In political science courses on our campus, for example, students must do a project that consists of several different pieces. First they select a political issue to follow throughout the term. They must subscribe to and read the *New York Times* daily and find a minimum of thirty articles concerning their issue. For each article they must write a brief summary. At the end of the term, they complete two additional tasks. First they write a policy statement and then they write a memo to an influential political figure about this issue. Students who fail to understand how to carry out the numerous pieces involved in this task have severe problems in doing well on a long-term project that is 30 percent of their grade.

Success at a Glance

Thinking About the Task

Type of Task + Level of Thinking = Task Knowledge

• Matching exam	**Memorization**
• Multiple choice	**Analysis**
• Essay/Short answer	**Synthesis**

Part Two: The Level of Thinking

Once you have identified the specific activities your professor expects, you're halfway there. The other part of task identification, and perhaps the more important part, is knowing what level of thinking is required to carry out that task. There are many types of thinking that a professor may want you to engage in.

Have you ever heard of *Bloom's taxonomy?** This classification provides a way to categorize the kinds of questions that students typically encounter in their classes. Knowing the level of questions your professor asks can help you choose appropriate learning and study strategies.

Bloom discusses six levels of questioning:

1. **Knowledge**—This includes knowledge of dates, events, major ideas, and bold-faced terms.

   Question Words: list, define, describe, identify, match, name, what, who, when, where

   Examples: When did the Tonkin Gulf incident occur?

   What does the term IQ stand for?

   Define *reliability*.

2. **Comprehension**—This includes grasping the meaning, explaining or summarizing, grouping, predicting outcomes, or inferring.

   Question Words: summarize, describe, interpret, distinguish, defend, explain, discuss, predict

   Examples: Which of the following is an example of a skill that someone with *componential intelligence* might excel in?

   Summarize the evolution of the Black Power party.

   Explain Gardner's theory of multiple intelligences.

3. **Application**—This level requires the ability to use the material in a new context, to solve problems, or to utilize rules, concepts, or theories.

   Question Words: apply, demonstrate, calculate, illustrate, show, relate, give an example of, solve

   Examples: If a plant with the genotype of BbCcDd was crossed with a plant that was BBCcdd, what are the chances of producing a plant with the genotype of BbCcDd?

   Illustrate how a school system might use Sternberg's Triarchic Theory of Intelligence.

4. **Analysis**—This involves understanding organization of parts, clarifying, concluding, or recognizing hidden meaning.

   Question Words: analyze, explain, compare and contrast, select, arrange, order

---

*Bloom, B. S. (1956). *Taxonomy of educational objectives: The classification of educational goals.* New York; Toronto: Longmans, Green.

Examples: Compare and contrast the characteristics of short-term memory and long-term memory.

Select the most appropriate method for solving this calculus problem.

5. **Synthesis**—This involves creating new ideas, relating knowledge from several sources of information, predicting, and drawing conclusions.

Question Words: combine, create, design, formulate, compose, integrate, rewrite, generalize

Examples: Rewrite the play *The Cherry Orchard* as if it were written by Ibsen.

Design a solution to the current parking problem on campus.

6. **Evaluation**—This relies on the ability to make choices based on evidence, to support stance with reasoning, to recognize subjectivity, and to assess value of theories.

Question Words: support, judge, discriminate, assess, recommend, measure, convince, conclude

Examples: How successful would the proposed federal income tax cut be in controlling inflation as well as decreasing unemployment?

Do you agree with President Johnson's decision to escalate the Vietnamese conflict? Why or why not?

TIMELY TIPS

Tasks After College

There are many tasks that college students have to do in addition to doing well in their courses. For example, to prepare for life after college, many career centers suggest that first-year students do the following three tasks:

1. **Visit the career center.** The staff can help you with choosing a major, planning for the future, exploring job options, and more.

2. **Start a résumé.** Many students struggle with creating a good résumé of their experience. By starting early, you can update it every term and graduate with a great tool for your job search.

3. **Find a summer internship.** These opportunities can be a great way to learn more about your field and in the future can set you apart from other applicants.

Most objective exams will have questions at each of these levels. Many students fail to think about this part of the task and concentrate their studying on the knowledge level, which often results in lower test grades and frustration. Another mistake that students, primarily first-year students, often make is that they believe that objective exams don't involve higher-level thinking. That is, they think that multiple-choice and true/false tests are basically memorization tasks. However, on most objective tests, some of the questions will be factual in nature, some will ask for examples, and some will require you to synthesize and analyze. Most essay questions require the highest level of thinking, but other subjective exams, such as identification items, could ask for just factual information. Remember, unless you know the task and the types of thinking expected, you will have a difficult time selecting the appropriate study strategies. In the next section, we will give you some hints about how to get more information about the task.

How Can You Get Information About the Task?

Now that you understand how important it is to know the task for each of your classes, you might ask the obvious question: How do I carry out the task? Because few professors will state the task precisely and completely, it becomes important for you to be able to piece together bits of information from a variety of sources in order to paint the picture for yourself.

1. **Attend Class Every Day.** The best place to begin, of course, is with what your professor says in class, especially in the early part of the term. Some professors spell out the task very neatly and clearly on the first day when they go over the syllabus. Others will give you a big picture of the task early in the term and then fill in the details as the course moves along. Still others, and perhaps most college professors fall into this category, give you a combination of implicit and explicit cues and expect you to pick up on those cues.

GET GOING

Go to Class

One of our favorite quotes comes from E. Jean Carroll who stated, "If Joan of Arc could turn the tide of an entire war before her eighteenth birthday, you can get out of bed." But we would like to add ". . . and go to class" to this quote. Attending every class is the most important thing you can do to help you not only stay on task, but also to better understand the specific tasks for each course.

2. **Write It Down.** It's just as important to take notes concerning what's expected of you as it is to take notes on the content. Students often think that they will remember how to structure an essay or the types of questions that will be on their exams. However, they discover two or three weeks later that they have only a faint recollection—or worse, no recollection at all—of some important piece of information that the professor had discussed in class. Go to class, listen carefully, and write down what your professor says about the task in your lecture notes.

3. **Consult Your Syllabus.** Read your syllabus carefully at the beginning of the course and then return to it on a regular basis. Look for any statements that tell you about course expectations. Examine your syllabus for the following information:

   - The number of tests you will have or papers you will have to write, and the approximate dates tests will be given or papers will be due.

   - Your professor's office hours and phone number (or e-mail address) so that you know how to make an appointment to talk with her.

   - Your professor's policies on make-up work and the consequences of missing an exam or another deadline.

   - Your professor's attendance policies (if any).

   - Your professor's philosophy on the course. This can give you insight into how your professor will approach the content and can go a long way in helping you define the task.

   - The course objectives. Reading these statements will tell you what the professor hopes you will learn in the course.

   All of these factors either directly or indirectly relate to task. Thus it is important not only to read your syllabus carefully at the beginning of the term, but also to refer to it often as the term progresses.

4. **Look at Old Exams.** Even if you think you have a clear understanding of what the task is, it's always a good idea to look over old exams as a way of confirming course requirements. Many professors routinely make old exams available to students, while others will provide example questions only when asked. Looking at old exams gives you lots of information, especially about the level of thinking required. You want to use these exams as ways of gathering information about the level of thinking, not about the actual content that you should study. Chances are your professor will write the same *types* of questions on future exams but probably will not ask the exact same questions.

Studying Smarter

If you have exhausted all efforts to figure out the task in a course, run, don't walk, to your professor's office, especially if you have already taken one test and performed poorly. Starting a conversation with your professor by explaining what you are doing and asking her for some advice about how to study may give you a lot more information about how she wants you to think about the course information.

5. **Ask Former Students.** Students who have already taken the course will be able to give you details about a course and a professor. But make sure that you ask former students the right questions. For example, asking someone, "Are Professor Smith's tests difficult?" is not the best way to pose the question because what is a difficult test to one person may not be difficult to another. Better questions would be: "What kind of tests does Professor Smith give?" "Can you remember examples of some questions?" "What kinds of structure does he expect for essay questions?" "Does he give you much guidance?" Questions such as these give you answers about the task.

Technology in College Classes

Most of your college professors will incorporate technology (specifically computers and the Internet) into their classes. But expect to find a wide range in the level of integration. Some professors will be from the old school—low-tech holdouts who won't even have an e-mail account. Other professors will use high-tech presentations during class with special effect extravaganzas. Most professors fall somewhere in the middle and use technology where they find it to be most beneficial for explaining course content and supporting classroom instruction. You can expect to see some or all of the following uses of technology as part of the tasks in your college courses:

- **Computerized Class Presentations (such as PowerPoint).** Many professors use computer slides to outline their lectures. They may use overheads of diagrams or show video clips to emphasize points. They may also display Web pages or other Internet sources of information during class.

- **Computerized Notes.** It is becoming more common for professors to put their notes on the Web. Web notes are best used as a supplement or guide for taking your own notes in class (see Chapter 14 for strategies on using Web notes effectively). You may also find yourself in a classroom equipped with computers or computer hookups that allow you to take notes on a laptop. This is a wonderful service and we suggest you take advantage of if it is available on your campus.

- **Computer Modules or CD-ROM Supplements.** Some professors place sample questions or problems on the Web so that students can evaluate their understanding of the course material as they prepare for exams. Other professors, especially in the sciences, provide supplementary material on CD-ROMs. These CDs generally contain information that cannot be depicted in a text format, such as a video of a chemical reaction, but enhances the information discussed in a lecture or in the text.

- **Computerized Course Management Systems (such as Web CT).** Professors using these course management systems find many creative uses for them. They may place their syllabi, quizzes, assignments, and other course information on there. They may also post student grades or have virtual chats with the class. We know a professor who conducts exam reviews online. If your professor uses these systems, plan to visit the site often to keep up with new assignments or important information.

- **Course Exams.** Some courses will require you to take exams on a computer. Many mathematics courses are moving toward computerized exams and many English courses require students to write in-class essays on computers. Taking an exam on a computer is a bit different than the old paper and pencil type. Still, you should not abandon your old-test taking strategies. Continue to read each question carefully and answer the items you know first. However, you should find out whether you can return to a question or if you must answer each item before moving on to the next one. Some students say that having exams on computers takes some getting used to, but once you have some experience, it is just like taking any other test.

- **Readings.** Your professors may assign readings that can be found only online. They may be from Web-based journals, supplied by the campus library's online service, or from any number of other sources. If you find you have trouble reading online, as many people do, we suggest you print it out in advance.

- **E-mail Assignments.** Professors may require you to turn in assignments via e-mail. If it is a short assignment, typing your response straight into the e-mail message is generally acceptable. If, however, you are required to turn in a longer assignment (more than one page), it is best to type it in a word processing program and send it as a file attachment. Be sure to use the file type requested by your professor. If you do not know how to do this, go to the nearest computer lab to get some help.

- **Group Presentations.** At some point in your college career, you will probably find yourself in a course that requires a group presentation that has a technology component. Some professors require a Web-based presentation or a presentation that utilizes several types of media. We suggest that you meet with your group early and often and try out the technology several times before presenting it in class to work out any problems.

- **Discussion Groups and Listservs.** These supports are used to generate discussion outside the class. Some professors require each student to post a certain number of messages each week to ensure that the listserv is used. You can ask questions or see what other people are thinking to gain multiple perspectives on the course information.

You will probably find several other ways that professors incorporate technology into their course tasks as new tools become available.

☐ REAL COLLEGE
Tina's Task

DIRECTIONS: Read the following "Real College" scenario and respond to the questions based on the information you learned in this chapter.

Tina decided that she could no longer put off taking a required history class, even though she "hates history with a passion." It's not that she hasn't done well in history. On the contrary, her grades in high school history classes were quite good. She sees herself as a good memorizer and since her high school history experience involved lots of memorization of names, dates, events, and the like, she tended to make good grades. She just doesn't like history, plain and simple.

As Tina looks over her class schedule for the term, she thinks about skipping the first class or two, because from her perspective, two less history classes to go to would be a good thing. But her roommate, who has already taken the course, advises her to attend every class—even the first one. Tina reluctantly takes her advice and actually finds the professor to be engaging and humorous.

Obviously, in order to earn a good grade in this course, Tina is going to have to figure out what the tasks are. On the first day, the professor said that there would be three essay exams as well as a cumulative final, but he didn't say much else about the tasks. Think about Tina's situation and respond to the following questions:

1. What additional information do you think Tina needs so that she can have a clearer idea of the task?

2. How should she go about gathering the necessary information?

☐ THINKING CRITICALLY
Something to Think About and Discuss

Most college students do not consciously sit down at the beginning of the term and say to themselves, "Gee, before I start doing my reading and studying for this class, I'd better figure out the task!" For students who intuitively understand that it is important to figure out the course demands, it's more of an unconscious effort. Think about yourself as a learner and respond to the following questions:

- Have you taken time this term to figure out the task in each of your classes? If not, how might you begin to gather that information this term and in future terms?

- Have you ever been in a class where you had a very difficult time understanding what the professor's expectations were? How did you handle that situation? What might you do differently now?

- Can you think of any other sources that might be able to give you task information? (We have mentioned your professor, syllabus, copies of old exams, and students who have already taken the course.)

- How might you organize your notes to draw attention to task information?

☐ ADD TO YOUR PORTFOLIO

For each of your classes this term, figure out the tasks. This is not always easy to do. Start by looking at the syllabus, e-mailing the professor, or talking to a TA. Then jot down how you figured out what the professor expects from you. What clues did you receive that helped you figure it out? Finally, think about how you will approach each course based on the task. How should you approach studying for each exam?

SELF MANAGEMENT: YOUR LEARNING CHARACTERISTICS

Part Two discusses how your characteristics as a learner affect your success in college. In Chapter 6, you learn strategies for managing yourself and your time, and learn how to create a schedule so that you can keep track of your college and personal obligations.

Chapter 7 discusses motivation, attitudes, and interests. You learn what motivates people as well as some strategies for maintaining your own motivation for learning. You also learn how your attitude toward college, your instructors, the topic, and toward yourself as a learner affect your learning. We also discuss ways to maintain a positive attitude.

Chapter 8 introduces five components of beliefs that influence learning. These components are discussed and you answer questions that assess your own beliefs about learning.

In Chapter 9, you learn about sources of stress in college and some strategies for reducing your stress levels. You also learn about strategies for coping with specific types of academic stress such as writing, math, and test anxiety.

CHAPTER 6

GETTING ORGANIZED

Managing Yourself and Your Time

Read this chapter to answer the following questions:

- Why do I need to manage my time?
- What is self-management?
- How can I create a schedule I can live with?
- How do I plan time to study for finals?

SELF-ASSESSMENT

DIRECTIONS: On a scale of 1 to 5, with 1 being "not at all effective," 3 being "somewhat effective," and 5 being "very effective," respond to each of the statements below. This evaluation should give you a good idea of your current time-management system.

Not at all ←——→ Very
effective   effective

1. How effective is your current system for managing time?   1   2   3   4   5

2. How effective is your current system for balancing your   1   2   3   4   5
   school, work, and social obligations?

3. How effective is your ability to get things done in an   1   2   3   4   5
   organized way?

4. How effective is your use of short periods of time (such   1   2   3   4   5
   as the time in between classes) to get things done?

If you scored mostly fives, then you are already finding success in your ability to manage yourself and your time. However, if your scores indicate that your current system is less than stellar, read on for some great time-management strategies.

Managing yourself and your time may be one of the most difficult challenges for you as a college student. If you are a returning student who has been in the workforce for a while, or if you are raising a family or holding a full-time job while attending college, you will face new challenges in juggling your many responsibilities. If you are a recent high school graduate, you are probably used to having most of your time managed for you. Your school and parents were responsible for setting a good deal of your daily schedule—you were in classes most of the day and after school you probably had set athletic, club, or family obligations, or perhaps you had a part-time job.

Studying Smarter
Write it down. Make a studying schedule and follow it to help you reach your academic goals.

In college, however, you are in class for fewer hours each day, which leaves you with big blocks of time to manage. The trick is to start out with a plan and not have to scramble to make up for lost time once you are already behind. You want to create a plan that will help you maximize your time so you can get everything done without falling behind.

Managing Yourself

Before you can manage your time effectively, you have to be able to manage yourself. We believe that the key to self-management is being able to organize and keep track of all the things that you have to do. College life is very hectic; you have class assignments, roommates to deal with, and tests to prepare for. If you are a returning student, you may also have a job to help pay your way through college or you may have daily family obligations. However, no matter what your situation, the secret to getting organized is to create a balance among school, home, work, and social life. In the past, you may have been taught about time management with an approach that suggested giving up your social life to focus only on studying. However, we believe that you should be able to take care of your class obligations and still have plenty of time for things you would like to do. We want you to be able to hang out with your friends and spend time with your family, but we also want you to be able to get the work done for your classes so that you can be academically successful and *stay* in college.

In order to create a balance between all the things you have to do and all the things you want to do, consider the following points:

- **Treat College Like a Full-Time Job.** If you are a full-time student, academic work should take up about forty hours each week. So for the next several years, consider college your full-time job. You might be in class only fifteen hours per week, but the other twenty-five hours should be spent studying and preparing for class. If you break it down, it is really not so bad. Each day, you will spend three to four hours in class and four to five hours reading, studying, and preparing for your assignments. The rest of the time is left for other activities or a part-time job. The good news is that unlike a full-time job, in college you have more control over when you want to schedule your classes and your study time. No one says that your studying must take place between 9:00 and 5:00 Monday through Friday—you are free to study whenever you want. In addition, you should think of your forty-hour week as more of a mind-set than as a fixed amount of time. In other words, when you have a full-time job, some weeks may require more than forty hours to get everything accomplished, but other weeks will require less. On the average, though, you should plan on putting in about forty hours.

- **Schedule Your Classes for Your Most Alert Times.** Are you a morning person? A late-afternoon person? An evening person? Are you up with the sun or are you lucky to be awake by noon? If you know you will never make it to an 8:00 A.M. class, don't schedule a class for that time, if possible. Likewise, if you are totally useless in the afternoon, try to schedule your courses before lunchtime. Many students don't consider their class times as an issue to think about when making their course schedule, but because you have the luxury of creating your own schedule, you should try to tailor it to your needs as much as possible. Certainly there will be times when you don't have the ideal schedule, but when it's possible, schedule your classes during the times you are most alert.

- **Go to Class.** Although many professors don't take attendance, most still believe that going to class is a very important part of learning. Students who skip a lot of classes miss out on the important information that they can only get in class. For example, some professors consider their syllabus a work in progress and modify it throughout the term. Suppose a professor assigned a paper that was mentioned only in class but was not on the syllabus. You would be responsible for turning in the paper, but the only way you would know it was assigned would be if you attended class. Also, as an added bonus, only by going to class each day will you know what the professor emphasized, which will help you when you study. So do yourself a favor and *go to class* every day.

NETWORKING

Using Notes from the Web

Some students believe that they can skip class because their professor puts her class notes on the Web. They think that they will be able to simply download the notes rather than take their own. Be advised that a professor's notes are generally meant to supplement those you take yourself. Sometimes the professor's notes are in skeletal form; you are expected to fill in the gaps during the lecture. So while downloading your professor's notes may be a good idea to supplement your own notes, they do not take the place of going to class and taking your own.

- **Don't Procrastinate.** Procrastination is intentionally and continually putting off work that needs to be done. This problem may actually be the toughest part of self-management for some students. Because you are in control of your own time, it is tempting to put off work until later. It's just human nature. But you quickly can become overwhelmed by all you need to do when you continually neglect your work. Almost everyone has a friend who has procrastinated until the last minute and must "read" an entire novel and write a five-page English paper all in one night. For some students, procrastination tends to become a bad habit and a way of life. Once you start procrastinating, it is difficult to get back on track. However, the strategies in the next section should help you avoid procrastination by helping you determine what you need to do each day.

TIMELY TIPS

Financial Management

Many campuses offer financial management workshops for students who are often bombarded with offers for credit cards the first month they hit college. We believe beginning to learn the complexity of money management is another way to learn to self-manage. Check out what your college offers before you break in that new credit card.

Managing Your Time

Effective time-management strategies can help you organize your responsibilities and reach your goals. To manage your time effectively you will need to determine three important pieces of information:

1. **What Do You Need to Accomplish?** Consider the classes you must attend each week, your work schedule, social commitments, class assignments, and so forth. One of the hardest problems to figure out is how much time an assignment will take. For example, when writing a paper you have to know if it will take you one hour or considerably longer to find what you need in the library or on the Web. Will you be able to write your paper in two days or will you need a full week? Some of the ability to know how long things will take comes with experience, but the following general rule may help you plan your time:

   Things always take longer than you think they will.

   Given this basic rule, try to plan more time than you think you will need. When you rush to get an assignment completed, you probably feel frustrated or angry when things take longer than planned. You may even give up without completing the assignment. So plan for things to take longer to avoid this problem.

2. **What Things Do You Currently Do That Waste Your Time?** Before you can figure out how to spend your time effectively, you need to find out if and how you are wasting time. To do this, think about how you currently spend your days. Are there some things you do that simply waste large amounts of time? For example, are you playing video games, watching TV, surfing the Net, napping, or hanging out with friends for hours on end? Everyone needs some unstructured time each day to simply do things they want to do. But if you find that your unstructured time bleeds over into your forty hours of being a student, you'll want to restructure your days.

3. **How Can I Keep Track of What I Need to Do?** Most people who manage their time successfully say that they can't live without their daily planner, calendar, or palm pilot. It helps them keep track of appointments, assignments, social commitments, and even important phone numbers. If you don't already use tools to help you schedule your time, invest in one today. Take your planner or pilot with you to class and be sure to mark down your assignments. But getting things down is only half the battle—you have to make a habit of checking your schedule every day to see what you need to do. To be really effective, schedule things that you must do first, things such as class time, family obligations, or meetings you must attend. Then schedule your study time. Finally, fill in unscheduled times with more flexible obligations such as doing laundry or going shopping. Because you have so many things to juggle in college, sometimes it is hard to find the time to study if you don't specifically add it to your schedule. Planning study sessions along with the rest of your responsibilities helps you stay on top of your school responsibilities.

Studying Smarter

If you tend to nap for long periods of time as a form of procrastination, try the twenty-minute power nap instead. Before you lie down to take your nap, set your alarm clock to go off in twenty minutes. Get up as soon as it goes off and get on with your day. If you find that you have not fallen asleep after twenty minutes, get up anyway. You probably didn't need a nap and will feel better just from lying down. We guarantee that you will feel refreshed and ready to tackle your next task.

Success at a Glance

Characteristics of Good and Poor Time Managers

Good Time Managers	Poor Time Managers
Study when they are most alert	Study whenever the mood strikes (even when they are dead tired)
Spend some time every day on each course	Study the night before each exam
Create a schedule that is specific	Do not schedule study times or do so only in a very general way

(continued)

Good Time Managers	Poor Time Managers
Make a reading schedule for each class	Read the night before the exam
Prioritize their work	Do the things they like to do first and put the rest off
Make "to do" lists to stay organized	Often find that they don't have assignments completed because they did not write them down
Use the time in between to get work done	Don't use small pockets of class time

Creating a Schedule You Can Live With

Creating a schedule that works is a challenge. Many students start out with good intentions, but ultimately end up with an unworkable schedule for a number of reasons. Some students create a schedule that is too rigid, so they don't have the flexibility they need. Others create a schedule that is not detailed enough to be of any use. Still others create a good schedule, but don't consult it regularly, so they forget what they need to do. In order to avoid falling into one of the time-management pitfalls, consider the tips in the "Success at a Glance" box above as you create you own schedule.

Timely Tips for Following Your Schedule

- **Plan to Study When You are Most Alert.** If you find that you are tired or you can't concentrate when you study, you probably are not studying at your most alert time. Try to find some blocks of time that are naturally best for you. Some students study best at night, others study best first thing in the morning. Test several times of the day to find out when you are the most ready to study. Experiment with times that you might not initially think are your best times of day—you just may surprise yourself and be a morning or night person after all.

- **Spend Some Time Every Day on Each Course You are Taking.** Even when you don't have an assignment due, plan some time each day to read the text, review your notes, and prepare for the next class. If you are taking classes that require problem solving such as math or chemistry, it is a good idea to work some problems each night. If you are taking a language class, plan to review new vocabulary, work on verb conjugation, or review grammar rules every day. By spending some time every day you won't have to cram for exams because you will always be caught up.

- **Be Specific.** The more specific you can be when planning your study schedule the better because you will know exactly what you need to do each time you study. When you create your schedule, don't just write down "study." Instead, write "Read psychology text pgs. 219–230." By creating a schedule that lists each specific task, you are more likely to remember to get everything done.

- **Make a Reading Schedule for Each Class.** One of the simplest, yet most effective, ways to manage your time and to stay on top of your reading assignments is to make a reading schedule for each class. To make a reading schedule simply add up the number of pages you need to read in the next week (some students prefer to add the pages in between each exam rather than weekly) and divide that number by five (or six or seven if you will read during the weekend). For example, Robert has the following reading assignments this week:

History	Read Chapters 3–4, 65 pages
Statistics	Read Chapter 5, 27 pages
	Complete 15 practice problems
Music	Read Chapters 4–5, 39 pages
Literature	Read 6 chapters of novel, 90 pages
Biology	Read Chapter 8, 29 pages

This equals 250 pages of text reading, which is about average, according to several college surveys. Thinking about reading 250 pages can be overwhelming, but when Robert divides the reading over five days he sees that he has only thirteen pages of history, six pages of statistics (and three practice problems), eight pages of music, eighteen pages of literature, and six pages of biology to read each day. And that sounds a lot more manageable. If he reads over six or seven days, his daily load is cut even more. To create you own reading schedule, survey your reading assignments (usually found on your syllabus) and divide up the reading in a way that makes sense. Use section breaks or headings to help you determine how to divide the readings so that you are not stopping in the middle of a concept.

- **Prioritize.** When you make your schedule, it is helpful to prioritize what you have to do. You might want to label your assignments as "high," "medium," or "low" priority. For example, reading your biology text before the lab might be a high priority, but starting on your history research paper that is due in three weeks might be lower. In general, start with high-priority tasks first so that you are sure to get them done. But don't ignore the medium and low priorities. That history research paper may be low priority now, but if nothing gets done in the next three weeks it will become high priority fast.

- **Make "To Do" Lists.** Sometimes when students begin to study they start to think about all the other things they need to do—call home, get a haircut, cancel a dental appointment. All of these thoughts are very distracting. To keep yourself on track and to avoid procrastination, keep a "to do" list next to you when you study. Write down all the things you think of, including course work, household chores (such as laundry), phone calls, e-mails to answer, and so forth. Cross items off as you complete them. Your to do list might look something like this:

Date: Oct. 2	What Do I Need to Do?	Priority (high, medium, low)
1.	Finish revising English paper	High
2.	Do laundry	High
3.	Read math pp. 81–97 and do the problems	Medium
4.	Call home	Medium
5.	Plan spring break trip	Low
6.	Think about topic for final history paper	Low

If you don't want to specify priorities as high, medium, or low, simply try to put your to do list in order, with the highest priority items at the top and the lowest ones at the bottom.

- **Set Aside One Hour a Week to Plan.** Our most successful students tell us that it takes them about one hour to really plan out what they hope to accomplish in the next week. We suggest taking some time on Sunday nights to review all of your syllabi as you make your reading schedule and to do lists for the coming week.

- **Borrow Time—Don't Steal It.** If you decide to go out for a pizza instead of spending an hour reading your psychology chapter—great. But remember that it's important to just borrow that time. If you decide to go out instead of following your schedule, be sure to add the activity you missed (that is, reading your psychology chapter) to your schedule (or to do list) for the next day so that you can make up that time. By having a schedule that is very specific, you'll know exactly what you have to do to catch up and you can easily make up for the lost time.

- **Use the Time Between Your Classes.** Many times students don't know where all of their time goes—an hour in between classes, two hours between school and work, fifteen minutes before classes begin—all of this time adds up and it is useful for getting your work done. You can read for class during hour breaks, review your notes while you are waiting for class to begin, use the time between lunch and class to review, or even meet with a study group in the laundromat. Plan to use short periods of time when making your schedule so this time does not get lost.

- **Schedule Studying Breaks.** If you plan to study for more than an hour at a time, schedule a ten- to fifteen-minute break for each hour and a half to two hours of study. You should also plan short breaks when switching from one topic to another to give yourself some time to refocus. When taking study breaks, you should avoid turning on the TV, going online, calling friends, "resting" your eyes, or engaging in any activity that could prolong what is supposed to be a brief break. You might get a snack, stretch, or go for a short walk—anything that will give your mind a brief rest.

- **Take Some Time Off.** Many students feel guilty when they take time off because they are always thinking about the things they should be doing, such as working on that chemistry lab assignment. But when you have a good schedule, you will be able to reward yourself by taking time off without guilt because you know that you have planned time to get all of your assignments done. So, relax and enjoy yourself after you finish your work—you deserve it. It is important to plan some free time when creating your schedule.

- **Don't Spin Your Wheels.** If you are having trouble in a course, seek help from a tutor, a professor, or a friend—anyone who might be able to help. There is nothing that gets in the way of managing your time more than wasting it by worrying rather than doing something productive so that you can be on top of things in a course that is difficult for you. It's important to get help if you need it and get back on track before you fall too far behind to catch up. We tell our students at the beginning of each fall semester not to wait until Thanksgiving to ask for help. Whether you are on a quarter or semester system, Thanksgiving is just too late.

TIMELY TIPS

Creating a Workable Schedule

Learning to manage your time is a skill that will help you in college and beyond. Start now, and by the time you enter the world of work, you will be a time-management veteran. Start this week. Consider the tips you just read to create a schedule. Use your schedule book to fill in your plan for the upcoming week in the following order:

1. Enter your class and lab times.
2. If you commute, enter the time it takes to travel to and from campus.

(continued)

3. Enter your work schedule.

4. Enter your meal times.

5. Enter all of your weekly personal activities (clubs, athletics, exercise).

6. Schedule your study times for each class. Include time for the following:
   • Reviewing your notes
   • Reading the text
   • Preparing for exams, writing papers, working on projects, etc.

7. Keep some time open so that your schedule is somewhat flexible.

8. Add any other things that you have to do this week.

Planning for Midterms and Finals

Every principle of time- and self-management discussed in this chapter usually goes into warp speed when you are preparing for midterms and finals. Generally, you will need to rethink your entire schedule to cope with the added pressures. In fact, you might even need to put in a few hours of overtime on your forty-hour work-week, but don't despair. By following the techniques outlined in this chapter you should get through it. In addition to the strategies we have already discussed, we add the following suggestions to help you cope with crunch exam time:

• **Plan Ahead.** Start to rehearse and review your notes and the texts *before* exam week so that you can cut down on your workload for the week. Start-ing early is essential for classes that have cumulative exams (exams that hold you responsible for topics covered over the entire term) because there is so much information to review.

• **Cut Down on Work or Other Commitments.** If you work part-time, ask for some time off or for fewer hours at your job and make sure that your family and friends understand that you will be extra busy. Try not to add any new commitments during midterm and final time.

• **Get Enough Sleep.** Pulling all-nighters for a big exam rarely pays off. Instead try to create your schedule for exam week in a way that leaves you adequate sleep time (try for at least six hours each night). You won't do well on an exam if you are falling asleep while taking it.

• **Study with a Partner.** Misery loves company and this is never truer than during midterms and finals. By the time midterms roll around you may have found a study partner or group that works. Study together to keep each other on schedule and motivated to work.

- **Don't Panic.** This point will be further discussed in Chapter 9, but to put it simply—midterms and finals are really just exams. The world will not stop and does not end because of midterms and finals. If you find that the pressure is getting to you, readjust your schedule to allow more break time and try to really relax during those breaks. If you find that you have excessive anxiety, get some help before it becomes a stumbling block to doing well.

In this chapter you have learned some strategies for managing yourself and your time. Try to make a schedule and follow it strictly for one week. Then make adjustments to suit your needs. Even if you do not consider yourself a "schedule person," it is imperative for you to find a way of keeping track of what you need to do. At the very least, having a schedule helps you organize and take control of your college career.

☐ REAL COLLEGE
Janice's Jam

DIRECTIONS: Read the following "Real College" scenario and respond to the question based on the information you learned in this chapter.

Janice is a college freshman. She loves her new freedom. A new town, her own place, new friends, and a great social life. Gone is the 10 P.M. curfew that her parents enforced in high school. Janice is living it up and having the time of her life, but she can't seem to make it to all of her classes and is falling way behind on her work.

Janice is taking five courses this term—American literature, accounting, sociology, history, and a chemistry course that involves lab projects. Her reading load is about 240 pages each week and she has at least one exam every other week. She never seems to be able to keep up with her reading or to find time to study. In addition, Janice is having trouble making it to her 8 A.M. accounting course. In fact, she missed both class periods last week. She has also missed several of her chemistry classes; she really enjoys them, but she just can't seem to make it to class on time.

Another concern is Janice's part-time job at a local video store. Although her hours are somewhat flexible, she always works at least two weeknights and one weekend day. She thinks that the fifteen hours spent at her job each week is really getting in the way of her studying, but she needs the money so she can't quit or cut back on hours.

She also finds her new social life to be a problem. It seems that no matter when she tries to study, someone is calling or stopping by her dorm room to ask her to go out. Janice really has a hard time saying no and ends up procrastinating on her work every time. She never had trouble in school before but now she is failing several courses, including chemistry, which she wants to major in. She knows that she needs to do things differently, but she just can't seem to find the time to get everything done.

Using the strategies you learned about time- and self-management, what advice would you give Janice to help her manage her time?

☐ THINKING CRITICALLY
Something to Think About and Discuss

- How do you think your current time management system is affecting your performance in college?

- Do you find yourself with a lot of time during which you do not get anything accomplished? If so, how can you adjust your current schedule to account for this wasted time?

- What kinds of obstacles currently make it hard to manage yourself as a college learner?

- How do you think your schedule will change when you are preparing for midterms and finals? How do you plan to make those changes successfully?

- If you have taken midterms or finals in the past, what obstacles did you find to managing yourself and your time? What do you plan to do differently this term?

☐ ADD TO YOUR PORTFOLIO

For one full week, keep a schedule of what you actually do. In your schedule book, jot down everything you do in half-hour increments. Evaluate your schedule to see if you have used your time wisely and accomplished everything in a timely fashion. Then create a schedule you can live with and follow that schedule for one week. Finally, reflect on your schedule by asking yourself the following questions:

1. Did you find that you accomplished more work?
2. What adjustments would you make to your schedule?
3. Have you left enough flexibility in your schedule for emergencies?
4. Are you studying during your most alert times?

CHAPTER 7

ACADEMIC ENERGY

Motivation for Learning, Attitudes, and Interests

Read this chapter to answer the following questions:

- What motivates people to learn?
- How do you get and stay motivated?
- How do attitudes and interests influence learning?
- How can you change your attitude and develop interest for topics you dislike?
- How can you maintain a positive attitude?

SELF-ASSESSMENT

DIRECTIONS: On a scale of 1 to 5 with 1 being "not at all true of me," 3 being "somewhat true of me," and 5 being "very true of me," respond to the following statements as honestly as you can. This assessment should give you a good idea of your motivation, attitudes, and interests.

	Not at all true of me ⟷ Very true of me				
1. I feel motivated for college learning.	1	2	3	4	5
2. I am more motivated to succeed in college than most of my peers.	1	2	3	4	5
3. I set and reach reasonable goals.	1	2	3	4	5
4. I am aware when I have reached my goals.	1	2	3	4	5
5. I have a positive attitude about attending college.	1	2	3	4	5
6. I have a positive attitude about many of the courses I am taking this term.	1	2	3	4	5
7. I tend to have a wide range of interests.	1	2	3	4	5
8. I can motivate myself even in courses I find uninteresting.	1	2	3	4	5
9. I know why I am attending college.	1	2	3	4	5
10. I am motivated to learn in all courses, not only in those in my major.	1	2	3	4	5

If you scored mostly fives, you probably have a positive attitude and are motivated for college learning. If, on the other hand, you scored mostly ones, you may want to pay extra careful attention to the strategies discussed in this chapter.

You already may have noticed that motivation, attitudes, and interests are tied together. It just makes sense that for courses in which you are interested or have a positive attitude about, you will be more motivated to learn. But let's try to separate these three important factors related to active learning to define what they are and how they interact to promote active learning and success in college. We'll begin with motivation.

Studying Smarter
Reward yourself for a job well done when you meet your goals.

What Influences Motivation?

Motivation is a combination of several factors including choice, desire for learning, value of learning, and personal control. Motivation is influenced by:

1. **The Amount of Choice You Have About What You Are Learning:** Sometimes your professors will offer you several projects to choose from, or sometimes they will even ask you to choose the topics that will be covered. Choices like these will help to increase your motivation. However, even if you are not given choices about the class content, college offers you many choices about what you will learn. You choose your major, and to a certain extent you choose the courses you will take and your course schedule.

2. **Your Desire to Learn:** It's likely that because you are currently enrolled in college you do want to learn, but sometimes you might be required to take courses that don't particularly interest you. For example, most colleges have a liberal arts requirement for all students, which means that regardless of their major, students must take courses in humanities, mathematics, and the sciences.

3. **How Much You Value the Subject to Be Learned:** As a general rule, the more you believe the subject to be worthwhile, the easier it will be to become motivated. For example, many colleges require students to take at least one foreign language course. If you believe that it is valuable to learn another language you will feel motivated—perhaps enough to take a second course. However, if you don't see it as valuable you may have a harder time motivating yourself to learn in your language course.

4. **The Extent to Which You Are Willing to Take Personal Control of Your Learning:** The degree to which you are motivated to learn depends in a large part on knowing the strategies to use and then taking control and applying those strategies. That is the "will" part of the skill versus will paradigm. Other individuals, such as teachers, peers, and parents, can expose you to skills that will lead to effective and efficient learning, but you must have the will to apply them.

In an ideal setting, you would have all of the components of motivation. However, you can learn successfully without choice, desire, and value, but learning will take more of a conscious effort from you.

What Motivates People?

You may not realize it, but you are always motivated. No matter where you are or what you are doing, *you are always motivated to do something* even if it's just sleeping. Focusing your motivation on learning, however, may be challenging sometimes.

It's important to understand right from the beginning that you are responsible for your own motivation, even in courses that you don't like. The current thinking on motivation can be summed up by saying that motivation is not something that is done to you. In other words, no one can motivate you but you. Others can provide you with stimuli, for example, explaining the reasons why it is important to learn biology even though you plan to major in literature, but in the end, the motivation must come from you. Thus, although an interesting instructor makes it easier for you to stay motivated, no one can directly motivate you to learn. But given that you are always motivated to do something and that you are primarily responsible for your motivation, there are some differences between students who are motivated to learn and students who are not.

You may have heard the terms *intrinsic* and *extrinsic*, especially as they relate to motivation. **Intrinsic motivation** occurs when the activity is its own reward. For example, some people read for the sheer enjoyment, others calculate numbers for the pleasure, and still others conduct experiments for the thrill of discovery. Think of intrinsic motivation as doing something you choose to do for sheer pleasure, challenge, or simply because it interests you.

Extrinsic motivation, on the other hand, occurs when your incentive is a reward, such as grades or praise or even money. Did your parents ever pay you to get good grades in elementary or middle school? You may have earned $5.00 for each A and $2.00 for each B. Money can be a very strong extrinsic motivator, as can automobiles or spring break trips for college students. You can think of extrinsic motivation as trying to get it done for some external reward, rather than for the sake of learning. For example, you may be failing organic chemistry, but when the professor offers an extra credit assignment, you decide to do it even though you are not motivated to learn in the course. In this case, you are extrinsically motivated to earn extra credit points that can boost your course grade rather than by learning organic chemistry for the sheer pleasure of it.

TIMELY TIPS

Adjusting Your Sleep Cycle

Some students tell us that their motivation is off kilter because they have gotten their sleep cycle out of whack. These students are napping for several hours each afternoon and then staying up until the wee hours of the morning. This cycle of sleeping during the day and then staying up all night leads them to miss a good deal of classes and to feel somewhat unconnected to the topics they are supposed to be learning. If you find yourself in this situation you will need to give up that long daytime nap to get your awake/asleep cycles back on track. You may be tired for a day or two as your body readjusts, but you should find a vast improvement in your motivation for learning.

The more you are intrinsically motivated to learn, the easier learning will be for you. The key to becoming intrinsically motivated, even in classes you don't particularly like, is to find *something* about the course that you find motivating and to focus on the positives rather than the negatives of the course. It also helps to focus more on understanding the concepts to be learned than on grades and to have a professor who can set the stage for intrinsic motivation.

Getting Motivated Through Goal Setting

Getting motivated is the first step toward staying motivated. One of the best ways to become motivated is to set learning goals. Your goals should be more than just "I want to make an A in the course," because grades are mainly an extrinsic motivator. In fact, students who focus only on grades to motivate themselves usually have a harder time maintaining their motivation as the term goes on. Students who set goals that focus on learning rather than grades tend not only to be more successful, but also can learn and remember more.

You probably have set goals before without even realizing it. For example, think about some New Year's resolutions you have made—to exercise more, to stop smoking, or to increase your GPA. How many of your resolutions have you kept? If you are like most people, your resolutions are long forgotten by Valentine's Day because most people do not set themselves up to achieve their New Year's goals. People tend to be unrealistic when they make New Year's resolutions. For example, although a goal of exercising more and getting in shape is a good resolution to make, it is unrealistic to expect to be in great shape right away if you have not been exercising regularly. Individuals who do not set short-term goals on their way to reaching long-term goals will soon find that their resolutions are not easily achievable and will give up on reaching their goals.

In addition, the goals you set should be conscious and deliberate. You should set your goals and make a plan to meet them only after you have given them some intentional thought. New Year's resolutions are easily forgotten because they are generally made with little thought. Most of the time we make resolutions in the middle of a party on New Year's Eve when someone might say, "So what's your New Year's resolution?" We may say the first thing that comes into our mind, which provides very little incentive to follow through. In order to set goals that can be achieved, your goals should be:

- **Realistic:** Can the goal be achieved? If not, how can the goal be divided into smaller goals? You should try to have short-term, intermediate, and long-term academic goals. A **short-term goal** is one that you will achieve within the next few days, such as "I will read Chapter 10 of my biology book tonight." **Intermediate goals** are ones that you will achieve within the next few weeks or months, such as "I will compare my notes to the text material each night to prepare for my cumulative psychology exam, which will be at the end of the semester." A **long-term goal** is one that will take longer still, perhaps a few months or even years to achieve, such as "I will begin to learn Spanish this year." An even longer-term goal is, "I want to graduate with a degree in marketing." Most people make the mistake of making only intermediate and long-term goals, but short-term goals are also important because they help you follow the progress you are making and they help you stay on track.

- **Believable:** Do you feel that you will be able to achieve your goal? Being confident about your ability to learn is crucial to your motivation. If you think that a task is too difficult for you to achieve, your motivation will decrease and you might give up before you even try. Some students believe that they can succeed only in certain disciplines. Students will say, "I'm good at math, but I'm terrible at English," or "I can learn history really well, but not science." These statements tell us that the students are motivated to learn one topic, but not another. If you find yourself making these kinds of statements, take a minute to reflect on how they are negatively affecting your motivation to learn in those courses.

- **Desirable:** How much do you want to reach your goal? When goals are desirable, you can provide reasons why you should work hard toward reaching the goal. Reasoning why it is important to accomplish a task helps to intrinsically motivate you. In order to succeed in reaching your goals, they should be goals that you really desire. Then, learning will be particularly rewarding or enjoyable to you and it will be easier to achieve. Your goal may be to graduate from college within four years and to land a good job in your field, but you must have the desire for success to reach that type of goal.

- **Measurable:** How will you know whether or when your goal has been met? Some goals are easy to measure. If your goal is to lose ten pounds, you will know whether your goal has been met when you weigh yourself. However, sometimes learning goals are not so easy to quantify, so you need to set some standards to help you measure your progress. This may be as simple as taking a few minutes to think about what you have learned after each study session or it may include a more in-depth assessment. In general, you will need more checks of your progress for long-term goals than for short-term goals.

Finally, it is a good idea to make your goals public. By public we mean sharing them with others—those you believe will encourage you to stay the course and might even help you achieve your goals. In addition, the fact that others know your goals, in some respects, holds you more accountable. For example, if your goal is to make the dean's list, share that with your roommate, members of your study group, or your best friend. Ask them to check in with you occasionally to see if you are on track. This puts some pressure on you, to be sure, but sometimes a little pressure can be a plus in helping you work toward your goals.

NETWORKING

Finding Motivation

Many sites on the Internet feature tips for getting and staying motivated. Some good sources include college counseling centers or freshman-year experience sites. Try the following keywords to find at least three motivation sites: motivation, college motivation, student motivation, or learning motivation. What kind of information did you find that will help you become more motivated or to maintain your motivation?

Staying Motivated

Getting motivated is one thing; staying motivated is another. We rarely see students at the beginning of a term who are not motivated. Almost everyone is excited about the prospect of a new term and, in a sense, starting with a clean slate. But as the term wears on, it is easy for motivation also to wane, especially in courses that are causing you trouble. In order to stay motivated you should give yourself checkpoints on the way to reaching your goals. These checkpoints might include:

- Monitor your motivation for learning just as you monitor your comprehension when you read. Each time you sit down to study, ask yourself about your level of motivation for the task. You have an internal body clock, which means that you will find that certain times of the day are more conducive to learning than others. (This idea was discussed in Chapter 6.) Listen to your body clock to find out when you are most motivated (first thing in the morning, late afternoons, evenings) and try to plan your study sessions around those times. In addition, try to get a handle on how you feel psychologically and physically when you begin to lose motivation. Because your thought processes tend to change when you lose motivation, you may experience less confidence in yourself and have more of a negative take on your life as a student. Physically, you may experience tiredness or an increased stress level, feelings that are not typical for you. Being in tune with yourself can often help you bounce back sooner and easier from a slump in motivation.

- Study the subjects you find the most difficult, or are least motivated to learn, first. Then move to the subjects that are easier or those that you enjoy more. In that way you will be more likely to stay motivated to study the subjects you find the most interesting.

- Plan some breaks in your study time—don't try to study for more than one hour without a short break because you will find it difficult to maintain your motivation. If possible, also try to change the type of tasks you do after each break. For example, if you have just spent an hour reading your psychology assignment, take a five or ten minute break, and come back and do the practice exercises for your French class.

But what if you find yourself losing motivation? It's important to have strategies to follow in this scenario as well. It might help if you:

- Take a break and come back to what you were doing at a later time.

- Switch topics every hour or so.

- Work with a study group. One key component of motivation is collaborating with others.

- Plan to study in the library or another quiet place if you find that your social life is interfering with studying. Find somewhere to study where you will be free from distractions and temptation.

- Use the best/worst case scenario technique. Imagine what will happen and how you will feel if you get your work done. Focusing on that positive image may help you find your motivation. On the other hand, picturing what will happen if the task is not completed is motivating for others. Thinking about the poor grade, or worse, being placed on academic probation is enough to get some students moving in the right direction.

Sometimes students find that they lose motivation as the term goes on. Some of this is natural—people are generally more motivated at the beginning and at the end of a term. So, if you experience a slight dip in your motivation toward the middle of a term or during the first nice spring day, you probably shouldn't be too concerned. Set some new goals to get back on track. However, sometimes losing motivation can be a sign of a bigger problem. If you think your loss of motivation may be a problem, reflect on the source of your lack of motivation. Can you pinpoint a reason for it? Or are you unsure why you are unmotivated? Sometimes students become unmotivated by poor grades in a particular course, or sometimes outside influences (for example, family, roommates, social situations, substance abuse, or health concerns) cause students to lose their motivation.

Another way to maintain your motivation is to figure out all of the tasks that you need to complete in your courses. By listing this information, you should be able to find something in the course that is motivating for you. You will also be able to determine the tasks you find unmotivating, which can help you psych yourself up to maintain your motivation. Before each exam (or paper, or project) for each of your courses this term, monitor your motivation by answering the questions in the accompanying "Success at a Glance" box.

Any method you find to renew your motivation is great. Try a few techniques to find out what works best. The motivation checkpoints in the "Success at a Glance" box should help you monitor your motivation in many different situations in all of your courses. It will help you discover the kinds of tasks you find particularly motivating and the kinds of tasks that you find less motivating. Once you know the kind of tasks that fail to motivate you, you can counter with some of the techniques discussed earlier.

SUCCESS AT A GLANCE

Motivation Checkpoints

When you are setting your goals, remember that achievable goals are:

Realistic

Believable

Desirable

Measurable

DIRECTIONS: For one of your courses this term answer the following questions.

What do I need to learn? What is the task (exam, paper, presentation, discussion, etc.)?

What sources will I need to use (text, labs, lecture, discussion, etc.)?

What is my level of motivation for beginning the task (high, medium, low)? Why?

What are my goals for completing this project? Include short-term, intermediate, and long-term goals.

(continued)

DIRECTIONS: For one of your courses this term answer the following questions.

What is my level of motivation for completing the task (high, medium, low). Why?

What, if any, adjustments do I need to make to reach my learning goals?

Changing Attitudes and Interests

Now that you understand the role that motivation plays in active learning, let's turn to attitudes and interest. As you read this portion of the chapter, reflect on how they relate to one another.

How many times have you dealt with a clerk in the grocery store, a family member, your advisor, a server in a restaurant, or even your best friend and walked away thinking, "Now there's a person with a bad attitude"? Everyone probably has a bad attitude about something at some time, which suggests that attitude, like motivation, is situational. Rarely are people positive about everything, nor are they negative about everything.

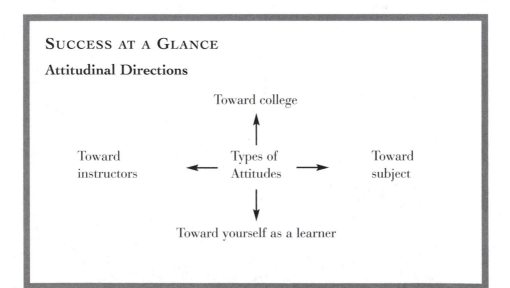

SUCCESS AT A GLANCE

Attitudinal Directions

Toward college

Toward instructors ← Types of Attitudes → Toward subject

Toward yourself as a learner

Likewise, interest is situational. Students generally aren't interested in everything. In most cases, individuals tend to show great interest in a limited number of areas, moderate interest in a greater number of topics, and low or no interest in many more. Everyone knows people who have a strong passion for something—computers, fly fishing, travel, photography, writing, basketball, history. And, more often than not, these passions are reflected in majors that students select and the careers they ultimately choose. Interests can't help but influence academic decisions students make and how actively they pursue certain goals.

Like motivation, attitudes and interests help define who you are as a learner. Moreover, each of these factors is either directly or indirectly a part of your personality, thus making them a bit more difficult to change than basic study habits.

Although everyone seems to know someone who has an overall bad or good attitude, attitudes actually can be thought of as emotional reactions to specific situations. Think of attitudes as:

- **Reflexive:** By reflexive we mean that you experience them without even thinking about it. For example, if your professor assigns you two extra chapters to read before a quiz on Friday and you already have every minute of your schedule between now and Friday planned, you may have an immediate negative reaction. However, that attitude may not be permanent. Perhaps a professor in another class cancels a test that was scheduled for Friday, or a date that you really didn't want to go on is canceled, causing your initial bad attitude to mellow. The bottom line is that most students' attitudes about things change. What you have a bad attitude about on Tuesday may be seen in another light by Wednesday.

- **An Influence on Your Motivation:** It makes sense that if you are motivated in a particular course your attitude would be more positive than if you were unmotivated.

- **Characteristics that Match Your Behavior:** For example, if you have a bad attitude toward learning a foreign language and believe that no matter what, you can't succeed, your behavior will follow suit. You won't work on the material on a daily basis, you won't say much in class, and you even may display a poor attitude toward your professor, even if she is a good teacher.

Types of Academic Attitudes

There are four types of academic attitudes you will encounter in college: (a) attitude toward college; (b) attitude toward your instructors; (c) attitude toward the subject and learning environment; and (d) attitude toward yourself as a learner. As you read about each one, think about yourself as a learner and the attitudes that you have.

Attitude Toward College   Students begin college with different attitudes for many different reasons. Some are happy with their school choice, others aren't, and still others don't care. Obviously, it's better to begin on the right foot—with a positive attitude about the college you are attending—but also remember that attitudes change. We've known many students who started college having one perception about what they would experience only to be either disappointed or elated later on. For whatever reason you chose to attend your current college, know that your general attitude about being in college and your expectations of what that college experience will be strongly influence the attitudes you will have. In turn, these attitudes influence your academic performance. Conflicts often occur when there is not a good match between expectations and the realities of college life. For example, if you attended a small high school where you knew everyone and had small classes and lots of individual attention, you may be overwhelmed by being on a campus with 30,000-plus students. In addition, sometimes college just isn't what students expected it would be. Large class sizes, classes that are difficult to get into, long lines, roommate problems, and homesickness are just a few of the many problems that can sour initially good attitudes.

Attitude Toward Your Instructors   Your attitude about your instructor also influences your academic performance. This is especially true for disciplines you don't particularly like. If you enroll in a mathematics course "hating" math and project that feeling onto your professor, you are probably going to have some problems. On the other hand, if you try to have the attitude that each instructor has something unique to offer you may have a totally different experience. We suggest that students try to get to know their professors and not to feel intimidated about talking with them. We know of a student who, at the beginning of every term, makes an appointment to see all of his professors. He takes only about fifteen minutes of their time introducing himself and talking with each of them about how to study in their courses. He says it helps him see his professors in a different light, and although he still has a better attitude toward some professors than others, the experience makes all his professors "human." Rarely does a professor turn down his request for an appointment, and in many cases, this initial contact makes it easier for him to approach a professor if he experiences problems with a course.

Attitude Toward the Subject and Learning Environment   When we think about attitudes toward subject matter, it's difficult to separate attitude from interest and motivation since most students have a more negative attitude toward subjects in which they are not interested and less motivated. For example, if you are strong in mathematics and science and have been successful in those courses in the past, you will most likely enter into these courses in college with a positive attitude toward learning the material. However, if you have little interest in math and science and fail to see any relevance in these courses to your future career choice, then you are more likely to have a bad attitude toward these classes. In fact, some students try to avoid subjects they dislike until the very end of their program. We know students who have delayed taking their lab science, history, or mathematics requirements until their senior year, only to find out that the course wasn't as bad as anticipated. It's also important to try hard not to have preconceived notions about a course. Even though you may have had an unpleasant experience in a similar past course, try to begin each course with an open mind. An open mind can go a long way in changing your attitude, helping you develop your interests and maintain motivation.

Attitude Toward Yourself as a Learner   The attitude that you have toward yourself as a learner may be the most important of the four because it is the sum total of the educational experiences you have accumulated in your twelve-plus years of schooling. If you have had teachers who encouraged you, if you have experienced academic success, and if you have parents who have been actively involved in your learning at home, you probably have a positive view of yourself in learning situations. That's not to say that students who have a positive attitude never doubt themselves. They do. But they know themselves well enough to identify what they will have to change and how they will do it in order to make things improve.

On the other hand, if school was not challenging, if you experienced only moderate academic success, and if your family had little involvement with your learning, you may have a more negative view of yourself and lack confidence academically. Students who fall into this category initially may have a more difficult time adjusting to college, but we have seen such students gain confidence in themselves when they begin to experience academic successes.

Maintaining a Positive Attitude

Few students begin college with a totally negative attitude. Thus, we suggest that your first step is to evaluate what it is you like about college. You may have a great roommate, you may have at least one class and professor that seems to be enjoyable, or maybe you are simply positive about having a new beginning. Whatever excites you and makes you feel positive should be what you concentrate on, especially during those first few days of a new term. Yes, things will go wrong. The new registration system touted by the registrar's office might crash just when you finally were making some progress in adding a class you wanted, the bursar's office may have lost proof that you paid your tuition, and the lines in the bookstore may go on forever. But you have no control over these things. Take a deep breath, count to ten (or fifty, if need be), and try not to let these negative happenings get in the way of your excitement and positiveness. We realize that this can be difficult, but it's important to learn early on that you need to develop patience with things in life that you have little or no control over. Don't let those things bring you down. Save your energy for staying on top of what you can control.

Another suggestion that students find helpful in maintaining a positive attitude is not to dwell on past mistakes. For example, if writing has always been a struggle for you, telling yourself, "I'm a terrible writer," will do little to help. Rather, concentrate on the positives such as, "I'm a good learner in general, so writing should not be impossible. I can get help at the writing center if I need it, so I know I can do it." Everyone has strong points and weak points. The secret of maintaining a positive attitude is one of balance. If you lack confidence in writing, for example, be sure to balance that writing course with another course that you will like and that will be less of a struggle for you. Also, try to give each course and each professor a chance. Enter each course with the attitude that you will do your best. In some courses, this may mean that you will not earn the best grade. There's nothing wrong with *earning* a C in a course that is particularly difficult for you. There is something wrong, however, in *settling* for a C because your attitude in that course was negative and you simply did not put in the necessary effort.

In addition, expect to learn something valuable in every course you take. We know that's often a difficult suggestion to follow, but if you try to think that parts of a course might be interesting and valuable, both your attitude and your motivation will be better. It's particularly difficult to follow this suggestion when you are a first-year student because we know that first-year students often get stuck taking leftover courses or core courses in which they haven't much interest. But no matter how uninteresting or boring you might find a course, look toward the positive. Think how you might use some of the information at a later date or how it might be related to other areas that do interest you and for which you already possess a positive attitude. Imagine how you might feel at the end of the term if you do well in a subject that either wasn't your favorite or that previously made you struggle.

The Role of Interests

As we mentioned earlier, attitudes and interests go hand in hand. If you have an interest in something, you also probably have a good attitude toward it. Likewise, when you're not interested in a topic or course, you may not have a very good attitude about having to learn it.

We have found that many students lack interest in a wide variety of areas, which puts limitations on the courses that they want to take. But not having a wide variety of interests doesn't mean that you can't develop them. As we suggested, every course has *something* interesting about it or people wouldn't spend their lives studying it. Students who have the most focused interests are usually those who have the most difficult time developing new interests. We have had conversations with students that go something like this:

Student: Why do I have to take this stuff—history, sociology, and drama, for goodness sakes! I'm a computer science major and none of this is important to me. I just want to be able to work with computers.

Professor: Well, I understand that, but you also have to take a series of core courses—courses that help you have a well-rounded education. Besides, they can help to develop other interests. One of the reasons for a college education is to give you a broader view of the world.

Student: (rolling her eyes) Maybe so, but I don't care about any of this. I'll do it because I have to, but I'm not going to like it.

The student shuffles off, unhappy, determined to get nothing from any course that isn't computer-related. Chances are that she will get into academic trouble simply because she is already convinced that there is nothing about these courses that could possibly be of interest. How different the scenario might have been if she thought about courses as a chance to develop new interests and learn new things.

There are also students who enter college with no overriding interest in any one particular area. Many of these students have not yet selected a major and hope to find something that interests them as a result of enrolling in general core courses. The best advice we can give to you if you fall into this category is to keep up with assignments. Do the reading, participate in discussion groups, study with others, and seek assistance when the going gets rough. Often a class that starts out slowly turns into an interesting course if you keep on top of things. It particularly helps if you create study groups to talk about the information, and it helps even more if at least one person in the group has more than a superficial interest in the course. What starts out as a way to try to earn a decent grade in a class can turn into an experience that creates an enormous amount of interest in a course.

A final suggestion about developing and maintaining interest in courses: Don't wait until the end of your college career to take all the courses you think you'll hate. Intersperse the good with the bad. Try to balance courses you know you'll be interested in with those that you think won't. And for those less interesting courses, select your instructors carefully. A good instructor can make or break your interest toward and attitude about a particular course.

It is easy to see that motivation, attitude, and interest are related to one another and difficult to separate. Unfortunately, lack of motivation, a poor attitude, and few interests usually go hand in hand. But everyone can make a conscious effort to develop interests, improve attitudes, and work on motivation.

☐ REAL COLLEGE
Martin's Misery

DIRECTIONS: Read the following "Real College" scenario and respond to the question based on the information you learned in this chapter.

Martin is a first-year student. Because Martin did very well in high school and also had high entrance exam scores, he had his pick of colleges and was courted by some of the top schools in the county. Martin's parents, who were very proud of their son's accomplishments, persuaded him to attend a large prestigious school. Martin wanted to go to a smaller school that had a good reputation in the sciences because he had a strong interest in majoring in biology. In fact, although he had been successful in all of his courses in high school, he really didn't want much to do with anything that wasn't in some way related to science. His career goal is to become a veterinarian.

When Martin arrived on campus, he immediately felt overwhelmed. The campus was too big, he didn't know anyone, and his classes were extremely difficult. He had no choice in his courses for the first term because his schedule was set for him. He was enrolled in five courses: World Literature I, Political Science, Calculus, Anthropology, and Computer Applications I. Martin became miserable—fast! For the first few days, he tried to maintain a positive attitude and a high level of motivation, but he kept asking himself, "Why am I here? Why did I let my parents talk me into this?" Before he knew it, he found himself with a general bad attitude about being in college and zero motivation.

Martin is bright and has long-term career plans, but it is also obvious that he's not motivated to do the work and has a bad attitude about school and his classes that may influence him negatively if he doesn't do something fast. Based on what you have read and what you know about the role that motivation, attitudes, and interests play in learning, what advice would you give Martin?

☐ THINKING CRITICALLY
Something to Think About and Discuss

DIRECTIONS: Discuss the following questions about your motivation, attitudes, and interests to learn in college with a partner or a small group. Summarize your answers to present to another group or the entire class.

- What do you want to get out of college?
- What do you want to get out of your courses this term (other than a good grade)?
- Why do you think you have to take courses that are outside your major?
- How would you describe your general level of motivation for learning in college?
- Why do you think some students have more developed interests than others?
- We stated that motivation and attitudes were situational. In what kinds of situations are you more motivated? In what kinds of situations do you have a poor attitude?

What small steps could you take to improve your attitude in a course this term? Could you get help from a tutor if you are having problems with the class? Could you join a study group? Would it help to talk things over with the professor? If these suggestions won't work, brainstorm some that will.

☐ ADD TO YOUR PORTFOLIO

1. Write down three short-term, one intermediate, and one long-term goal for the rest of this year. Before you begin working on these goals, share them with a class-mate or friend to help you determine if your goals are realistic, desirable, believ-able, and measurable. As the year progresses, periodically evaluate those goals.

2. In each of your courses, monitor your motivation throughout the term. What activities do you find particularly motivating? Which do you find fail to motivate? What strategies do you find helpful in regaining your motivation? How can you use these strategies in other situations to help you get or stay motivated?

CHAPTER 8

JUST WHAT DO YOU BELIEVE, ANYWAY?

Read this chapter to answer the following questions:

- How is your learning affected by your beliefs?
- What are the five belief components that influence learning?

SELF-ASSESSMENT

DIRECTIONS: Read the following scenario and answer the questions honestly. The purpose of this scenario is to help you to identify and think about your beliefs, in terms of the five components of beliefs covered in this chapter. Remember that there are no right or wrong responses.

Chris is taking Introductory Biology. He studies hard for the class, but he has failed his first two exams. When he studies, he tries to focus on the material covered in the lectures, but he really doesn't read the text. He does try to memorize almost all of the bold-faced terms in the text by writing them on three-by-five inch index cards and flipping through them until he has memorized the definitions. After the last exam, he tried studying with friends, but he didn't find it helpful because his friends explained the information differently than the professor had. He wasn't sure they knew what they were talking about and didn't want to get confused.

Chris believes that science is really just memorization and that most science problems have only one answer, so if he looks at the material enough he should do fine. Even though he doesn't spend a lot of time studying, he feels that he puts in hard work and effort and, therefore, he should be receiving high grades. Chris thinks his poor grades could be due to the new professor teaching the course. Professor Smith tries to have class discussions, despite the fact that there are 250 students enrolled in the class. She also tries to tell the class about all sides to each issue. When there are competing scientific theories, she is sure to discuss each one, because she wants to give an unbiased lecture each time. However, Chris knows that science is based on proven facts and finds all these theories confusing. When Chris went to her office asking which theory is the right one, or which one he needed to know for the exam, she told him that all of the theories have some merit and that he must decide for himself what he will believe. Chris believes that it is the professor's responsibility to make sure that the students learn in class. However, this professor often asks exam questions over topics that were covered in the text but not during the lectures. Chris is beginning to believe that he is failing the class because he is not able to learn science.

	Strongly disagree ⟷ Strongly agree
1. I agree with Chris that science is based on proven facts.	1 2 3 4 5
2. I agree with Chris that the students should only be responsible for the scientific theories that the professor discusses in class.	1 2 3 4 5
3. Like Chris, I believe that there must be one theory that is more correct than others.	1 2 3 4 5
4. I agree with Chris that the professor is responsible for student learning.	1 2 3 4 5

	Strongly disagree ◄───► Strongly agree
5. I agree with Chris that if I don't do well on my biology exam it is because I am not able to learn science.	1 2 3 4 5
6. Like Chris, I believe that I don't have to read the text as long as I listen in class because the professor goes over all of the important information.	1 2 3 4 5
7. I agree with Chris that learning competing science theories is too confusing for students.	1 2 3 4 5
8. I agree with Chris that there is usually only one right answer to a science problem.	1 2 3 4 5
9. I believe that some people will do fine in Chris's class because they are good learners, but others have a limited ability to learn science.	1 2 3 4 5
10. Like Chris, I believe that I will only do well in this class if I can learn information quickly.	1 2 3 4 5
11. Chris's plan of taking good notes and trying to memorize facts should be all it takes to get a good grade in Introductory Biology.	1 2 3 4 5
12. Chris will be able to understand the complex processes involved in biology if he memorizes definitions.	1 2 3 4 5
13. If Chris tried to understand every theory it would take him too much time to read a chapter.	1 2 3 4 5
14. Like Chris, I believe that no matter how much time and effort is put in to it, some people will never be able to learn biology.	1 2 3 4 5
15. I believe that if I am going to understand my biology text, it will make sense the first time I read it— rereading will not help me understand any better.	1 2 3 4 5

To find how the five components of personal beliefs that influence learning apply to you, add your scores to the following questions together.

Component 1: Certain Knowledge   1_____ + 3 _____ + 8 _____ = _____

Component 2: Simple Knowledge   7_____ +11 _____ +12 _____ = _____

Component 3: Responsibility for   2_____ + 4 _____ + 6 _____ = _____
                Learning

Source: Adapted from Holschuh, J. L. (1998). *Epistemological beliefs in introductory biology: Addressing measurement concerns and exploring the relationship with strategy use.* Unpublished doctoral dissertation, University of Georgia, Athens.

| Component 4: Speed of Learning | 10_____ +13 _____+ 15 _____ = _____ |
| Component 5: Ability | 5 _____ + 9 _____ +14 _____ = _____ |

Assessing Your Personal Theory

Your score on each component can range from 3 to 15. Look at where your scores fall on each component. The way the scale is structured, the higher your score on a component, the more strongly you hold a belief that may get in the way of your academic success. The lower your score on a component, the more strongly you hold a belief that research has shown leads to academic success. Because no one is completely consistent in her beliefs, chances are you hold a strong belief on some components (as indicated by either high or low scores), but are more in the middle on other components.

Studying Smarter
Take responsibility for your own learning by finding out about your beliefs about knowledge.

The Five Components of Beliefs That Influence Learning

Many different kinds of beliefs affect your life everyday. People have different religious beliefs, moral beliefs, political beliefs, and so on. You may have thought a lot about those kinds of beliefs, but have you ever thought about your beliefs about learning? Have you ever considered how you gain knowledge or what knowledge is? If you are like most students, you probably haven't thought much about where knowledge comes from, but your beliefs about knowledge do impact what and how you learn.

As you read this chapter, consider your own beliefs about learning. Where do your beliefs fall? How might these beliefs affect your learning in college courses? Remember that to get off on the right foot in college you may need to reevaluate your beliefs and the role they play in your academic success.

Component 1: Certainty of Knowledge

Some students believe that knowledge is continually changing based on current information. When they are in class, they think about what they already know about the topic and may change their beliefs about a topic by adding new information to what they already know. For example, a student might enter a physics class believing that when a bullet is shot from a gun, it falls to the ground faster than a bullet that is simply dropped. However, she might change her beliefs based on new information after learning about the laws of gravity.

SUCCESS AT A GLANCE

The Five Components of Beliefs

Component 1:	Certainty of Knowledge	Can range from the belief that knowledge is fact, to the belief that knowledge is continually changing.
Component 2:	Simple Knowledge	Can range from the belief that knowledge is made up of isolated bits of information, to the belief that knowledge is complex.
Component 3:	Responsibility for Learning	Can range from the belief that it is the professor's responsibility to ensure that students learn, to the belief that it is the individual's responsibility to learn information.
Component 4:	Speed of Learning	Can range from the belief that learning happens fast or not at all, to the belief that learning is a gradual process that takes time.
Component 5:	Ability	Can range from the belief that the ability to learn is fixed, to the belief that people can learn how to learn.

Source: Schommer, M. (1990). Effects of beliefs about the nature of knowledge on comprehension. *Journal of Educational Psychology, 82,* 498–504.

Other students believe that there are absolute answers and there is a definite right or wrong solution to every problem. These students approach learning by trying to find the truth in all situations. In the same physics class, another student may have trouble understanding that scientists believe that physics is based on theories, not truth, and that these theories are in a constant state of change based on new research.

Additionally, although experts are continually reassessing what they know, students are often encouraged only to look for the facts in their textbooks. They may approach reading history by focusing strictly on names, dates, and places because that was what was important in their previous experience. But most college courses require you to do more than learn facts. Professors tend to view their disciplines as dynamic and constantly changing; to memorize only "facts" would be a waste of time. Instead, most professors not only want you to be able to understand what is currently known, but also want to prepare you for future learning. Professors expect students to question what they read and be willing to live with the idea that there may not be a solution or definite answer to every problem or question.

Component 2: Simple Knowledge

Some students believe that knowledge is complex and consists of highly interconnected concepts, but other students believe that knowledge consists of a series of unrelated bits of information. Students who believe that knowledge is complex look for relationships between ideas as they learn. They try to see the big picture and the relationships among the small pieces of information within that big picture.

On the other hand, students who have a strong belief that knowledge is simple tend to break information down into very small isolated parts and never put it back together again. Although breaking information into smaller chunks is a great strategy for some tasks, for example when learning something you must memorize such as the periodic table of the elements, a student who learns *only* isolated pieces of information will miss the big ideas. If a student in history class only memorized dates and names, she would be unprepared for an essay question that asked her to compare and contrast ideas about the larger concepts. Likewise, a student who memorizes bold-faced terms in biology would not be able to explain more complex science processes. Because most of the assignments you will experience require you to apply what you have learned, you need to go beyond memorizing small bits of information and begin to see how the information is connected.

Component 3: Responsibility for Learning

Beliefs about knowledge also depend on your perception about who is responsible for your learning in college. Some students believe that it is the professor's responsibility to ensure that all students learn the information. Other students believe that although the professor guides their learning, they are ultimately responsible for their own learning.

Get Going

Taking Responsibility for Learning

The ability to take responsibility for your own learning is a helpful skill to learn in college because when you enter the workforce you will be expected to draw on your ability to direct your own learning (look at the number of help-wanted ads looking for a "self-starter"), which includes making decisions and creating new solutions. So the next time you find yourself putting the responsibility on others ("I can only learn when I have a good professor," "I didn't do well on the test because my roommate made too much noise for me to study"), think about ways to take responsibility for the situation.

In high school, your teacher probably took a lot of the responsibility for your learning in class. You most likely had little choice in the subjects you studied, what you learned, or the way you were assessed (e.g., tests, papers, labs, etc.). In fact, the teacher may have even gone over all of the relevant information in class, which left you little to learn on your own. However, you may have already noticed that college professors have different assumptions about who is responsible for learning.

Professors expect students to take responsibility for a good deal of their own learning. They expect students to be able figure out information on their own, and they also may expect students to be able to pull together information from a variety of sources.

Component 4: Speed of Learning

Some students believe that learning is a gradual and ongoing process, but other students believe that if learning is going to happen, it happens quickly or not at all. In other words, some people believe that most things worth knowing take a long time to learn, but other people think that if they don't get it right away, they never will.

Students who believe that learning takes time are better prepared for college tasks, while students who believe that learning should happen quickly are often frustrated in college when they are faced with complex information. Many college students believe that learning should happen quickly because of their experiences in high school (and elementary and middle school, too). In fact, research has shown that in high school mathematics classes, most problems that students answered could be solved in less than two minutes. It's no wonder that many students are unprepared for more difficult tasks in college and why some students get frustrated or just give up when faced with challenging problems.

TIMELY TIPS

Time on Task

Most students hold beliefs about how long it should take to complete a task. For example, the student who has only encountered math problems that could be solved in two minutes would likely believe that all mathematics problems can be solved that quickly. Students have similar beliefs about how long it should take to read a textbook chapter, write a paper, or study for an exam. The next time you find yourself unmotivated or frustrated in your classes, think about your own beliefs about the speed of learning. Are your expectations holding you back from giving the task the time it requires?

Component 5: The Role of Ability

Some students believe that people can learn how to learn, but others believe that the ability to learn is fixed and that they are naturally good at some things but will never be able to do other things. For example, a student may say, "I am good at math and science, but not history or English."

Students who believe that the ability to learn is fixed tend to talk to themselves in a negative way. A student may say, "I will never be able to do this," or " I am too dumb to learn this," when in fact this student may be just giving up too easily.

Studying Smarter
What is important is to keep learning, to enjoy challenge, and to tolerate ambiguity. In the end there are no certain answers.

**— Martina Horner,
President of Radcliffe College**

On the other hand, students who believe that people can learn how to learn tend to view difficult tasks as challenges that can be met. Instead of giving up, these students will try different strategies for learning and will ask for help from the professor or their friends if they need it.

There are probably people in your classes who make learning look easy, but students who appear to learn "naturally" most likely spend time and effort in activities, such as reading and reflecting, that promote academic success.

Based on what you have read about beliefs, you probably have figured out that students who believe that knowledge is changeable, that knowledge consists of interrelated concepts, that learning is under the control of the student, and that learning may take time and effort are expected to have more success in college than students who hold the opposite beliefs.

NETWORKING

Deciding What to Believe

You may have noticed that some of the information you find on the Internet seems to contradict other information. Your personal theory of beliefs will influence how you decide which information to believe. Find three sites that give you different perspectives about the same topic. For example, you might look at three reviews of the same movie or three political essays about an issue from a Democratic, Republican, and Independent perspective. Think about how you will decide which one to believe. How do your beliefs about knowledge affect your decision?

Changing Your Beliefs

After evaluating the components of personal beliefs using the scale at the beginning of this chapter, you may have found that you have some beliefs that need to be altered because they may negatively affect your success in college. This section will present some strategies for promoting change.

Your beliefs about learning influence the strategies you use to study, which is part of the reason why beliefs are related to college performance. For example, if you believe that knowledge is simple, then you will select a strategy that reflects your belief, such as making flash cards to memorize definitions of key terms even when your professor expects you to integrate ideas. Thus, when you have all of the terms memorized, you will feel prepared for the exam. If you do not pass the exam, you may not understand what you did wrong, because according to your beliefs about learning, you were adequately prepared. The question, then, is: If you currently hold beliefs that may make academic success more difficult, how do you go about changing those beliefs?

- **Be Aware of Your Beliefs.** If you have beliefs that are getting in the way of your learning, consider changing them. However, before you can change a belief, you must first be unsatisfied with your current beliefs about learning. For example, when you find yourself giving up on an assignment too quickly or trying to merely memorize when the task requires you to understand and apply difficult concepts, you can reflect on your beliefs, rethink your approach, and take the time to really learn the information.

- **Look for the Big Picture.** Instead of just memorizing a lot of separate facts, make a conscious effort to relate ideas to what you already know and to other ideas discussed in class. Many of the strategies in *College Success Strategies* help you to integrate and synthesize ideas as you read.

- **Learn to Live with Uncertainty.** It is sometimes difficult to accept that there are no right answers to some questions. For example, in a statistics class, you may want to know the "right" way to solve a problem, and although there are some ways that are better than others, chances are that if you ask three statisticians how to solve the problem you will get three different answers.

- **Don't Compare Your Ability with That of Others.** Worrying that you are not as good as your roommate in math will not get you anywhere. Focus instead on how to improve your ability to learn in the subjects that you find difficult. You can find a tutor to work with or form a study group to help you learn. It may take you longer to get there, but remember that college learning is more like an endurance sport than a sprint.

- **Realize That Learning Takes Time.** If you begin your assignments with the expectation that they will take time to fully understand and complete, you are likely to experience less frustration and more understanding. Don't expect to learn complex concepts the first time you encounter them. Instead, plan to spread out your study time so you can review difficult material several times.

Now that you know about how beliefs affect your learning, you can begin to examine your own beliefs in the many learning situations you encounter. Your beliefs about learning will change because of your college experiences, and being aware of your own beliefs can help you learn more effectively.

Evaluating Internet Information

One real-world example of how your beliefs about knowledge impact your everyday life is in how you perceive information you obtain online.

You can find it all on the Internet, from world-class thinking to pure garbage to blatant lies. Anyone can put up a Web page that looks good. But a well-designed site doesn't mean that the content is good. How can you decide what to believe? There are several ways to evaluate the credibility and quality of the information you find online. Consider the following criteria each time you surf the Web:

- **Source.** Who is the author of this information? Is it a noted expert in the field, a high school student doing a report for school, a fan, a business, or an organization? Your answer to this question will tell you a lot about the quality of the information. In general, it is best to trust the information from the authority in the field over a fan or hobbyist.

- **Purpose.** What is the reason for this site to exist? Is it trying to educate, inform, or is it trying to market a product? Although commercial Web sites can sound very persuasive, if they are trying to sell you something, you need to take that into consideration when evaluating the information you find.

- **Corroboration.** How does this information compare with other Web sites? Usually there is a good deal of overlap, but if you find a site that is claiming ideas that no one else is discussing, that should send up a red flag for credibility. Try to check out a few sources to help you determine corroboration.

- **Accuracy.** Is the information you find correct? Several of the criteria on this list should help you determine the truthfulness of the information you are finding. One idea that applies in this case is that if the information sounds too good to be true then it probably is false.

- **Timeliness.** How current is the information? Because the Web is an ever-changing source of information, in general, the more current the source, the better. Most Web pages tell you the last time the site was updated. If no one has updated it in a long time, you might want to visit a more current site.

- **Bias.** Does the information seem to present a particular point of view or is it trying to present an unbiased view? Most sites will contain some sort of bias. Your job is to use the other criteria on this list to figure out what it is.

REAL COLLEGE
College Knowledge

DIRECTIONS: Read the following "Real College" scenario about the beliefs of four college students. Respond to the questions based on what you learned in this chapter about beliefs about knowledge.

Pat is taking history mostly because it is required. In this history class, he finds that the professor often asks exam questions about topics that were not covered in class. Pat doesn't think that is fair because he doesn't know how he is supposed to figure out what to study if the professor doesn't tell him what is important.

Alysha believes that she will be successful in biology because she has always done well in science classes. She believes a scientist, if he or she tries hard enough, can find the answers to almost anything. One problem she has is that her professor tries to tell the class about too many science theories, which Alysha finds confusing.

David was a good English student in high school. He was always able to quickly understand concepts and didn't need to spend a lot of time on homework. When he started his literature class, the readings were familiar and he didn't really spend much time outside of class reading or studying. However, he found that he did not do well on the first essay exam and that the new concepts were confusing. He still believes that he should be able to learn the information quickly and is unsure why he is having so much trouble.

Li believes that she is the type of person who can't do math. She sees that some students just seem to get it because they are naturally good at learning calculus.

She wishes that the college would understand that some people just can't learn math and that it shouldn't be a requirement for all students.

Answer the following questions and then discuss your responses with a partner or small group.

1. How are these students' beliefs similar to yours? How do they differ?
2. How do you think these beliefs will affect the students' performance in their classes?
3. What advice would you give these students?

☐ THINKING CRITICALLY
Something to Think About and Discuss

- What have you observed about your own beliefs that may make learning easier for you?
- What have you observed about your own beliefs that may make learning harder for you?
- How are your beliefs affecting how you approach and carry out the tasks in your courses?
- Are your beliefs leading you toward academic success? Why or why not?

☐ ADD TO YOUR PORTFOLIO

1. Reflect on your self-assessment scores from pages 96–97. Is this an accurate reflection of you? Why or why not? Which components of beliefs do you think are negatively impacting your academic career? Brainstorm and write down three changes you can make this semester to these components.
2. At the end of this semester, retake the self-assessment (found on pages 95–97). How have your beliefs changed in the past year? What experiences have helped you make the changes you have had?
3. At the end of the semester, reflect on the three changes you sought to make. How successful have your efforts been? What do you think you still need to work on in the future?

CHAPTER 9

DEALING WITH STRESS

Read this chapter to answer the following questions:

- What are common sources of stress?
- What is academic stress?
- How do you control or reduce stress?

SELF-ASSESSMENT

DIRECTIONS: Take the following assessment of stressful situations to determine your current stress level. Check the events you have experienced in the past six months or are likely to experience in the next six months. This assessment will help you determine whether you are currently experiencing an unhealthy amount of stress. Remember, some stress is necessary and even productive for everyday life, but if you are experiencing an overwhelming amount of stress, look for ways to reduce it and seek help if necessary.

Student Stress Scale[*]

1. Death of a family member	_____ 100
2. Death of a friend	_____ 73
3. Divorce between parents	_____ 65
4. Jail term	_____ 63
5. Major injury or illness	_____ 63
6. Marriage	_____ 58
7. Fired from job	_____ 50
8. Failed important course	_____ 47
9. Change in health of a family member	_____ 45
10. Pregnancy	_____ 45
11. Sex problems	_____ 44
12. Serious argument with a close friend	_____ 40
13. Change in financial status	_____ 39
14. Change of major	_____ 39
15. Trouble with parents	_____ 39
16. New girl or boyfriend	_____ 38
17. Increased workload	_____ 37
18. Outstanding personal achievement	_____ 36
19. First quarter/semester in college	_____ 35
20. Change in living conditions	_____ 31
21. Argument with instructor	_____ 30
22. Lower grades than expected	_____ 29
23. Change in sleeping habits	_____ 29
24. Change in social activities	_____ 29
25. Change in eating habits	_____ 28
26. Chronic car trouble	_____ 26

27. Change in number of family get-togethers	_____ 26
28. Too many missed classes	_____ 25
29. Change of college	_____ 24
30. Dropped more than one class	_____ 23
31. Minor traffic violations	_____ 20
TOTAL	_____

SCORING: A score of 300 or higher indicates an extremely high stress life; a score of 200–299 indicates a high stress life; a score between 100–199 indicates a moderate stress life; and a score below 100 indicates a low stress life. If you find that you are having a very high stress life, you might want to seek help from a counselor, friend, or family member.

*The Stress Scale was adapted from:

DeMeuse, K., The relationship between life events and indices of classroom performance, *Teaching of Psychology*, *12*, (1985, 146–149).

Holmes, T. H., & Rahe, R. H., The social readjustment rating scale, *Journal of Psychosomatic Research*, *11*, (1967, 213–218).

Insel, P., & Roth, W., *Core concepts in health*, (Palo Alto, CA: Mayfield Publishing, 1985).

Sources of Stress

Believe us when we say that as a college student you will experience many different types of stress including social pressures, financial burdens, and academic competition.

Studying Smarter
Keep your stress levels under control by creating a plan to cope with stressful issues.

In fact, stress levels in college tend to ebb and flow—you might feel more stress at the beginning of a term when everything is new, less stress in the middle of the term (until midterms, of course), and more stress again at the end of the term when you have to take final exams. Usually we think of stress as something to be avoided, but actually that's not always true. Stress is a normal part of life and at least some of the stress you experience in college is helpful and stimulating—without stress we would lead a rather boring existence. The problem comes when you have an extremely high stress life.

Generally, college stress can be broken down into six categories: prior academic record, social influences, family, finances, career direction, and situational problems (such as illness or drug problems). Most students think that stress is caused by outside factors. They might say that a test, a professor, or a paper is "stressing them out." But stress is largely an internal process. Therefore, it's important to recognize the things that are causing your own stress in order to put your reactions to it in perspective. As you read about the six categories of stress, remember that stress is natural, it is internal, it is often an overreaction to a specific situation, and *it can be controlled.*

1. **Prior Academic Record.** Interestingly, both good and poor academic records can cause students to feel stress. Students who have a shaky academic past may believe that they can't succeed in college. On the other hand, students who have a 4.0 average may feel stress to sustain their stellar grade point average. Either way, your past history as a learner affects your stress level.

2. **Social Influences.** You probably have realized that dealing with your friends can often be stressful. A fight with your roommate, feeling lonely, missing your old friends, breaking up with a boyfriend or girlfriend, meeting new people—all of these situations can be stressful. In fact, even situations we would consider to be positive social factors, such as falling in love or socializing with really good friends, can cause a stressful reaction. Having too good of a social life can cause stress, because you may worry about the academic work that is not getting done. Overall, however, having good friends and social support will actually reduce your stress levels because you have someone to confide in.

3. **Family.** You may feel pressure to do well in college in order to make your family proud, you may feel stress because you have moved away from your family, or because of family crises that arise. Returning students may feel stress because college is taking away time that they spend with their family. But like social influences, your family can also be a source of support to help you when you experience a lot of stress. Let your family know what they can do to help you in these situations.

4. **Finances.** Financial stress usually begins in college because students may take out loans to attend college, get jobs to help pay for college, or have to maintain a certain grade point average to keep their scholarships. Many college students are also responsible for paying bills and are gaining responsibility for their own financial security. In addition, college students get their own credit cards, which can lead to great financial stress if used excessively. We know many college students who graduate not only with a diploma, but also with student loans and a stack of credit card debt. All of these things can cause stress, especially for students who are handling their own finances for the first time.

5. **Career Direction.** "So what's your major? What the heck are you going to do with a degree in that?" You may have heard similar comments from friends and relatives. Everyone, perhaps yourself included, wants to know what you will do with your life after college. The less sure you are about your career direction, the more stress you might feel about it. You may even be concerned that you'll never find your direction. On the other hand, students who have already decided on a career might also feel stress because they are concerned about achieving their goals.

6. **Situational Problems.** Certain stresses are unexpected and sometimes devastating. You may become ill during the term, experience the death of someone

close to you, realize you have a drug or alcohol problem, or cope with an eating disorder. As with all of the categories of stress, if you feel overwhelmed by situational problems, seek help from a counselor on campus or someone you can talk to about these concerns.

Strategies for Reducing Stress

Now that you know what stress is and what causes stress for most students, you will be happy to know that there are many ways to control or even reduce your stress levels. But it is important to take some sort of action before you start to feel overwhelmed. Consider the following strategies for reducing your stress.

- **Relax.** You should make relaxation a regular part of your day. If you don't know how to go about relaxing, there are numerous paperback self-help books available that offer great techniques and advice. At the very least, try deep breathing or meditation for a few minutes each day to help you unwind. If you find yourself "stressing out," stop whatever you are doing, close your eyes, and focus on your breathing for a few minutes. This should help you relax so that you can return to what you were doing, feeling in more control of the situation.

- **Exercise.** Working out daily is a great stress buster. Physical activity helps take your mind off of your stress and the chemicals your body releases during exercise actually boost your ability to handle stressful situations. If you are feeling especially stressed, try taking a walk or a jog to clear your head.

- **Take Charge.** You are in control of your own situation and you have to accept that responsibility. By taking charge, you can control the amount of stress you feel by remembering that stress is an internal reaction to situations, and it is often really an overreaction. However, if stress gets out of control, you can also take charge of the situation by seeking help.

- **Put Problems in Perspective.** Sometimes it helps to talk to a good friend or a family member who has been in a similar situation to help put your problems in a more realistic light. Don't allow yourself to get carried away imagining all the things that could go wrong in a situation—focus instead on the positives. Think about how this particular situation will affect you five years from now. Will it affect your life or will it really not matter much?

- **Be Flexible.** Everyone makes mistakes, and learning from your mistakes will help reduce your stress levels. But if you are too set in the way you do things or the way you view the world, you may end up causing yourself additional stress. It pays to have an open mind and to try new approaches.

- **Develop Interests.** Join a club on campus, meet with others who share similar interests, or find some new interests on your own. By experiencing life outside of schoolwork, you will be able to enjoy yourself and relax during your time off from studying. Developing new interests also helps you in the class-room because you tend to do better in subjects that interest you.

- **Seek Help.** Seek out campus resources to help you through stressful times. In fact, it is a good idea to seek out the people and places that can support you *before* you need them. Often problems can be solved easily if you ask for assistance before a small problem balloons into a major one.

- **Enjoy Yourself.** Take a walk, read a good book, see a movie, call a friend. Do something you like to do before you start feeling overwhelmed. Remember, if you manage your life well, you should have plenty of time for studying and engaging in activities for fun.

SUCCESS AT A GLANCE

Strategies for Reducing Stress

Relax

Exercise

Take Charge

Put Problems in Perspective

Be Flexible

Develop Interests

Seek Help

Enjoy Yourself

Academic Stress: Anxieties

The stress students feel about college, or what we refer to as academic stress, is due to many different factors and is a part of the general stress you feel every day. You want to do well in your classes, you want to gain valuable experience, and you want to be a success in life. However, there are four common types of academic stress or anxieties that can actually get in the way of these goals: public speaking anxiety, writing anxiety, math anxiety, and test anxiety. If you have experienced one of these stresses you know how harmful it can be. In this section we discuss the four types of academic stress and strategies for coping with each.

Get Going

Monitoring Your Stress Level

Many students find that experiencing academic stress impacts motivation for learning. For some, feeling academic stress leads students to overcome procrastination and get their work done. For others, academic stress leads them to feel paralyzed and they become unable to concentrate or work well at all. We believe that you should take the time to monitor both your motivation and stress levels for a few days. Does it seem like stress helps or hinders? Which academic tasks seem to cause the most stress for you? By identifying your own reaction to stress, you will be better able to create ways to cope with your academic stress.

Public Speaking Anxiety

Public speaking causes people to react in strange ways. They may find that their hands get sweaty, that their mouths are dry, or that they forget what they were going to say. In fact, research has found that some people fear public speaking more than death. In college, there will be many times when you are required to speak in public, whether it is making a comment in a large lecture class or giving a presentation or speech to a class.

Coping with Public Speaking Anxiety   The best way to cope with a fear of public speaking is to be prepared. Practice your presentation out loud several times before presenting it to your class. Practice in front of a mirror, or better yet, recruit some friends to listen to your speech. Have them record your time to be sure that you are on track and ask them to critique your speaking style using the following questions:

- **Are You Speaking Too Fast?** Sometimes when people are nervous they talk very fast, which makes it difficult for the audience to follow. Don't rush through your talk. Instead, try to use a conversational tone.

- **Are You Using Good Inflection?** When people are nervous they sometimes speak in a monotone, which is difficult to listen to for an extended period of time. Try to speak confidently and with enthusiasm.

- **Are You Jittery?** You may find yourself moving from side to side or wringing your hands when you are nervous. It is good to move a little, such as using hand gestures or walking around to include the audience, but too much nervous movement can be distracting to your audience.

- **Are You Making Eye Contact?** When you are giving your presentation it may help to focus on one or two friendly faces in the room and "present" to them. You should be sure to make eye contact with the other people in the room, of course. But concentrate mostly on those two people. This strategy should help calm your fear of speaking in front of a large group.

- **Have You Jotted Down Some Notes?** Having some notes to follow during your presentation makes you feel more secure and confident. Even if you have rehearsed your talk and have a good idea of what you will cover, you should have notes to glance at just in case you need a reminder of what you are going to say.

Writing Anxiety

Many students experience a great deal of stress when asked to write something for a class, especially if they are asked to write during class with the added pressure of time limitations. Students might be anxious about having to think up a good idea, flesh the idea out, and then have their writing evaluated by their instructor. They sit staring at a blank page waiting for the words to come. This is sometimes called writer's block and it is a very frustrating experience. Just about every writer, the authors of this book included, has had an experience when finding the words to write has been difficult. However, writing anxiety becomes harmful when students experience writer's block almost every time they try to write. When students are anxious about writing, they try to avoid it as much as possible because they find it such a stressful activity. The problem is that in college (and in most careers after college) you are often asked to express your ideas in writing.

Coping with Writing Anxiety   We offer the following suggestions for dealing with writing anxiety.

- **Write Often.** Like any skill, your ability to write will improve with practice. You may want to keep a daily journal in which you record you experiences. Or you might want to do some "free writing" by giving yourself a fixed amount of time (perhaps five to ten minutes) to write about whatever you want. Another alternative is to sit on a bus or in a coffee shop and write some character sketches about the people you see.

- **Work from a Plan.** It's helpful to make a list of the points you want to make and then use your list to guide you when you are writing your paper. If you are having trouble organizing the points you want to make, talk to a classmate or a tutor about your ideas. Most campuses have a writing center or a place where students can talk to a tutor about their papers at any stage, from choosing a topic, to reading rough drafts, to critiquing final drafts.

- **For Essay Tests, Predict Questions.** This idea will be covered in greater detail in Chapter 18, but in brief, use your class notes and topics emphasized in the text to predict the kinds of questions that might be asked. You might want to look at your professor's old exams to help you predict good essay questions.

- **Start Early.** Because students who experience writing anxiety try to avoid writing, they often procrastinate. These students sometimes believe that they can write only under pressure, but they are fooling themselves because they are actually making their stress level greater by waiting until the last minute. If they do not make a good grade on the paper, they tend to blame it on the fact that they have trouble writing instead of the fact that they churned it out quickly.

Mathematics Anxiety

As with writing, some students feel stress when they encounter anything that has to do with numbers. Students who experience math anxiety usually try to avoid taking math or math-related courses. For most students, math anxiety usually results from previous experiences in math classes. You may have had some trouble with a particular topic, such as word problems in algebra, and have told yourself, "I can't do math" ever since. For some reason, math anxiety seems to be the most traumatic and widespread. However, just like any other type of stress, math anxiety is an overreaction to a situation and, therefore, you can change your response to mathematics.

Coping with Mathematics Anxiety   The following suggestions will help you deal with mathematics anxiety.

- **Face It Head-On.** Don't wait until your senior year to take your math courses—take them early and overcome your fears. In fact, waiting until later in your college career might cause you to forget more of what you had learned in high school math classes.

- **Take a Class That is at Your Level.** Don't try to get into calculus if you have never had a precalculus course. If your college recommends a particular course based on exam scores or placement tests, take that course instead of one that is a higher level.

- **Read the Textbook and Do the Practice Problems Each Day.** Going to class is not enough, because you must be able to apply what you have learned to new situations. Additionally, the more times you work with the material, the better you will remember it.

- **Talk the Problems Through.** One of the best strategies for learning math is to solve problems with words. That is, explain in words how to solve the problem rather than just trying to plug in numbers.

- **Get Help Early On.** If you find that you are having trouble learning math concepts, seek help as soon as you need it. Get help from a classmate or the instructor, and plan to work with a tutor weekly if necessary. In math classes, the information you are learning usually builds on itself so if you don't understand what you learned in Chapter 2 you will have even more trouble learning the material in Chapter 6.

- **Use Positive Talk.** Don't say, "I can't," or "I'll never," to yourself because these thoughts can be self-defeating. Instead, try to focus on the positives. Reward yourself for figuring out a tough problem and keep trying to do your best.

TIMELY TIPS

Learning Life Skills

Are you wondering why you have to take courses that are not really related to your major? Think about what you really need to learn in college. We believe that the time spent learning in college is more than just mastering academic content. In fact, most employers are looking for people who can speak well, write well, think critically, and problem solve effectively. Work on honing these skills while you are in college, even in those classes you may dislike.

General Test Anxiety

Test anxiety is similar to writing and math anxiety, except it is a feeling of stress when studying for or taking an exam, regardless of the subject. You might worry about the types of questions that will be on the test, forgetting about and missing the test, or studying the wrong material. Students who experience test anxiety are often paralyzed with fear when faced with a test situation and they can end up missing questions they know.

Many different experiences can lead to test anxiety. It might be caused by past test-taking experiences, such as blanking on answers or failing an exam. It could be caused by inadequate test preparation. If you know that you are not prepared to take an exam, it's natural to be anxious about it. Test anxiety can also be caused by competition with your friends or classmates. If you are focusing on how others are doing, you might cause yourself undue stress. In addition, test anxiety can be caused by a lack of confidence in yourself as a learner. When students believe that they are not good learners, they tend to become more anxious about testing situations. If you find that you are talking negatively to yourself about your ability to learn, you may actually be causing yourself greater anxiety.

Coping with Test Anxiety   To cope with general test anxiety, try the following suggestions:

- **Be Prepared.** If you monitor your learning to the point where you know which concepts you understand and which concepts are giving you problems, you will feel more confident. Allow enough time for studying, so that you are sure you have prepared the best you can. In addition, gather all of the things you need for the test. Do you need a pencil, calculator, student ID, notes, or anything else? You don't want to be tracking these things down right before the test, so be ready to go the night before.

- **Understand the Task.** Talk to the professor about what the exams will be like. Even better, try to look at some of the professor's old exams. Examining retired tests will give you an idea of what kinds of questions the professor asks and will also help you become familiar with the professor's questioning style. It is also a good idea to talk to the professor or to students who have taken the class about the content and format of the exams.

- **Arrive to Take the Test a Bit Early.** Get organized and practice some deep breathing techniques to relax. Take a few deep breaths; think of something you find comforting—the sound of the ocean, a walk in the woods. Concentrate on and relax each of your muscle groups.

- **Have an Approach in Mind.** If you find you blank out on exams, try to make jot lists as soon as you get the test. Read each question and just jot down everything you know about it in the margin of the test. Don't look at any answers if it is a multiple-choice test, just write everything you know before you blank out.

- **Focus on You.** Ignore other students who finish the exam before you. Just because they finish earlier does not mean that they know more than you do. It might be that they are done so soon because they *don't* know the answers. But either way, don't worry about what other students are doing.

- **Get Help in Controlling Your Anxiety.** There are usually several resource areas on campus that can help you. You might need some tutoring on course content, some counseling to deal with your anxiety, or you might be eligible for alternate testing situations, such as increased time for tests.

- **Visualize Your Success.** Think about how well you will do before you walk into the classroom and remind yourself that you are well prepared and ready to go as the test is being handed out. The more positive you can be, the less anxiety you'll feel.

NETWORKING

Plagiarism Taboos

With more and more students gaining access to Internet information, campuses have seen an increase in student plagiarism. We believe that this is partially due to the fact that many students do not

(continued)

have a complete understanding of what plagiarism is. So let's lay it out for you, because being accused of cheating when you did not know it was wrong is extremely stress inducing. Plagiarism is taking someone else's ideas and representing them as your own. This includes a theory or idea, a direct quote, a paraphrase of an idea, or pieces of information that are not common knowledge. To avoid plagiarism, be sure to give credit to the author whenever you use someone else's ideas in your own work.

Of course, plagiarism also includes direct cheating, such as buying a paper online, turning in another person's work as your own, or copying directly out of another text without quoting the author. It is easy to avoid this type of plagiarism—just don't do it. When you find information on the Internet, or from any other source, be sure to report where that information came from.

Three Important Tips for Reducing Academic Stress

In addition to the ways to cope with math, writing, and test anxiety, here are three tips for coping with the general academic pressures that you experience every day.

1. **Don't Procrastinate.** This sounds simple enough, but probably most of the academic stress students experience comes from waiting until the last minute to get their assignments done. As we discussed in Chapter 6, you are much better off starting early and doing some work each night rather than waiting until right before it is due to begin working on it.

2. **Don't Listen to Other Students Right Before the Test.** Listening to your classmates discuss something you have not studied will just make you more nervous. Simply take your seat, gather your thoughts, take a few deep breaths, and wait for the test to begin. Many students who experience academic stress madly rush through their notes as they are waiting for the exams to be passed out, but this too can increase stress if you find a topic that you don't remember. It is much better to use the time before the exam to relax.

Studying Smarter
An "A" is an "A." We know many students who worry needlessly when they receive anything less than the highest scores. In high school, there may have been a difference between a 99 and a 90, but unless your college uses a plus/minus grading system, both of those scores would be recorded as an A.

3. **Learn to Say No.** Many students experience academic stress because they have too much to do. Don't take on too much added responsibility beyond your classes. You might be

offered some interesting opportunities, but if you wind up with too much to do your grades and your health could suffer. Learn to say no to some things if you find you have too much to handle.

☐ REAL COLLEGE
Andrea's Anxiety

DIRECTIONS: Read the following "Real College" scenario and respond to the questions based on what you learned in this chapter.

Andrea is a first-year college student. She is the first person in her family to attend college and she is trying hard to make her parents proud, but she is worried that she won't make it. Every day she wakes up with a pounding headache and sometimes she even has trouble sleeping because she is so stressed out. Part of the problem is that she is very homesick for her family and her friends. She is also worried about her relationship with her boyfriend who still lives at home—six hours away. He gets upset if she doesn't come home every weekend and it seems likely that they will break up soon. In addition, although Andrea is starting to meet new friends in college, they are not like her old friends from high school—she just doesn't have anyone she can really confide in yet.

Another problem is that Andrea was forced to register for a math class because it was the only course open and she hates math. Every time she studies for an exam, she gets so nervous that her palms get sweaty and she can't really concentrate on what she is doing. She is sure that she will fail the course, but she doesn't know what to do about it because she believes that there is no way she will ever be able to learn math. She is thinking about dropping out of school because she's afraid that she is not smart enough.

Use what you have learned about coping with and reducing stress to help Andrea figure out what to do.

1. List three to five strategies Andrea should use to reduce her general stress about her social and family relationships.

2. How do you think these strategies will help Andrea's situation?

3. List three to five strategies Andrea should use to reduce her math anxiety.

4. How do you think these strategies will help Andrea's situation?

☐ THINKING CRITICALLY
Something to Think About and Discuss

- What kinds of academic tasks (e.g., essays, mathematics, standardized tests) cause you to feel the most stress? Why do you think you experience anxiety when faced with those tasks? What can you do to reduce your anxiety in those situations?

- How can you tell the difference between being really stressed out and having normal, productive stress?

☐ ADD TO YOUR PORTFOLIO

For three to five days this week, keep a stress diary where you record your reactions to stressful events.

- What stresses you out?
- How do you react to this stress?
- What can you do to keep your stress levels in check?

Try to use at least two of strategies presented in this chapter to help you cope with those stressful situations.

PART THREE

STRATEGIES FOR COLLEGE LEARNING

Part Three introduces a wide variety of strategies for active learning. We have included two chapters from college-level texts for practicing these strategies as appendixes to this book. The first piece, a history chapter, discusses the Vietnam conflict and social conflict that occurred between 1964 and 1971. The second chapter, from a psychology text, focuses on cognition and intelligence. The information from these text chapters is used throughout the remainder of *College Success Strategies* as we present the learning and study strategies.

In Chapter 10, you learn about strategies for gearing up and for concentrating as you read and about the importance of creating a good environment for learning. Chapter 11 introduces you to strategies for staying active and concentrating during reading.

In Chapter 12, you learn about the importance of rehearsal. We discuss strategies for both verbal and written rehearsal to help you remember and retrieve what you have studied. Chapter 13 presents strategies to help you organize information to review as you prepare for exams.

CHAPTER 10

PREREADING STRATEGIES

Read this chapter to answer the following questions:

- How can you create a positive learning environment?
- Why do you need to gear up during reading?
- What are some strategies for gearing up?

SELF-ASSESSMENT

DIRECTIONS: Answer each of the following questions by answering yes or no. This will give you an idea of how you get ready to read your textbooks.

	Yes	No
1. Do you read in an environment that is relatively free of distractions?	_____	_____
2. Do you have an idea of the concepts that are presented in the chapter before you start to read?	_____	_____
3. Do you set goals prior to reading?	_____	_____
4. Do you reflect on what you are going to read?	_____	_____
5. Do you skim through your reading and pay attention to chapter headings and boldface terms before you read the chapter?	_____	_____

If you answered yes to most of these questions, you are doing a good job of "warming up" prior to reading. If you answered no to most of the questions, this chapter will help you learn some prereading techniques.

Gearing Up for Reading

As a college student, reading is something that you have to do everyday. But are you getting what you need out of your textbook reading, or are you just spinning your wheels? Do you find that your first half-hour is unproductive because you are not concentrating on what you are doing? Do you have a difficult time motivating yourself to get started? Do you get lost if the reading assignment is long? If so, maybe the problem is that you have not geared up for reading.

Studying Smarter
To make the most of your study sessions, take some time to warm up before reading and then read actively.

Picture a track meet at a local college. The athletes pile out of a van just as the first race begins. They throw off their sweats and start running. Would that ever happen? Of course not. Just as an athlete would never run a race or even practice "cold" you should not expect to start reading or studying without warming up. Athletes warm up to get their muscles ready to perform. Students, on the other hand, need to warm up their brains so that they will be more efficient and productive and remember more of what they read.

There are several activities you can engage in in order to gear up for reading. You should:

1. **Create a Good Learning Environment.** Think about the place where you currently read and study by asking yourself the following questions: Do you study

in a setting that allows you to concentrate and study effectively? Are you constantly distracted by people, noise, or other diversions? Your learning environment can help you in a positive way when reading or studying or, if you do not have a good setting, it can actually hinder your efforts. You need to create a place that is free from distractions and allows you to maximize your studying time, so consider these factors:

- **Noise Level.** Some students say that they need complete quiet to study. Even hearing a clock ticking in the background is enough to distract them. Other students say that they study best in a crowded, noisy room because the noise actually helps them concentrate. Some study most successfully when they are in familiar surroundings such as their bedroom; for others, familiar surroundings do not make a difference. Some students like quiet music playing; others do not. The point is, you should know the level of noise that is optimal for your own studying. However, one general rule for all students is that the television seems to be more of a distraction than music or other background noise, so we suggest you leave the TV off when you are reading or studying. In fact, we believe that the fewer distractions the better. This means turning off your cell phone and saving Internet surfing or playing computer games as rewards when you have finished studying. If you are convinced you need noise in order to study, we suggest "white noise"—the hum of an air conditioner or the sound of an electric fan—noise that drowns out more distracting sounds.

- **Your Special "Learning" Place.** Your ideal learning place is one where the only thing you do there is study. If you have a desk, set it up so that you have everything handy—pens and pencils, a tablet of paper, calculator, your books and notes or anything else you need to study. If everything is right at hand, you won't have an excuse to get up and interrupt your studying. If you find that you cannot create an effective learning environment in your home because there are too many distractions, try to find a quiet place on campus to study, such as the library or the student union. You can also concentrate better when you read or study in a straight-backed chair, such as a desk or kitchen chair. Keep in mind that the absolute worst possible place to study is on your bed. Students who attempt to study on their bed usually wind up doing more sleeping than studying.

2. **Survey Your Textbooks.** After setting up your learning environment at the beginning of the term, the next step in gearing up is examining your textbooks for each course. Most textbooks are written and formatted in a way that is very reader friendly. Such textbooks have some or all of the following features:

   - An introduction at the beginning of the book that outlines the book's features, organization, and format.
   - Tips for studying and learning the discipline.
   - Preview questions or an organizer at the beginning of each chapter to help readers focus on what they are about to learn.

- Diagrams, pictures, and figures to give readers a better perspective of the topic.
- **Bold-faced** or *italicized* words to emphasize key terms.
- Summary or review questions at the end of each chapter.
- Large margins so that readers have room to write notes as they read.
- A CD-ROM or other supplementary materials.

In order to determine if your textbooks are reader friendly, examine the way they are arranged. If you find that your books are not reader friendly, you will have to use additional strategies in order to get the most out of them. Surveying your texts will help you:

- **Familiarize yourself with the topics** to be covered so that you can activate what you already know. One of the keys to being an efficient and effective reader is to make links to new information using what you already know. Students who do this are able to concentrate their studying efforts in a more productive manner.

NETWORKING

Building Background Knowledge

You can use the Internet to help you build your background knowledge of the content for your college courses. For one of your classes this semester, choose a topic that interests you and then visit several sites on the Web to find out more about it. Often getting some additional information before you even begin to read the chapter will help you understand difficult material, and can even help you become more motivated to learn in the class.

- **Increase your interest** in reading the chapters. If you have an idea of what you are going to read, you may be more interested in the material and remember it better in the long term. You can think about tying information to current events and to personal situations.
- **Give yourself time to gear up** for reading effectively. Unless you have some information about the average chapter length, the difficulty, and format of the text you are going to read, you will not be able to plan your time wisely. For example, taking a small amount of time to preview each chapter can save you a considerable amount of actual reading time.

GET GOING

Staying Motivated Through Previewing

Sometimes just getting started is half the battle. Because previewing takes such a small amount of time and has such a big payoff, it may be the motivator you need to keep up with your reading assignments. Once you have spent ten minutes previewing, you just might be able to stick with it a while longer to get some reading completed.

3. **Preview Your Reading Assignments.** You have found a quiet place to study and you have all of your studying tools at your fingertips. Now you're ready to gear up for the day's reading by previewing. Previewing the chapter doesn't take very long, but just as surveying your entire textbook helped you gear up for each course, previewing what you will read today will help to activate your prior knowledge and build your interest in the specific topics. Previewing consists of the following steps:

- **Read the Chapter Title.** The title tells you about the overall topic of the chapter and may clue you in to the author's intent. The title can also help you activate what you know about the topic so that you can begin to make links.

- **Read the Headings and Subheadings.** The headings and subheadings will tell you about the specific focus in the chapter and may suggest the author's approach to the topic. For example, a subheading in your history text called "The Horrors of War" would introduce very different material than a subheading called "War: Benefits and Advances." The headings and subheadings also provide organization to the chapter to help understand its flow.

- **Read the Boldfaced or Italicized Terms.** These terms will clue you in to ideas that will be emphasized in the text and will point out new vocabulary or content-specific terms that will be discussed in the chapter. You can also begin to get a better understanding of which terms go with which headings and subheadings for more efficient studying and learning.

- **Note the Typographical Aids.** Besides boldfaced or italicized words, many texts use graphs, charts, tables, or illustrations to emphasize key ideas. Read the captions that accompany these text aids as another way of determining what is important in the chapter.

Studying Smarter

Part of studying smarter is not only being an effective learner but also an efficient learner. Previewing helps with efficiency because it gets your mind "wired" for reading and helps you concentrate.

- **Read the Introduction.** If your textbook offers chapter introductions, it is a good idea to read this section when you preview the chapter. Introductions provide a global idea of what the topic is about and the scope of information that will be covered in the chapter.

- **Read the Summary.** If your textbook contains chapter summaries, it is a good idea to read this section *before* you actually read the chapter. The summary section outlines the key information you should have learned when reading the chapter and focuses your attention to the most important concepts in the chapter.

- **Read the End of the Chapter Material.** This may include study questions, vocabulary lists, or application exercises. The end material will also provide cues about what the author deems as the most important information in the chapter. Look for overlap between the summary and the end of chapter material as a way of identifying what you should pay particular attention to when you read the chapter in its entirety.

SUCCESS AT A GLANCE

Examining Your Textbooks

Examine the textbooks you are reading this term. Which of the following features do they contain?

	Textbook 1 Subject:	Textbook 2 Subject:	Textbook 3 Subject:	Textbook 4 Subject:	Textbook 5 Subject:
Preview Questions					
Boldfaced Terms					
Summaries					
Diagrams					
Formulas					

(continued)

	Textbook 1 Subject:	Textbook 2 Subject:	Textbook 3 Subject:	Textbook 4 Subject:	Textbook 5 Subject:
Glossaries					
Application Activities					
Large Margins					
Review Questions					

Although this might sound like a lot to do before reading, previewing actually takes a only few minutes to accomplish because you are not getting bogged down in the details of the chapter. Your purpose in previewing is to get a general idea of the concepts that will be covered in the chapter, not to read and digest it totally. Previewing should serve as your warm up to reading.

4. **Determine Your Reading Purpose.** As you preview a chapter you should begin to think of some questions about the key topics. For example, in previewing the "The Nation Divides: The Vietnam War and Social Conflict, 1964–1971," which includes the excerpt on the Great Society, you might ask yourself these questions: What was Johnson's vision of the Great Society? What was the purpose of the program? How was it carried out? How did the Great Society improve the quality of people's lives? By asking questions, you are starting to think about the key ideas contained in the text, which will make your reading more effective. Jot down your questions and try to answer them as you read.

It is always a good idea to read with a purpose in mind. When you are reading your textbooks for a class, your primary purpose is to learn the information contained in each chapter. However, this is a tall order. If you tried to learn every idea contained in every chapter, you probably would have a difficult time. What you need to do is identify and learn the key ideas contained in each chapter. A good way to help you determine what's important is to use your class syllabus and lecture notes as a guide.

TIMELY TIPS

Saving Time Through Previewing

For some reason, many students often balk at previewing a chapter before they begin to read it, believing that previewing just wastes time. Nothing could be further from the truth. The ten or fifteen minutes that it takes to preview actually saves you time in the long run and can be a real motivator to reading the assignment. Previewing also can create interest, which also makes the reading more pleasant.

☐ REAL COLLEGE
Fast Frank

DIRECTIONS: Read the following "Real College" scenario and respond to the question based on what you learned in this chapter.

Frank has always had the attitude that "the quickest way is the best way," which is how he got the nickname Fast Frank. Although this may be a good motto to follow in some things—Frank could always find the quickest way to work, the fastest Internet connection, the shortest line at the grocery store—when it came to studying and learning, the quickest way often didn't pan out.

Frank had been a fairly conscientious student in high school. He did what he needed to do to make good grades and he was able to do it at warp speed. He really never had to read his high school textbooks because his teachers gave him study guides and other studying supports that didn't make reading necessary. But things changed when Frank got to college. He was excellent at finding the quickest route to his classes, but his quickness didn't pay off when it came to reading his textbooks. Because he never had to read much in high school, he thought if he just sat down and tried to plow through the assigned reading of his textbooks he would get it done. Read it fast and move on. He found out very quickly that his approach wasn't going to work. He was getting through with the reading fast, but it was wasted time. He couldn't remember anything that he read and had a difficult time making connections between ideas presented in the chapters.

What advice would you give Frank about what he can do before he reads so that his actual reading time might be effective as well as efficient?

☐ THINKING CRITICALLY
Something to Think About and Discuss

- Discuss three benefits you see to engaging in prereading activities.
- Discuss three concerns you have about engaging in prereading activities.

☐ ADD TO YOUR PORTFOLIO

1. Select one of the courses you are taking this semester and preview your next reading assignment. How did you preview the chapter? Did your previewing help motivate you to read the chapter? Did your previewing enable you to get a good grasp of the concepts presented in the chapter? How might you modify your previewing for different courses?

2. Do a reading tolerance test. For each of your courses you probably have a set amount of time for which you can read without losing concentration—we call this your reading tolerance level. Your reading tolerance level will depend on the course, the textbook, your background knowledge, and your interest in the topic. To build your reading tolerance you must first know your starting point: When you read in each of your textbooks this week, time yourself. How long can you go before you lose your concentration? Write down your time for each text. Then, with each subsequent time you read, try to build your tolerance by adding two to five minutes to your total reading time. Even if you lose concentration you can generally get yourself back into it for just another few minutes. Aim to get your reading tolerance to forty-five to sixty minutes for each class.

3. Think about your current learning environment when responding to these questions.

   Where do you currently study? Check all that apply.

   _____ Bedroom

   _____ Library

   _____ Living room

   _____ Desk

   _____ Bed

   _____ Kitchen table

   _____ No set studying place

   _____ Other _____

Which of these best describes your learning environment? Check all that apply.

_____ TV on

_____ Music playing

_____ Complete quiet

_____ Roommates/others talking

_____ Roommates/others studying

_____ Other _____

What are the greatest distractors to your studying? What changes do you need to make to create a more effective learning environment?

_____

_____

_____

CHAPTER 11
STRATEGIC READING

Read this chapter to answer the following questions:

- What is the difference between active and passive reading?
- What are some strategies for concentrating on textbook reading?

SELF-ASSESSMENT

DIRECTIONS: Answer each of the following questions by answering yes or no. This will give you an idea of how actively you read your textbooks.

	Yes	No
1. Do you try to personalize your reading to help you understand it better?	_____	_____
2. Do you write in your textbooks when you read?	_____	_____
3. Do you try to put important text information in your own words?	_____	_____
4. Do you think about the visual aids in the chapter?	_____	_____
5. Do you try to summarize what you have read?	_____	_____
6. Do you reflect on ideas during reading?	_____	_____
7. Do you understand most of what you have read?	_____	_____
8. Do you ask for clarification when you don't understand what you have read?	_____	_____
9. Do you keep up with your reading?	_____	_____

If you answered yes to most of these questions, you are off to a good start. If you answered no to most of these questions, this chapter should help you get on track.

Reading Done "Write": Staying Active During Reading

Have you ever finished reading a text chapter only to realize that you don't remember anything you just read? If so, chances are you were not reading actively. Because reading textbooks rarely tops any student's list of favorite activities, and also because reading textbooks is one of the most common college tasks, it is important to learn strategies that enable you to understand and remember what you read. If you finish "reading" ten pages of text and can't summarize what you have read, you have just wasted valuable time. So where do you begin?

Studying Smarter

In order to improve concentration and remember more of what you read, never read without a pen or pencil in hand. Have the attitude that writing in your textbooks is a positive activity and a part of sound studying practice.

Put Away Your Highlighters

When we ask students how they go about reading their textbooks, many students tell us that they try to pull out key ideas by highlighting or underlining during read-

GET GOING

Breaking the Highlighting Habit

Some students just gasp when we tell them to get rid of their highlighters. They believe that highlighting is the strategy of choice for most college students. As we try to change their minds and talk more about text annotation, we have them make the transition from highlighting to annotating by purchasing a pen with a highlighter on one end. Such pens are commonly found in college bookstores and office supply stores. We get them into the annotating mode, but when they feel this absolute need to highlight and annotate, they have everything they need right there.

ing. Although this is a popular strategy, highlighting is actually a very passive activity because students do not really understand the ideas they are highlighting. Many students actually put off reading for understanding until after they have highlighted the text. In other words, they skim the text looking for important information, highlight entire sections that seem important, and plan to return to those sections later when they study for the exam. Or, they do the opposite, highlighting only key words that are already either in bold print or italics. Neither approach is very strategic and both encourage passive reading.

When students mark their texts through highlighting, they are not being very selective; sometimes entire pages are highlighted in bright pink or yellow or blue. Students who highlight most everything have not been very discriminating about what to mark. They will have just as much information to cope with when they begin to study—and they will have to go fishing in a pink, yellow, or blue sea in order to find the key points.

On the other hand, some students highlight too little. If these students tried to rely on their highlighting for their test review, they would not have adequate information and would probably end up rereading entire chapters or just memorizing small bits and pieces of information. Our advice is to put away your highlighters because you will want to use strategies that promote greater active involvement in reading and learning.

Make a Note of It

As we discussed in Chapter 10, active readers gear up to read by previewing and then they are ready to focus on their reading. One way to be sure that you are concentrating on and understanding what you read is to annotate your text, which requires you to write in your books. We realize this might take a bit of adjusting to because most of you were not allowed to write in your textbooks in high school. But in college, you buy your own books. Be sure you get your money's worth and "write on."

NETWORKING

Learning from Web Pages

Many colleges and universities offer advice for learning from text on their Web pages. First, try to locate these resources at your own institution by looking at an academic assistance or learning center page. Then, seek out advice from learning centers at other institutions using the following keywords: learning center, tutoring center, study strategies, study skills, textbook reading.

What Is Annotation?

In a nutshell, annotation is summing up the important information in your text by briefly writing the key ideas in the margin. Unlike highlighting, which promotes passivity, annotation requires that you understand what you are reading. It requires you to actively make decisions about what is important because you are putting the ideas in your own words. As shown on the next page, an annotated piece of text includes key ideas as well as examples, definitions, and other important details about the concepts.

In order to annotate properly, you need to think about what you read before you write. If you find that your mind is wandering or that you are not concentrating, you have to get back on track. Because you stop reading after a paragraph or two to annotate what you have read, you will be able to reconnect with the reading.

Why Annotate Your Text?

Annotating your text is an effective strategy for several reasons. Annotation helps you:

- **Isolate Information.** By annotating your texts, you are selecting important information that you want to remember. Much of what is written in textbooks is filler so your job is to whittle down the information to just the key information, details, and examples.

- **Reduce Information.** You reduce the information you need to study into more manageable amounts.

- **Organize Information.** Sometimes your textbooks fail to do a good job of organizing information. Through annotation you can reorganize the material in a way that is meaningful for you, which makes it easier for you to remember what you have read and to prepare for exams.

Model Annotations of a History Text

"Great society" = War on poverty: ⅕ lived ↓ pov. line

Measures to combat pov.
1. ↑ $ + food stamps through welfare pgrms.

2. raised social security
3. Improved educational opp.
  - Head Start
  - Elem. + Sec. Ed. Act
  - expanded student loans
  - job care for employee training
  - VISTA

Race Issues— LBJ changes position on race due to
1. ≠ weaked US competition w/ China + USSR
2. AA struggle in South had reached a very hostile stage

The Great Society: Fighting Poverty and Discrimination

In pursuit of what he called the Great Society, Johnson first declared a "War on Poverty." No citizen in the richest nation on earth should live in squalor, he believed. More than one out of five Americans still lived below the conservatively estimated official poverty line ($3,022 for a nonfarm family of four in 1960), and 70 percent of these were white.

The president and a large congressional majority passed several measures to alleviate poverty. They sharply in-creased the availability of money and food stamps through the Aid to Families with Dependent Children ("welfare") program, and they raised Social Security payments to older Americans. Several programs focused on improving educational opportunities as an avenue out of poverty: Head Start offered preschool education and meals for youngsters, the Elementary and Secondary Education Act sent federal funds to the least affluent school districts, and an expanded system of student loans facilitated access to college. The Job Corps provided employment training, and Volunteers in Service to America (VISTA) served as a domestic Peace Corps, funneling people with education and skills into poor communities to serve as teachers and providers of other social services.

No barrier to opportunity in the early 1960s was higher than the color bar. Both opportunist and idealist, Johnson as president shed his segregationist voting record (necessary for election in Texas before 1960) and became the most vocal proponent of racial equality ever to occupy the Oval Office. Two factors facilitated his change in position. Blatant inequalities for American citizens weakened the United States in its competition with the Soviets and Chinese for the loyalty of the nonwhite Third World majority. Moreover, the African American freedom struggle in the South had reached a boiling point. Black frustration was mounting over white brutality and the seeming indifference or even hostility of the national government.

- **Identify Key Concepts.** Annotation also helps you differentiate between major concepts and supporting ideas. Although for most courses you will have to know something about both major concepts and supporting details, by determining what is really important you will know how to focus your studying. Annotation helps you study concepts rather than small bits of information.

- **Monitor Your Learning.** Because you annotate in your own words, you can monitor your understanding of what you are reading. If you are unable to put the information in your own words, you are alerted to the fact that your comprehension is breaking down.

Studying Smarter
Different types of text call for different approaches to annotation. Previewing will help you figure out the most effective way to annotate your text.

How Do You Annotate?

There are some basic guidelines to follow regardless of the type of text you are annotating. Although you might have to modify these guidelines slightly for special kinds of texts, they will work in a majority of instances.

- **Read First, Then Annotate.** To help you decide what to annotate, read a section and then think about what would be important if you were going to teach the material to someone else. When students try to read and annotate at the same time, they end up writing either too much or too little. We generally suggest that if your text does not have clearly defined sections, read at least two or three paragraphs before stopping to annotate. Another alternative is to keep reading until the text seems to move to a new topic. When you first begin to annotate, it's okay to read just one paragraph and then write down the key information. However, as you become a seasoned annotator, you should be able to read more before you begin to do your annotations.

- **Write Your Annotations in Your Own Words.** Don't copy directly from the book, unless you are annotating something that must be learned exactly as it is stated in the book, such as a chemistry or statistics formula. When you are annotating definitions, you will want to simply paraphrase the author's words so that you don't change the meaning of the definition. Otherwise, put all information into your own words. (See the accompanying table for examples of the difference between paraphrasing and writing in your own words.) Keep in mind that stating things in your own words is a good way of monitoring what you understand. Information that is not understood should not be skipped over. Ask for help from another student or from your professor.

Difference Between Paraphrasing and Writing in Your Own Words

	Your text states . . .	Your annotations . . .
Paraphrasing	The term intelligence refers to individuals' abilities to understand complex ideas, to adapt effectively to the environment, to learn from experience, to engage in various forms of reasoning, to overcome obstacles by careful thought.	*Intelligence=how one understands ideas, adapts, learns fr. experience, reasons, solves problems through thinking*
Writing in Your Own Words	Johnson's vision of the Great Society extended to the broader quality of life in the United States. Health care was perhaps the most fundamental issue for citizens' sense of personal security. After 1965, the new Medicare system paid for the medical needs of Americans age sixty-five and older, and Medicaid underwrote health care services for the indigent.	*LBJ's Great Society-extended quality of life, esp. in health care* *EX. Medicare for seniors & Medicaid for the poor*

■   ■   ■

What Type of Information Should You Annotate?

Remember that the purpose of annotation is to isolate information that you will need to study and remember. Although disciplines are different in terms of the types of concepts you will need to focus on, you should look for the following types of information whenever you annotate:

- **Definitions,** especially content-specific terms and concepts. Content-specific terms are words you find in that particular subject. For example, *triarchic theory* (page 253) is a content-specific term in the psychology chapter, as is *the Great Society* (page 277) from the history chapter. *Catapulted* (page 277), also from the history chapter, is not a content-specific word. If you did not know the definition for catapulted, you might look it up in the dictionary, but you would not include it in your annotations.

- **Examples** are also important to annotate because they depict specific instances, theories, experiments, cases, and so forth. Text examples often show up on your tests, so it is crucial to note them. You also should include personal examples when you can, because relating the information to what you already know will help you better remember the information. If the text does not provide an example, but you can think of one that helps you, add that information to your annotations.

- **Predicted test questions** are also an important consideration. When you read, try to predict likely test questions about the material. Be sure to ask higher-level questions as well as questions that connect your reading to the class lecture. Higher-level questions require more than just memorization of facts; they require application of the concept. You can begin the prediction process when you preview and then hone those questions during annotation.

- **People, dates, places, and events** are important in history, social science, and political science courses. However, this should not be the only type of information you annotate. The types of questions you will usually be asked in college require you to think at a higher level about the significance of the names, dates, and events. The only reason you annotate this type of information is to get a chronology of events. Be sure that you think about how the information fits into the larger context of the material.

- **Numbered lists or characteristics** contained in your text should also be annotated. If your text states that "there are three major causes of," or "reasons for," or "factors that contribute to" a certain idea, annotate them by numbering them in the margin. In this way, you are connecting and learning those ideas together. Reader-friendly texts generally cue you to how many reasons or characteristics you should annotate, but less friendly texts do not. Even though the text may not point out how many there are, you should be aware and number the lists.

TIMELY TIPS

Annotation Pays Off

One of the major complaints that students have when they first begin to annotate is that it takes too long. However, if you stick with it and try different approaches to annotation, there is a huge pay-off in the end. And, in the long run, annotation actually ends up saving time since you are able to remember and understand much more of what you read and annotate as you prepare for exams.

- **Relationships between concepts,** such as cause/effect or comparison/contrast, are important to note. When you read your text, look for relationships between concepts, even if the text doesn't explicitly point them out. They will help you reorganize the information in a meaningful way.

- **Graphs, charts, diagrams,** and other visuals are important to annotate because they often contain information that is not anywhere else in the text. In addition, graphs and diagrams can also provide good examples of the concepts presented.

Studying Your Annotations

If you have done a good job of annotating, studying from your annotations is actually quite simple. To use your annotations to help you study, cover up the text with your hand or a piece of notebook paper. Read over your annotations a few times to be sure that you understand the concepts. When you feel comfortable with your understanding of the material and that your annotations are complete, talk through the major points in your annotations without looking at the text. You should be able to talk about each topic that is annotated and you should be able to give examples and details as well. If you find that there is a section that you don't know, then reread your annotations. If you still don't understand, then reread that section in the text, ask a friend, look at your lecture notes, or ask your professor.

When you talk through your annotations, be sure that you are precise and complete in your explanations. Preciseness means that what you are saying is accurate information, that the conclusions you are drawing are logical, and that you can see relationships between ideas. Completeness means that you know all of the important information, not just the main point. It's also important to know examples, explanations, and, in many cases, details. For example, you should understand the why's and how's of the Vietnam conflict, not just the chronology of dates or events.

It's also a good idea to review your annotations a little bit each day so that when you are ready to study for an exam, you already know a lot of the material. These review sessions are a good time to link your lecture notes, secondary texts, and discussion group notes to your annotations. Pulling everything together as you go along makes studying from your annotations an active approach that is efficient and effective.

Another effective way to study your annotations is by asking yourself questions based on what you have written. Be careful not to simply ask "what" questions or questions that require one-word answers. You will want to be sure that some of your questions begin with "why," "how," and "explain."

Annotation Pitfalls

We turn now to three major problems students can experience when they are learning to annotate.* In order to help you avoid these pitfalls and to assess your own annotations, we will outline these pitfalls and offer some suggestions for overcoming them.

1. **"Medieval Monk" Syndrome.** This happens when a student annotates by copying the text almost word for word. Sometimes students fall into this trap because they are trying to memorize information instead of really learning it. Students who write too much in the margins may be afraid that they will leave out something important if they try to paraphrase. However, with practice, you should be able to tell the difference between key ideas and details. If you find yourself experiencing the medieval monk syndrome, be sure to do a thorough job of previewing the text before you read so that you are somewhat familiar with the chapter contents. Read longer sections at a time before marking. After reading each section think about what would be important information to tell someone about the material you just read and write it in your own words.

2. **"Nothin' Here" Syndrome.** Students who use this approach do not annotate very much at all. They may have random words annotated, or may just copy the heading or bold-faced words in the margin. This is a problem because if there is not enough information annotated in the margins there is little content to study. It leads students to believe that they have learned all the important material when, in fact, they have not. Sometimes students don't annotate enough because they feel that the strategy takes too much time. If this is a concern you have, try annotation with one course this term. You will probably find that it actually *saves* you time when you go to study because you have already thought about the information and organized it in some way. Occasionally, students do not annotate enough because the margins in the text are very small. If this is a problem, use post-it notes to annotate and stick them in the margins to give you more room to write.

3. **"Rest of the Story" Syndrome.** Students who demonstrate this pitfall may identify the key topics but do not annotate complete ideas. Sometimes students only partially mark ideas to save time, but because they do not pull out entire ideas, they will have trouble using their annotations to help them study.

---

*This section draws from Simpson, M. L., & Nist, S. L., Textbook annotation: An effective and efficient study strategy for college students, *Journal of Reading, 34,* (1990, 122–129).

SUCCESS AT A GLANCE

Annotation Pitfalls and Models

Medieval Monk	Nothin' Here Syndrome	Rest of the Story
To eliminate cultural bias from IQ tests, psychologists design culture-fair tests	Culture fair tests-items	Culture fair tests-eliminate bias
Attempt to include only items to which all groups have exposure; usually nonverbal in nature		
EX. In Raven Progressive Matrices, which consists of 60 matrices of varying difficulty; each has a logical pattern and missing design; test focuses on fluid intelligence which is our abilities to form concepts, reason, and identify similarities.	Raven Progressive Matrices	Ex. Raven Progressive Matrices
	Tests for fluid intelligence	based on idea of fluid intelligence
Less likely to be biased but don't know if problem is totally eliminated.		

This is especially a problem in courses that give cumulative finals. If you did not annotate in enough detail, you may have to resort to rereading just to make sense of the information. Sometimes, students try to annotate only the information they don't know. In other words, when they come across a topic that they know a little bit about, they will only annotate the new information.

Model Annotations	Passage

Culture-fair tests =
designed to help do
away with cultural bias
- Include items
  that are nonverbal
- Useful with all
  races and ethnicity
- EX. Raven
  Progressive Matrices
  Has 60 matrices
  of varying diff.
  Ind. must choose
  which missing
  piece complete
  matrix
  Focuses on fluid
  intell. Ability to
  form concepts,
  reason, and find
  similarities
- Probably doesn't
  totally do away
  with bias

In an effort to eliminate cultural bias from
intelligence tests, psychologists have attempted
to design *culture-fair* tests. Such tests attempt
to include only items to which all groups,
regardless of ethnic or racial background,
have been exposed. Because many minority
children are exposed to languages other than
standard English, these tests tend to be nonverbal in nature. One of these, the *Raven Progressive Matrices* (Raven, 1977), is illustrated
in Figure 7.22. This test consists of sixty matrices of varying difficulty, each containing a
logical pattern or design with a missing part.
Individuals select the item that completes the
pattern from several different choices. Because
the Raven test and ones like it focus primarily
on *fluid intelligence*—our basic abilities to form
concepts, reason, and identify similarities—
these tests seem less likely to be subject to cultural bias than other kinds of intelligence
tests. However, it is not clear that these tests,
or any others, totally eliminate the problem of
subtle built-in bias.

However, one of the benefits of annotation is that it helps you connect new
ideas with prior knowledge, which helps you remember the new information.
A student who doesn't link the information together will be less likely to
remember it on an exam. To overcome this pitfall, write everything you think
you will need to remember, even if the information seems common sense now.

Read over your annotations to be sure that they are complete and that they make sense. One way to know whether they are complete is to ask yourself—and be honest about this—if you were allowed to use only your annotations to prepare for an exam over the material, would you be able to do well based on what you have selected to annotate?

Practicing text annotation will help you become better at locating the key information and pulling out complete ideas. By taking the time to create good, quality annotations, you will save yourself time when you go to study the information. However, doing a halfhearted job will not be much help come exam time.

Some Common Concerns About Annotation

Annotation is a strategy that many students find is one of the best ways to help them focus on their reading. However, many students have concerns about their annotations.

- **How Do You Know What is Important to Mark?** Deciding what is important to annotate is sometimes tricky. Obviously, you want to note what the text emphasizes, but you also want to annotate information the professor stresses in class. You can often tell what is important by looking at the headings and subheadings in your book. Most students find that the more they annotate in a textbook, the more familiar they become with how the text is written and what the professor thinks is important. Therefore, even if you are having trouble organizing the information right now, eventually you should feel more confident about it.

- **Doesn't This Take a Lot of Time?** Yes, in the beginning annotation does take more time than reading alone. Maybe even twice as long. However, if you have annotated properly, you have already taken a big step in preparing for exams. When you annotate, you have pulled out all of the information you will need to study, so you shouldn't have to reread the material unless you need some clarification about a specific concept. In addition, because you have actively studied the text material from the start, you will be able to remember more. This will cut your study time prior to an exam. Most students say that they find that the extra time spent annotating is worth it when they go back to study because they are sure they understand the material.

- **How Can You Be Sure That You are Annotating the Information That Will Be on the Exam?** By listening to class lectures and discussion, you should be able to determine most of the important information. However, the goal of annotation is to learn the concepts that are presented in the text, not to guess exactly what will be on the exam. If you understand all of the information in the text, you will be prepared for almost any exam question on that topic.

☐ REAL COLLEGE
Hillary's Highlighter

DIRECTIONS: Read the following "Real College" scenario and respond to the questions based on what you learned in this chapter.

Hillary is a returning student. After twenty years she has decided to quit her job and return to school full-time. Because she wants to get off to a good start, she bought herself all the supplies she thought she would need—pencils, notebooks, pens, and especially highlighters. Hillary doesn't see how she could study without her highlighter. Her approach is to open her textbook to the assigned chapter and immediately put her highlighter to work. Her daughter jokes that most of the pages in her books are now bright yellow.

For Hillary's sociology class she must read her textbook and the local newspaper. When she reads the text, she tries to highlight everything that seems important. One problem is that it *all* seems important so she sometimes ends up highlighting whole pages. There are so many details in the textbook that she is not sure what the professor will focus on for the exam. She is especially careful to note every name and date discussed in the book, but she doesn't spend a lot of time reading the newspaper because the professor barely mentions the newspaper in class. Basically, she just skims the articles for the facts. Hillary did not do well on the first essay exam even though she studied for hours because it seemed to focus on relating the sociology topics to the newspaper articles. She knows that she needs a new approach to learning because when she studies, she finds that she rereads almost every chapter because it was all highlighted. She hardly has time to read all of her text once, much less twice.

Using what you know about annotations, what advice would you give Hillary about switching from highlighting to annotation?. What insight would you give Hillary about how she should approach annotating her sociology readings?

☐ THINKING CRITICALLY
Something to Think About and Discuss

- Examine the textbooks you are reading this term. Which of the following features do they contain?
- Discuss three benefits you see to using annotation.
- Discuss three concerns you have about using annotation.

☐ ADD TO YOUR PORTFOLIO

1. Annotate the history chapter, which begins on page 275. How might you annotate this text differently than you would the psychology chapter?

2. Annotate the text for one of your classes for one week. Remember to annotate in your own words and to mark all of the important information contained in the text.

3. Reflect on your learning of the material you previewed and annotated. Do you remember the concepts in the chapters you annotated better than the concepts in other chapters? How do you feel the strategy will benefit you when you begin to study for your exam?

CHAPTER 12

REHEARSING AFTER READING

Read this chapter to answer the following questions:

- What are rehearsal strategies?
- Why is it important to know how to use a variety of rehearsal strategies?
- When is it appropriate to use the different types of rehearsal strategies?

DIRECTIONS: Think about the types of rehearsal strategies you currently use. Answer yes or no for each of the following questions. Do you:

	Yes	No
1. Create CARDS, concept maps, or charts to rehearse information?	_____	_____
2. Vary your studying techniques depending on the course?	_____	_____
3. Create a study plan before each exam?	_____	_____
4. Connect ideas together as you study?	_____	_____
5. Study with the intent to really learn the information?	_____	_____
6. Self-test as a way of monitoring what you know?	_____	_____
7. Use all of your senses when you learn?	_____	_____

If you answered yes to most of these questions, you are on the right track and doing what you need to in order to complete the studying process. Read the chapter to discover additional rehearsal strategies you might use. If you answered no to several of these questions, rethink how you rehearse information as you read this chapter.

What Is Rehearsal?

Just as actors rehearse their lines to remember them, so students must rehearse what they want to learn. Rehearsal means engaging in activities, either written or spoken, that will help you learn information from a variety of sources. You might say the information out loud, write down the information in an organized fashion, or discuss it with a classmate. We present many ways that you can go about rehearsing later in the chapter. What's important at this point is that you understand what rehearsal is and why it is important to your academic success.

Studying Smarter
Don't be a one-trick pony! Use different rehearsal strategies for different content areas.

Rehearsal strategies help you organize the concepts that your professor expects you to learn. In Chapter 10, we stressed the importance of engaging your mind before you begin to read by prereading. This warm-up activity, which gets the mind ready for mental exercise, enables you to actively read and annotate. You're putting the information in your own words and beginning to see how the concepts relate. If everything goes well, you understand what you have read. Well, sort of. You have comprehended it, but you just can't remember all of it. This is where the next step—rehearsal—enters the picture. Rehearsal helps you to actually learn and remember the material. You organize the information from your text and lectures, make it meaningful in some way, write it, and then say it to yourself. Rehearsal allows you to use more of your senses in learning, which will help you retrieve or have access to the information at exam time.

Why Is Rehearsal Important?

We already touched on why rehearsal is important, but let's think about this a little more by reviewing how memory works. In Chapter 3, we discussed two theories of memory—the parts theory and the levels of processing theory. It matters little which theory you believe more accurately reflects how memory actually works. What does matter, however, is that in order to get information into LTM or to process it deeply, you must rehearse in some meaningful way. Just reading over the material is not enough. At the rehearsal stage of learning, it's time to further organize by pulling out key ideas and supporting concepts and to personalize or *elaborate* on the ideas to the point where you have not just memorized—you have conceptualized and truly understand.

Written and Verbal Rehearsal Strategies

Now that you have an idea of what rehearsal is and why it is important to use rehearsal strategies, let's think about two different types of rehearsal strategies: written strategies and verbal strategies.

1. **Written Strategies.** When you use written strategies, you record the important information in an organized fashion. The way you organize depends on the task your professor expects from you, the texts you are using, and the particular way that you learn best. In other words, because the tasks and materials vary from course to course, the written strategies that work well for you in biology will probably be very different from those that work for you in political science. Likewise, what works well for you may not work for the person sitting next to you. Specific written strategies, which we will present and discuss in detail, include: CARDS, concept maps, concept charts, questions and answers, and time lines.

2. **Verbal Strategies.** Verbal strategies are those rehearsal strategies that require talking rather than writing. They work well for students who are more auditory learners, meaning those who learn better through hearing rather than by reading or writing information. You say the information out loud and then check your accuracy. Like written strategies, the verbal strategies you select depend on all the other factors that impact learning—your characteristics, the task, and the text—although we believe that talk-throughs benefit all students because saying the information out loud will help you recall the information come test time. The specific verbal rehearsal strategies that will be presented are reciprocal questioning and talk-throughs.

It is important to understand that there is no single best strategy, either written or verbal. The best rehearsal strategies are those that work for you in a particular situation. And the best students know and appropriately use a variety of strategies, both written and verbal.

Components of Good Rehearsal Strategies

When you were in high school you may have used rehearsal strategies without even knowing it. Perhaps you made outlines after you read your text or put vocabulary words or foreign language terms on index cards. You may have had a family member or friend ask you questions before a test. All of these are examples of rehearsal strategies, some of which are better than others. It is our hope that you learn to distinguish good strategies from those that are less effective. Use the following guidelines to help make this distinction.

Good rehearsal strategies:

- **Allow for Self-Testing.** When you self-test, you rehearse without actually looking at the answer. For example, if you need to learn the different theories on human intelligence for a psychology exam you would want to say the theories to yourself or out loud, and then immediately check your rehearsal strategy to see whether you were correct. This process differs greatly from looking over or reading though information and having no real idea of whether or not you know the material. Good rehearsal strategies allow you to monitor what you know and allow for the element of self-testing.

- **Include Complete and Precise Information.** Have you have ever taken a test, particularly a multiple-choice test, when the information seemed familiar, yet you had a difficult time selecting the correct answer? If so, you probably didn't rehearse completely and precisely. Like good text annotations, good rehearsal strategies require you to say or write *all* the information related to a concept and to see relationships among ideas.

- **Are Organized.** Good strategies have some structure to isolate the information in a way that makes sense and helps you remember it. Your brain files information very much as a computer does. That is, concepts are stored in a logical way. Likewise, your rehearsal strategies need to have a logical flow as well.

- **State the Ideas in Your Own Words.** Few professors test you over verbatim information from text or lectures. Rather, they paraphrase and synthesize concepts—they put them in their own words. Thus, trying to memorize material straight from the text or lecture will cause problems at test time when the exam questions are written in another way. If you are confused by the text questions, or if after a test you find yourself thinking, "The professor never talked about the information that way in class," you probably need to put the information in your own words as you study.

Written Rehearsal Strategies

CARDS: Cognitive Aids for Rehearsing Difficult Subjects

Of all the rehearsal strategies we will present in this chapter, you are probably most familiar with CARDS: *Cognitive Aids for Rehearsing Difficult Subjects.* You may have called this strategy "flash cards" if you used it in high school. But there are a few key differences. Like flash cards, CARDS is a strategy that uses three-by-five-inch index cards. As shown in the CARDS example, you write the key concept on the front of the card. Then you write another word or phrase, called an organizing term, in the top right-hand corner. This is an important element of CARDS because it allows you to see how ideas are grouped by this organizing term. In the example CARDS for *heritability,* the organizing term is *heredity and intelligence.* This suggests that *heritability* is only one of the ideas related to heredity and intelligence and that it is linked to other ideas. Also write the source of the information—the text page, date of the lecture, documentary notes, and so forth—on the front of the card.

On the back of the CARDS you write all of the material you want to learn about this particular concept in an organized fashion *and* in your own words. Notice that the example has not only a definition of heritability, but also some examples. Because most college professors expect you to go beyond memorization, you should include examples, links to other concepts, and a general synthesis of the key points you need to remember about the concept.

CARDS has several major advantages.

- **They Are Easy to Carry Around.** You can stick them in your backpack or pocket, and then easily pull them out when you have a few minutes to rehearse, such as while you are standing in line at the bookstore or waiting for class to begin. When you rehearse ten minutes here or fifteen minutes there, the additional study time quickly adds up.

- **They Are Versatile.** CARDS works well in classes that require you to learn numerous terms, and if composed correctly, can help you to see connections among ideas. For example, suppose you were in a biology course and you were reading a chapter on meiosis. Many terms go with this overriding concept. Rather than making just one card with a weak definition of meiosis, you would use meiosis as the organizing term and write it in the upper right hand corner of all the cards relating to meiosis. Then you would clip all of your meiosis cards together so that you could see how the different terms relating to meiosis connect. CARDS also works well for learning vocabulary, rules, conjugations, and so forth in foreign languages or in mathematics, statistics, or chemistry where you have to learn and apply formulas.

Heredity and intelligence

Heritability

Chapter 7—p. 277

Front of CARDS

Def. The proportion of variance in intelligence that can be linked to genetic factors.

—Seems to increase with age (ex. 35% in childhood to 75% in adulthood)

ex. IQs of twins raised together or apart are nearly identical. This supports theory of heritability of intelligence

---

Back of CARDS

How Do You Use CARDS?   Follow these steps to use CARDS to study.

1. **Organize the CARDS.** Use the organizing term in the upper right hand corner to group all like terms together.

2. **Start with One Organizing Term.** Read the key concept on the front of the first card, flip it over to the back, and read the information through a couple of times.

Flip the card back over to the front and see how much of the information you can say to yourself without actually looking at it. Turn the card to the back again, and see how much you remembered. Repeat with each concept. Then return to the organizing term. Think about how all of the concepts you just learned relate not only to the organizing term, but also to each other. Try to group the CARDS by their organizing term so that you can study the topic as a whole.

3. **Separate What You Have Learned.** Review your CARDS each day, using those small pockets of time. Separate the CARDS you have learned from those you need to spend more time on. Spend more time concentrating on the concepts that are giving you the most trouble.

4. **Review with a Classmate.** Once you feel that you know most of the material on your CARDS, have a classmate ask you the term and then check to see how much of the material you are able to say accurately and precisely. Then exchange roles. (See the section on reciprocal questioning later in the chapter for some tips on how to quiz each other effectively.) Be sure that you can clearly discuss how the smaller concepts relate to larger ones and how the larger concepts relate to each other.

Concept Maps

As shown in the accompanying examples, concept maps are visual representations of information, and thus these strategies are very useful for students who tend to learn visually. A concept map is organized in such a way that it is easy to see the major concept that is being mapped, related concepts, and how everything is related; this is seen in the sample concept maps below.

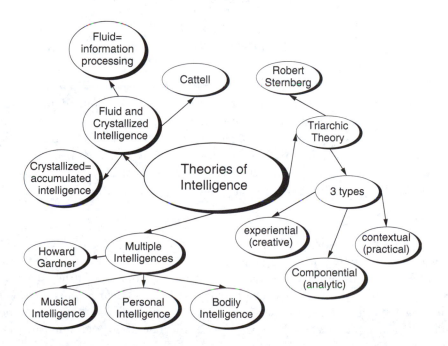

Concept mapping works well when it is important to see the relationship between complex concepts and it works particularly well in the sciences, where many ideas tend to be related and tend to interconnect. For example, mapping might work well to see the relationship between hormones of the endocrine system or the different stages of meiosis and mitosis. Mapping is especially useful for students who like to personalize strategies, because there is no right or wrong way to map. The important thing is that the way ideas are linked together be clearly shown in your concept map. The second sample concept map depicts the events and fall-out of the Tet Offensive; note that the structure differs from the previous example, yet the map still presents the information in an organized fashion.

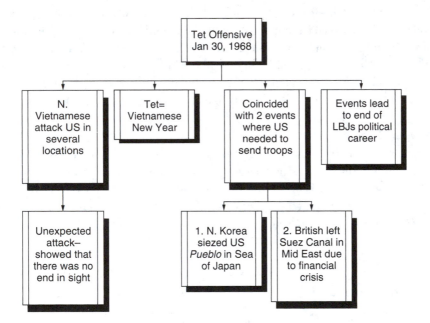

How Do You Use Maps in Studying?   When you study your map, you can rehearse one concept at a time, then cover up everything except the main concept, and begin to talk the information through. Say the related material and then check your accuracy. Focus on how the concepts are related to each other because that is the major strength of mapping. Rather than viewing ideas one at a time, as is the case with CARDS, mapping enables you to understand how these ideas fit together.

Charting

Charting is similar to mapping but is useful in different kinds of situations. As shown in the accompanying example, charting helps you synthesize information and is especially helpful when you are asked to compare and contrast ideas. For example, suppose you were in a chemistry class where you learned about covalent and ionic molecules. Knowing that there was a strong possibility that this question would be asked on the exam, you would want to think about the similarities and differences between the two types of molecules. Start by making a jot list as seen in the example. Then from your jot list, use those categories to create your chart as shown in the example.

Sample Jot List
Molecular Bonds

Covalent	Ionic
Molecules	Positive and negative ions
Shared electrons— covalent bonds	Ions held together by electrostatic attraction
Solids, liquids, or gases (water, ice, vapor)	Crystalline solids (salt)
Small electronegativity differences	High electronegativity differences
Lower melting and boiling points	High melting and boiling points

Sample Chart
Molecular Bonds

	Covalent	Ionic
Composition	Discrete particles—molecules. Molecules made up of atoms held together by covalent bonds (shared electrons).	Pos (+) and neg (-) ions. Ions held together by electrostatic attraction— ionic bond (opposites attract).
Forms	Can exist as liquid, solid, or gas.	Exists as crystalline solids.
Example	H_2O, water (can be ice, water, or vapor).	NaCl, salt.
Properties	Lower melting and boiling points. Small electronegativity differences.	Higher melting and boiling points. High electronegativity differences.

How Do You Use Charts in Studying? You can study your chart by the categories either on the horizontal or vertical axis. In fact, it is best to study charts both ways. Using the chart example, you would talk through the characteristics of covalent bonds thinking about composition, forms, examples, and properties. Then, you would talk though ionic bonds in the same fashion. Next, you would then study your chart horizontally by comparing and contrasting the properties of covalent and ionic bonds across the different categories.

TIMELY TIPS

Organizing Lots of Information

You may ask yourself, "How am I going to find the time to learn all of this stuff? It is just too much material." This is the perfect time to use a map or a chart to help you organize the massive amounts of information and see the distinctions between ideas that may seem to be very similar.

Question/Answer Strategy

Remember the study guides that your high school teachers gave you? These study guides were intended to help focus your thinking for a test, usually by posing a series of questions. The premise was that if you could answer the questions on the study guide, you would be able to do well on the test. The question/answer strategy uses a similar premise, except you are the active learner who is creating both the questions and the answers. You think about the important information in the text and lectures, pose questions that cover the material, and then answer each of the questions you pose.

The format of the accompanying question/answer strategy example probably looks different from what your previous teachers used. For this question/answer strategy, you write your question on the left-hand side of the paper. The right-hand space is to answer the question and is wider and longer than the left side. This format should give you a clue that the questions you pose should require more than a one-word answer.

When you are posing your questions, think about Bloom's taxonomy (discussed in Chapter 5). Try to create questions that focus on the higher levels, questions that typically begin with *why* or *how*. By higher level, we mean questions that encourage synthesis of the information to be learned. Try to ask questions that require you to understand the entire concept—not just the small pieces. Most importantly, the questions you write should reflect the kinds of information that your professor expects you to learn.

The example here shows you the difference between writing primarily memory-level questions and asking higher-level items. The numbered questions show how you would word your questions if you know that your professor gives multiple-choice exams that have numerous application and synthesis questions. If, on the other hand, your professor simply expects you to memorize information, the questions posed in the parentheses may be sufficient for your rehearsal; notice, however that these questions do not require that you fully understand the concepts. Also note that the questions you pose using the question/answer strategy are more focused than those you predicted during the prereading stage when you were unfamiliar with the important information in the text chapter.

Question/Answer Strategy

Questions	Answers
1. Explain how processing speed is related to measuring intelligence. (What is processing speed?)	1. _____ _____
2. How does one's environment affect intelligence? (What is environmental deprivation?)	2. _____ _____
3. How does heredity affect one's intelligence? (What is heritability?)	3. _____ _____

To answer the questions, you would read your text annotations and lecture notes. As with all of the strategies, your question/answer strategy will not be effective if you leave out important information or include information that is wrong or incomplete. Also, whenever possible, put the material in your own words to help you remember it better.

How Do You Use the Question/Answer Strategy in Studying?   When you study using the question/answer strategy, fold your paper so that just your questions are showing. Ask yourself or get someone else to ask you a question. Then answer it by saying the information out loud. Check to see how much of the material you remembered correctly. If your answer matches what you wrote, repeat the process with the next question. If your answer is incomplete or wrong, read the correct answer several times and try to say it again before moving on to the next question. In addition, because the questions on the exam will most certainly be in random order, don't always begin with your first question and work your way through to the end. Instead, vary the order—start with the last question, do every other question, or use some other pattern.

Time Lines

Unlike the other strategies we have discussed, time lines are appropriate only in specific situations. Basically, you can use time lines when it is important to know chronology—the order of something that happened over a period of time. For example, you might use time lines in a history course when it's important to know the chronology of the Vietnam conflict, in an art appreciation class when you need to be able to compare and contrast major artistic movements, or in a geology course when you're expected to trace the evolution of the earth's crust over millions of years. Hence, you can use time lines in many different disciplines but they do have a very specific function.

Time lines are flexible in that they can be constructed in a variety of ways. The accompanying example shows the time line of acts passed during the time of LBJ's Great Society. Your textbooks may depict other types of time lines to show longer spans of time.

TIME LINE EXAMPLE

LBJ's Great Society

1964	• Clean Air Act
	• War on Poverty
	• Food stamps
	• Civil Rights Act
	• Headstart
	• National Endowment for Arts and Humanities
	• Job Corps
1965	• Voting Rights Act
	• Medicare signed into law
	• PBS TV began
	• Cigarette Labeling Act
	• Housing and Urban Development Act
1966	• Clean Waters Act
	• Child Nutrition Act
	• Fair Packaging and Labeling Act
1968	• Wild and Scenic Rivers Act
	• Open Housing Act

In the majority of studying situations, time lines should be supplemented with other strategies such as CARDS, concept maps, or charts. For example, a time line portraying the major acts passed during the Great Society indicates only the chronology—which events happened when. But that would be insufficient knowledge to have when preparing for an exam. For example, you would need to know *why* Johnson felt the need for the Great Society, *what* the impact of these acts were, and *what* the details of each act entailed. This information cannot be gleaned from the time line alone.

Studying Smarter
We often think that when we have completed our study of one, we know all about two, because "two" is "one and one." We forget that we have still to make of a study of "and."
—**Sir Arthur Eddington**

How Do You Use Time Lines in studying? When you study with time lines, use the dates only as the cue. Talk through the important events, laws, battles, and so forth that occurred on that date. At the same time, use your other strategies to talk through the nature of each of the events, thinking about cause and effect, or how one event influenced another when appropriate. Use newspaper questions—who, what, where, when, why, and how—to be certain that you are fully describing each event. In addition, it's important to understand how events are related, so be sure that you see the big picture as well.

Verbal Rehearsal Strategies

Verbal rehearsal strategies are those that involve talk in some way—talking out loud, to yourself, or to a study partner. Although it may seem odd to talk to yourself as you study and learn, saying information out loud is a powerful tool because it is a form of active learning that keeps you connected with what you are learning. Talking and listening as you study helps you use other senses as well, and remember, the more senses you use when you study, the easier learning will be. We will discuss two different verbal strategies: reciprocal questioning and talk-throughs. Each of these strategies is a form of verbal summarization and each is generally used along with written strategies.

Reciprocal Questioning

Reciprocal questioning involves two learners, one who takes the role of the teacher, and the other who takes the role of the student. The "teacher" asks a question from one of the written strategies described earlier in the question/answer strategy, from text annotations, or from lecture notes. Most should be questions that elicit higher-level or critical thinking rather than those that promote memorization or one-word answers. The "student" answers the question and the teacher checks his answer against the written strategy. If the student answers the question correctly, the teacher asks the next question. If the question is not answered adequately, the teacher gives some hints and tries to guide the student to the answer. The goal is to help the student learn the material rather than just provide the correct response. Those questions that were missed should be asked again at the end of the study session.

After all of the questions have been asked and answered, and if necessary, reviewed, the "student" becomes the teacher and asks the questions and the "teacher" becomes the student and answers them. The new teacher should be sure that she asks the questions in a different order and adds new questions.

The accompanying example about the Johnson administration gives you an idea of the difference between good and poor questions. Notice that most of the questions in the "Poor" column require only a one-word answer or simple memorization. The questions in the "Good" column are questions that require critical thinking, synthesis, and analysis.

Good Questions	Poor Questions
How did the Great Society aim to fight poverty?	What is the Great Society?
Discuss the impact of the Supreme Court's decisions under Justice Warren.	Name three decisions made by the Supreme Court in the 1960s.
Why did the Tet Offensive play such a pivotal role in the conflict in Vietnam?	What was the Tet Offensive?

Reciprocal questioning can be a powerful strategy for several reasons.

- **It Brings More Senses Into Play.** You have read the information using the visual sense, you have written important concepts down in an organized fashion using the kinesthetic sense, and you are now hearing the information using the auditory sense. Using more than one sense helps you remember better because it makes you a more active learner.

- **It Encourages Multiple Perspectives.** The old adage "two heads are better than one" is true in this situation. One person may be very strong in understanding concept A and the other very knowledgeable about concept B. Pulling the ideas of two people together generally makes for clearer, more precise learning for both.

- **It Encourages You to Use Your Own Words.** Because professors rarely write questions that come exactly from the text, it's important to put information in your own words so that you will recognize it in a slightly different form on the test. When you have two people putting it in their own words, you begin to think outside of the textbook, and you get another perspective of how the information might be phrased.

- **It Helps You to Monitor Your Learning.** When you are asked a question and then provide the answer, you get immediate feedback about your knowledge on that particular topic. This helps you monitor what concepts you know and on what concepts you need more work.

Talk-Throughs

As the name of this strategy suggests, talk-throughs involve saying the information (talking it through) to yourself, either silently or out loud to monitor your learning. When you talk through the concepts you become both the student and the teacher, because rather than having someone ask you questions or ask you to explain concepts, you fill both roles. Start by making a talk-through list on an index card. As seen in the accompanying example, a talk-through card simply lists, in an organized fashion, the concepts you need to learn and remember. Notice that the supporting ideas are indented so that it is easy to see which ideas are connected in some way. For example, in this talk-through card, it is easy to see that there are three main types of intelligence tests covered under the heading "Measuring Intelligence." In this case, the text's headings and subheadings were the basis for organizing the talk-through card and these headings are further supplemented with key terms. Although this is not always the case, headings and subheadings are a good place to start because they give you the overall big picture of the chapter.

Talk-Through Card Example

Measuring Intelligence

1. Tests

   Stanford-Binet Test
   IQ
   Wechsler Scales
   Group vs. individual tests

2. Cognitive Basis

   Processing speed
   Inspection time

3. Neural Basis

   Nerve conduction
   Competency

After you make your talk-through card, begin rehearsal by saying what you know about the first major concept. Talk it through, looking back at your written strategies, if necessary, including text annotations and lecture notes. In fact, after you have said the information silently or out loud, it is a good idea to go back to your strategy and read over the information again to be sure that you are complete and precise. As you learn each piece of information, also be sure that you can make connections between the major concepts and the supporting details. Explain to yourself how the pieces fit together.

Strategy Selection

The strategies you select depend on a variety of factors: the task your professor asks you to do, the course for which you are studying, and how you learn best. This will be discussed further in Chapter 15, but the accompanying chart summarizes the rehearsal strategies presented in this chapter and suggests when they might be most effective. However, remember: Active learners can modify strategies so that they can be used in situations other than those outlined here.

SUCCESS AT A GLANCE

Summary Table of Rehearsal Strategies

Rehearsal Strategies	Use in:	Types of Questions
CARDS	Hard sciences, foreign languages, mathematics, statistics, any course where you have to learn many new terms	Best with objective questions; can be modified for use with either memory-level or higher-level questions
Concept Maps and Charts	Hard sciences and social sciences, history; if you are a visual learner; when you need to see relationships	Can be used for both objective and essay questions; best for higher-level questions that require you to see the big picture
Question/ Answers	All courses	Best for objective test questions unless you plan to modify it to predict essay questions

(continued)

Rehearsal Strategies	Use in:	Types of Questions
Time Lines	History, art history, music history, anthropology, any course where you need to know chronology	Memory level questions; can supplement this strategy with other such as concept maps, charts, or CARDS
Reciprocal Questioning	All courses	All types of questions but works well when rehearsing answers to higher-level questions
Talk-Throughs	All courses	All types of questions; helps you concentrate on key concepts rather than small details

☐ REAL COLLEGE
Conrad's Confusion

DIRECTIONS: Read the following "Real College" scenario and respond to the questions based on what you learned in this chapter.

Conrad is a first-year college student who is pretty nervous about doing well in his courses. He is particularly unhappy with his inability to see the big picture in some of his courses and is surprised that his classes seem to require him to study in different ways in order to do well.

In high school, Conrad simply skimmed the parts of his texts to answer questions on the study guides that most of his teachers provided. He would memorize this information and do well on almost every exam. But in college, three of his professors expect him to conceptualize information. That is, he has to understand scientific processes in biology, he is expected "to put information in a historical perspective" in history, and he has to think about how character development and use of language relate to the plot in short stories in literature class.

Conrad doesn't even know where to start studying for these courses. In high school, he used to put lots of information on index cards and sometimes he would make complex outlines, but he doesn't know any other study strategies to consider.

What would your advice to Conrad be? What rehearsal and review strategies would you recommend for each of his courses and why?

☐ THINKING CRITICALLY
Something to Think About and Discuss

- In the past, how have you rehearsed and reviewed information?
- Do the rehearsal strategies you currently use have the characteristics of good rehearsal strategies outlined in this chapter?
- What might you do to improve the quality of your rehearsal strategies?

☐ ADD TO YOUR PORTFOLIO

1. Construct a set of ten questions/answers for a chapter for a course in which you are currently enrolled. Be sure to ask some higher-level questions that begin with the words "how" and "why."
2. Construct one of the following strategies for a course in which you are currently enrolled. Be sure to consider the task before you select your strategy.

   - Twenty CARDS
   - One concept map
   - One chart

CHAPTER 13

REVIEWING STRATEGIES

Read this chapter to answer the following questions:

- What are the differences between rehearsal and review strategies?
- Why is it important to be able to say material out loud?
- How can study groups promote learning?
- Why is it important to have a specific study plan?

Think about the types of review you currently engage in for your textbook, lecture notes, and other course material. Answer yes or no for each of the following questions. Do you review:

1. On a daily basis?	Yes_____	No_____
2. When you have small pockets of time?	Yes_____	No_____
3. Several days before an exam?	Yes_____	No_____
4. More than once before an exam?	Yes_____	No_____
5. At the beginning of each study session?	Yes_____	No_____
6. At the end of each study session?	Yes_____	No_____
7. With classmates?	Yes_____	No_____
8. By self-questioning?	Yes_____	No_____

If you answered yes to most of these questions, you are probably on the right track and doing what you need to in order to complete the studying process. Read the remainder of the chapter to discover additional reviewing strategies. If you answered no to several of these questions, rethink how you review as you read the remainder of this chapter.

Reviewing

Reviewing is the step you take after you rehearse. In Chapter 12, you learned that rehearsal enables you to learn the information after you have read. It not only helps you store the concepts you need to learn, but it also helps you to retrieve the material at test time. When you rehearse, you write, say, and listen to the information until you know it very well. You look for connections between ideas and understand how concepts are related. Reviewing, on the other hand, is a way of making sure that the important information has been learned in such a way that it is complete, organized, and precise. Reviewing ensures that the information will stay fixed in your memory. By reviewing daily, you remember about three times more than if you had not reviewed. Thus, there is a tremendous payoff in review.

Studying Smarter

The more senses you involve in your learning the better you remember. As you review, try to read, write, and talk about the information so that you will process it more deeply.

You can use reviewing at various times during the studying process. For example, when you read Chapter 14, you will learn about taking effective lecture notes. In that chapter we emphasize the importance of reviewing notes daily. Getting to class ten minutes early and using those ten minutes to read over your notes is a form of reviewing. This type of review refreshes your memory of what happened in the last class and prepares your mind to receive new information, making it easier to connect ideas. But the kind of reviewing that we focus on in this chapter is generally done as a final phase of studying and test preparation. You review by self-testing to monitor your learning and gain a better understanding of the information you know very well and the information that requires further study through additional rehearsal.

Using Your Talk-Through Card for Reviewing

Think about the talk-through card we discussed in Chapter 12. Talk-through cards simply list the concepts you want to rehearse and learn as you study the material. Remember that you start with the first concept on the card, rehearse by reading the information through a couple of times, and then see whether you can say it without looking at your notes or rehearsal strategies. As you work through your list of key points, you think about connections and relationships between ideas. By the end of your study session, you should have learned at least a portion of the major concepts on your talk-through card. You repeat this same procedure with other concepts in other study sessions until you know and understand each one.

You can also use your talk-through card to review. Start with the first concept and completely and accurately talk through the key points. If you know all the information related to that concept, check it off and go on to the next. If you have trouble remembering the material, return to your annotations or rehearsal strategies and say the information again. Keep in mind that if rehearsal has been done properly, reviewing should just be a matter of keeping the information retrievable in your memory and seeing which concepts still give you problems. It is hoped that you will remember most of the important information and see links between concepts when you are reviewing. By the time you get to the reviewing stage, the information should be stored in your memory. You are simply checking to see that you remember it and will be able to retrieve it at test time.

Making a Specific Study Plan

We have talked in other chapters about the importance of planning. Rather than having a random approach to test preparation, think about how much time you will spend studying and what you will do during those study sessions. It's particularly important to structure specific study and review sessions as the time for the exam draws closer. That's why we suggest that you develop a Specific Study Plan or SSP for each exam you take. Although some students get to the point where they know what they are going to do in each study session just by writing a few notes, it has been our experience that most students benefit from creating a more structured plan. Therefore, we suggest that you write out a study plan and clip it in your daily planner.

Construct your study plan about a week before the exam. Think about your goals by asking yourself a series of questions:

1. What grade do I want to earn on the exam? (Note: Do not automatically say an "A" in response to this question. Instead, think about how much time and effort you are willing to invest to earn the grade you desire.)

2. How much time do I need to invest in order to make this grade?

3. Where will I find the extra time? Will I have to give up other activities in order to carve out time to study?

4. What kind of exam is it? Multiple-choice? Essay? What kinds of problems do I usually have when I take tests of this nature?

5. Do I know the balance of items? Is this a memorization task or will I be expected to answer higher-level questions? What proportion of questions will come from the text and the lectures?

6. What kinds of rehearsal strategies will I need to create because they will work best for this exam?

After you have answered these questions, you are ready to construct your SSP. As shown in the accompanying example, an SSP outlines what you will do in each particular study session. It shows which rehearsal or review strategies you will use, which concepts you will study, and approximately how long each study session will last. It's easy to see that the student in the example has three study sessions (1, 2, and 3) and two specific sessions set aside just to review with her classmates (4 and 6). One session (5) is set aside for self-testing as a way of getting a handle on concepts that may still be problematic. Also note that each study session begins with a review of information that was rehearsed in the previous session. Each session should also end with a review of what was learned in the current session.

An Example SSP for an Exam Covering Both Text Chapters and Lecture Notes

Session	What I'll Do:	Strategies I'll Use:	Reflection and Evaluation
#1 Sunday pm: 6:00–7:00	Study all concepts related to "covalent bonds"	CARDS, concept maps, lecture notes	Took more than 1 hour (actual 6–7:45)
#2 Monday pm: 4:40–6:30	Review "covalent bonds"; study all concepts related to "water molecules"	CARDS, concept maps, lecture notes	Too tired to study right after class. Need to plan a different time. zzzzzzz

(continued)

Session	What I'll Do:	Strategies I'll Use:	Reflection and Evaluation
#3 Tuesday pm: 7:00–9:30	Review "water molecules" and "covalent bonds"; study all concepts related to "atoms and molecules"	CARDS, concept maps, lecture notes	This is a much better study time for me.
#4 Wednesday pm: 7:30–9:00	Review with study group	question/answer, reciprocal teaching	Great study session. Really feel like I am starting to get this stuff!
#5 Thursday pm: 9:00–10:30	Self-test	question/answer, talk-through card	I actually didn't need to use this entire time. I really understand.
#6 Thursday pm: 7:30–9:00	Review with study group	talk-through card, oral question/answer	I feel ready to go

EXAM FRIDAY!

■   ■   ■

As you construct your SSP and think about the time you will need to rehearse and review the material, remember the principles discussed in Chapter 6: You should always allow more time than you think you will need. If you block out two hours for a study session to learn a set of concepts, and it takes you only an hour and a half, you have gained a half-hour in which you can do something else. But if you set aside the same two hours and it actually ends up taking you three hours to feel comfortable with the concepts, you have lost an hour. It's important to have some flexibility in your schedule that allows for additional time should you need it.

When you complete each study session, check it off, evaluate how long it actually took you, and determine any specific problems you had that you might need to return to in your next session. Did you exceed the amount of time you allotted or did you need less time? Did you plan your study sessions for times when you are most alert? The answers to these questions will help you as you develop an SSP for the next exam in this course.

Another thing to note about the SSP is that it specifies different types of review for specific times.

1. **Begin** each session with a review of what you learned previously. Using your talk-through card as a guide, say what you remember from the earlier study session. If there's material that is still giving you problems, begin the current study session with it.

2. **End** each session with a review of only those concepts you concentrated on in the current session. This type of review serves as a monitoring device to let you know what you actually remember from the session. If you start this review and find that you are having problems, you can return to those concepts immediately and rehearse some more. This is the monitoring part of your review when you discover whether you will need to devote more time to the study session than you originally planned.

3. **In the day or two before the test,** continue to monitor your understanding of all of the concepts you will be tested over. Concentrate the time you have left on the material that you understand least. Many students make the mistake of spending equal amounts of time on everything before an exam, even information that they know fairly well. Learn from their mistakes. The closer the exam, the more you want to concentrate on concepts you don't know well.

Setting some goals for yourself and making an SSP for each exam helps you stay on track with both rehearsing and reviewing. Note that it is important to focus on learning specific concepts, not on the amount of time you actually have allotted for studying. For example, if you were studying for the test outlined in the example, you would want to learn all of the information related to the concept "covalent bonds" in your first study session. It is usually ineffective to go over all the information in every study session. Students who plan around time rather than around mastery of the information can easily go into a testing situation unprepared.

TIMELY TIPS

Especially for Working Students

If you are holding down a job or returning to college after several years, you may find the SSP to be an invaluable strategy. When you are juggling work (even part time), family needs, and your other responsibilities, creating a studying plan that lets you know exactly how much time you will need to prepare can help you find a balance in your busy life.

Forming Study Groups

One of the best ways to review is by forming study groups. Some students establish study groups that meet weekly to talk about and review what went on in class that week. Other students form study groups just before an exam to review and perhaps get a new or different perspective on what they have learned. Either way, study groups have big advantages if they are done right.

Perhaps the biggest advantage of being part of a study group is that it allows you to listen to information in another person's voice, which can provide insights that you may not have considered. In a traditional course, you listen to your professor's interpretation of the information during lectures, you read the text for another interpretation, and through these two sources, you come up with your own interpretation or meaning. You have listened to, read, and written down material, so you have used several of your senses. All of this interaction should help you gain a greater degree of understanding of the material. It stands to reason, then, that by listening to and talking with others who are also trying to understand the course information, you could gain a deeper understanding, be able to remember the concepts better, and subsequently do better on the exams.

NETWORKING

Virtual Study Groups

Try to set up an online review session prior to an exam in one of your classes. You and your classmates can review by sending questions to one another via e-mail. Each of you can answer questions posed by the others and provide feedback as to the completeness and accuracy of your answers. You can also plan to "meet" online to use instant messaging as a means of discussing specific concepts.

It's important to think about the characteristics of *good* study groups. Just meeting with people in the same course does not necessarily make a study group. Productive study groups have the following characteristics:

- **Everyone Comes Prepared.** Study groups do not replace studying on your own. Everyone should come to the group prepared to review the information, pose and answer possible test questions, and voice questions about material they don't understand. If the study group members have to spend all of their time trying to teach a large portion of the course material to someone who didn't even attempt to learn it on her own, most members will not benefit.

- **Everyone Can Talk Through a Difficult Idea with the Group.** Divide the material among the group members. It helps if everyone selects something complex or confusing to discuss. During the study group, each member will lead the discussion on his topic. As you are reviewing your understanding of the concept, others who may understand it better than you should be encouraged to offer additional explanation. Don't shy away from discussing information that you don't know very well; it defeats the purpose of the group.

- **Members of the Study Group Should Be Classmates, but Not Necessarily Friends.** Everyone knows what can happen when friends get together to study: Everything goes fine for the first few minutes, but it's easy to get off track. It's much better to recruit serious students, who all have the goal of doing well, into your study group rather than just including friends. That's not to say that studying with friends will never work; it's simply harder to study with friends than it is with classmates working toward a common goal.

- **Meet at a Place That Is Conducive to Studying.** Campus libraries often have study rooms set aside for just this purpose. Such rooms are generally small and soundproof so that normal conversation and discussion can be carried out with ease. If your library doesn't have study rooms, dorms often have common areas equipped with study rooms. Empty classrooms or a local coffee shop also can work well. If your only alternative is to study in someone's room or at someone's home or apartment, remind yourself that the purpose of the session is to review the course material for a test, not to socialize.

- **Have Clear Goals and Structure.** When you initially form a study group, you should have a more specific goal than to get together and study. Most groups meet at regular times. We know of a study group in a statistics course that meets weekly to review the important ideas presented that week, and then also meets a couple of times right before the exam to review what they know and to predict and solve possible test questions. At each session, the members predict some possible test questions that review the concepts presented that week. Groups that have a game plan before they come together are generally the most successful. Along those lines, if you're really serious about having a good study group, it doesn't hurt to set some ground rules right from the beginning to prevent difficulties later on. For example, what will happen if someone comes to the group without doing any preparation on his own?

GET GOING

Motivation and Collaboration

One of the best ways to improve motivation is to work with others. If you find that your motivation has been lagging, forming a study group may be just what you need. Try to create a regularly scheduled time for your group to maintain the collaboration over the entire term.

Almost everyone can benefit from belonging to a study group at one time or another, but study groups work particularly well for students who learn better auditorily and through discussion and for students in courses they find problematic. We don't know of any student who is in a study group for *every* class, but if you are taking a particularly difficult course, it often helps to have the opinion and input of others.

SUCCESS AT A GLANCE

Elements of Successful Review

Regardless of which reviewing strategy you select, your studying sessions should include the following elements of review. Review sessions should:

- Focus on fixing concepts in your memory
- Aid in organizing the information in your mind
- Allow you to see relationships between ideas
- Help to monitor your understanding of the concepts
- Center on testing yourself over the material
- Employ several senses in learning

Improving Your Memory Through Reviewing

Reviewing can help you remember almost three times as much of the information. You can maximize the amount you remember, thereby improving your memory, if you keep in mind five basic reviewing principles.

1. **Organize.** Research indicates that people tend to remember information the way that they have organized it. So, the first step you should take as you begin to rehearse and review course material is to be sure that it is organized, and therefore stored, in an easily retrievable way. Decide how the concepts can be best organized and then learn them in that way. Remember, you don't have to organize the material the in same way the text or your professor does. Create an organization that will work for you.

2. **Use Images and Other Mnemonics.** The word *mnemonics* comes from the Greek word for "mindful" and mnemonics are memory devices—little tricks you can use to help you remember specific kinds of information. As discussed in Chapter 3, one way you can use mnemonics is to learn a list by taking the first letter of each item you are trying to memorize and making them spell something. Your mnemonic device doesn't have to make sense to anyone but you. In fact, the more outrageous the memory device, the easier it generally is to remember. For example, a mnemonic used by physics students to remember the Maxwell relations in thermodynamics is "*G*ood *P*hysicists *H*ave *S*tudied *U*nder

*V*ery *F*ine *T*eachers," which helps them remember the order of the variables in the square, in clockwise direction.

3. **Say It Rather Than Reread It.** We have stated more than once that rehearsal is a much more effective way to learn information than rereading. This is true for three reasons. First, few students have time to reread large portions of text. Second, when students reread, they pick up very little additional information. Third, students who only reread get overly dependent on the wording used in the text. If the professor asks questions in even a slightly different way, they often get confused because they have not thought through the items on their own. When you say the information, however, you tend to summarize the key points in your own words. This makes verbalization particularly effective for review. If you ask yourself questions (or get someone else to ask them) and then answer the questions, you will remember considerably more than if you simply tried to reread the material.

4. **Have Several Review Sessions.** Research indicates that students who read, rehearse, and review in a short time frame do not do as well as those who spread their study out over time, even when the amount of time engaged in learning is about the same. Therefore, we would expect the student who studied five hours spread out over a period of four days prior to the exam to do better than the student who spent five hours "studying" the night before an exam. Students who space their learning by using several study sessions tend to get less tired and can concentrate better during studying, thus improving the amount they can recall on test day.

5. **Overlearn.** We add this suggestion to make you aware of the difference between "kinda" knowing something and learning it to the point at which it is almost automatic. When you overlearn something you know it so well that you don't even have to think about it. We have all overlearned things as schoolchildren—the Pledge of Allegiance, "The Star Spangled Banner," nursery rhymes, the lyrics to popular music. At a sporting event, we stand to sing the National Anthem without seemingly having to do much to recall the lyrics. If you could just could remember the information for your biology or anthropology exam in the same way. The reason you can remember some information so easily is that you have been exposed to it over and over and over again. You know it so well that it is almost second nature to you. Contrast that with the feeling you have when you have studied, but you know that you do not know the information very well. If you feel as though you "kinda" know the material, you are probably not going to do very well on an exam. By reviewing course information from test to test, you will become more familiar with it. And although you probably will not have overlearned the concepts to the

---

Studying Smarter
Say not, when I have leisure I will study; you may not have leisure.
                    —The Mishnah

point at which they are second nature to you, reviewing will give you a greater sense of knowing—somewhere between "kinda" and overlearning.

In this chapter, we have stressed the importance of reviewing as a final step in the active learning process. Reviewing can be done alone or with study groups or partners. Whichever way you choose to review, keep in mind the importance of self-testing as a way to monitor your learning. Make an SSP and stick to it and make a conscious effort to work on improving your memory.

☐ REAL COLLEGE
Enrico's Excuses

DIRECTIONS: Read the following "Real College" scenario and respond to the questions. This activity is a little different from those in previous chapters in that we ask you to begin to pull together the studying issues we have been discussing throughout *College Success Strategies*.

By his own admission, Enrico is a slacker. In fact, he really prides himself on being a laid-back, low-stress guy. He has been fairly lucky so far in that he at least isn't failing any of his classes. He puts in the minimum amount of work possible to try to maintain what he calls "average" performance—no less than a D in any course for Enrico! But all of this is starting to wear on him, and on top of that, he's running out of excuses for his parents and he's running out of time. The semester is now two-thirds over and he finds himself worried and anxious that he might actually fail his courses this term.

Enrico uses every excuse in the book for not following a study regimen: "There's lots of time left." "I have a photographic memory so I don't have to study and review." "I'll study over the weekend when I have more time." "I don't like this course and the professor is so boring. I'll do better next term when I can take something I like." "I work best under pressure. That's why I study at the last minute." He's even told one professor that "The dog ate my homework" and another that he missed the 3 p.m. class because "My alarm clock didn't go off."

Enrico has decided to try to turn over a new leaf. His roommate encouraged him to make an appointment at the campus learning center where someone might be able to help him move from making excuses to taking positive action to get back on track. Reluctantly, he made an appointment and he actually showed up—a little late, but he did make it.

Given what you have read about Enrico, put yourself in the place of the person in the learning center assigned to help him. What kind of advice would you give Enrico if it were your job to help him get his studying life together? What strategies would you tell him to use so that he could get on a studying cycle? In particular, how might you encourage him to use daily reviewing as a way of promoting active learning? What "quick-start" tips might help Enrico see the light?

☐ THINKING CRITICALLY
Something to Think About and Discuss

- What are the advantages of saying information out loud as you review?
- What makes a study group successful? What makes a study group unsuccessful?
- What are the benefits of studying with classmates?
- In which courses would study groups benefit you the most?

☐ ADD TO YOUR PORTFOLIO

For the next exam in one of your classes, set goals by answering the following goal-related questions. Then construct an SSP. Refer to pages 168–169 to create your SSP chart. Remember to set aside time in your SSP for rehearsal and review. Also remember to begin and end each study session with review.

My goals and SSP for _____ test.

1. What grade do I want to earn on the exam?
2. How much time do I need to invest in order to make this grade?
3. Where will I find the extra time? Will I have to give up other activities in order to carve out time to study?
4. What kind of exam is it? Multiple choice? Essay? What kinds of problems do I usually have when I take tests of this nature?
5. Do I know the balance of items? Are there more text or lecture questions? Is this a memorization task or will I be expected to answer higher level questions?
6. What kinds of rehearsal strategies will work best for this exam? Will I need to begin by reformatting or constructing any strategies that I have already made?

CHAPTER 14

Take Note! Lectures

A Different Kind of Text

Read this chapter to answer the following questions:

- Why is it important to take good lecture notes?
- What should I do before, during, and after class to take good notes?
- How can I use my notes to self-test?

SELF-ASSESSMENT

DIRECTIONS: Examine your notes from one of your classes and evaluate them on a scale of 1 to 5, from 1 being "hardly ever" to 5 being "almost always."

	Hardly ever ⟷	Almost always
1. My notes are organized.	1 2 3	4 5
2. My notes distinguish main points from details.	1 2 3	4 5
3. My notes include examples.	1 2 3	4 5
4. I take notes over class discussions.	1 2 3	4 5
5. I test myself over my notes.	1 2 3	4 5
6. My notes accurately reflect the content of the lecture.	1 2 3	4 5
7. My notes contain abbreviations.	1 2 3	4 5
8. I review my notes as soon after class as possible.	1 2 3	4 5
9. I read my text assignments before lectures.	1 2 3	4 5
10. I compare my notes to the text when I study.	1 2 3	4 5

The more fives you marked, the better. Many students find that they need more efficient strategies for note taking. Read on to find out how to improve your note-taking skills.

The Importance and Characteristics of Good Lecture Notes

In college, a large percentage of information will be conveyed to you through lecture. In the traditional lecture format, professors explain information that they believe is important for you to learn. Most professors expect you to take notes in an organized fashion so that you can study and review the notes throughout the course. Note taking isn't too difficult if you have a professor who speaks slowly and clearly and lectures in an organized fashion. But many professors aren't the world's most top-notch, engaging lecturers. Therefore, students should be able to supply their own organization, to get down the important points, and to fill in the gaps when necessary.

Studying Smarter
Stay actively involved during lectures by writing for the full period. Then, review your notes as soon after class as possible.

It's important to be able to take good lecture notes for a variety of reasons:

- They serve as a record of what goes on in class each day. Without a complete record, it's difficult to have all the information you need to prepare for subsequent classes or exams.

- If your notes are organized, they can help you to identify patterns in your professor's lectures. Once you see patterns, you get a better idea of what your professor believes is important.
- Your notes will help you to spot overlap between your text and the professor's lecture. These overlaps are fertile ground for test questions.

What distinguishes good notes from poor notes? As you will see, good notes are more than just readable. As you read about the characteristics of good notes, look at the following examples. These examples show good, weak, and very weak lecture notes related to a portion of the text entitled "Cognition and Intelligence." We will refer to these examples throughout the chapter.

Example 1: Good Lecture Notes

	Intelligence	Nov. 15

Intelligence- differing views
Def.= -ability to understand complex ideas
      -adapt to environment
      -reason effectively
      -overcome problems through thought

What is the def. of intelligence?

Related to mastering new ideas, school + job success, getting along w/ others; however other factors play a role in life outcomes.

What is intel. related to?

Differing views

Explain the dif. b/t unitary & multifaceted views.

1. Unitary view= single dimension (Spearman)-how one did on a cog. task depended on a general (g) factor; based on idea that subscores on IQ tests correlate highly ∴ IQ was related to 1 factor

2. Multifaceted view= IQ consists of many unique abilites that operate independently; can be high on some + low on others (Thurstone said IQ was composed of 7 mental abilities
    EX. verbal, number, + space abilities)

How do the 2 views relate to the modern view?

Modern view is somewhere in between- could be a general factor BUT intelligence is expressed in diff. ways.

Explain Garner's Theory of X intell.

Garner's Theory of X intell.
-Theory= study persons at extremes of intell. rather than just who is in middle as has been done
-Believes there are several types of intell. impt. to understand all of them
    Quest. Does a talented gymnast have a certain kind of intell. that enables her to perform those moves?

Example 2: Weak Lecture Notes

Intelligence

Intelligence includes understanding ideas, reasoning + adapting.
Main views are unitary and multifaceted (Spearman and Thurstone).
Garner's is more like multifaceted; it has several levels of intelligence.

Example 3: Very Weak Notes

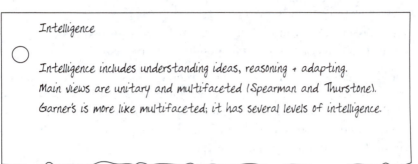

Intelligence
Understanding stuff blah, blah, blah
think about it differently
Spearman
—Spear man! ha!
IQ I am smart!
Garner's theory
soooooo...boring!!!
z-z-z-z
Call Chris later
CHRIS

Characteristics of good notes include the following.

- **Good Notes Are Organized.** When you look at the three examples of lecture notes, it is easy to see which one is best organized. The notes in the first example use organizational strategies such as underlining the main points, indenting details, noting examples, and numbering viewpoints. This differs dramatically from the notes in the second and third examples. In the second example, it's difficult to tell where one idea stops and another begins or what is a main point and what is a detail. Much of the information written in the notes in the second example is lost or difficult to link together. And what can we say about the notes in example three except that some students actually have notes that are this bad! Incomplete notes—those that are inadequate as well as imprecise—occur most frequently in courses that students find uninteresting or for students who have not yet mastered the art of active learning.

- **Good Notes Distinguish Main Points from Details.** Every lecture has both main points and details. The main points might be reasons, characteristics, or theories. Details include information that supports or explains the main points. It's important to write your notes in such a way that the main points are distinguishable from the details. If the information runs together or if you have only written down the main points and excluded the details, your notes will be of less use for studying.

- **Good Notes Include Examples.** Often when professors get to the point in the lecture at which they are giving examples, students are nodding off or thinking about what they plan to have for lunch. But examples often surface on exams, so it's crucial to write down every example of a particular main point that the professor provides. These examples should stand out in some way so that as you study, you know what they illustrate.

- **Good Notes Clearly Indicate Lecture Patterns.** Most professors use the same pattern in all of their lectures. The two most common are the *deductive* pattern and the in *inductive* pattern. **Deductive lectures** begin with the generalization ("There are three main reasons for . . .") and then fill in the reasons, details, and examples. **Inductive lectures** do the opposite. They progress from the specific to the general. For example, an inductive lecturer would provide a series of reasons or characteristics and conclude with a statement such as, "So, all of this means . . ." This concluding statement is the generalization that helps make sense of the lecture. It is generally easier to follow lectures when they are presented in a deductive manner. Moreover, different disciplines may lend themselves better to one type than the other. The style your professor uses should become apparent to you after the first few class sessions and your notes will need to reflect this lecture pattern.

- **Good Notes Allow for Self-Testing.** Students don't usually think about how the way they take notes will influence the way they study. Most students merely read over their notes. However, this approach often gives them a false sense of knowing the information when, in fact, they do not. Instead, try writing questions or key words in the margin of your notes to help you test yourself. Note the difference between the notes in the three earlier examples. The notes in the first example have questions in the margins that you can ask yourself, which will help you determine your knowledge of the material. (We will discuss self-questioning of lecture notes, or self-testing, in more detail later in the chapter.)

- **Good Notes Stand the Test of Time.** Because your notes are a daily record of what is said in class each day, they should make sense to you long after class is over. You should be able to read through your notes and annotations two days, two weeks, or two months later and find they are still understandable.

Because of the way memory works, you will be unable to remember everything your professor says in class every day. That's why you take notes to begin with. It's important, then, to be sure that your notes are organized in such a way that they will make sense down the line and that they include as much detail as you can reasonably get on paper.

- **Good Notes Use Abbreviations.** Because most professors speak faster than you can write, it's important to use abbreviations that make sense to you. For example, if your professor is lecturing on the Industrial Revolution, it would be too time consuming to write both words out every time they were mentioned. Using *Ind. Rev.* or even *IR* saves a considerable amount of time. It is also a good idea to develop a series of abbreviations for common and high-use words. See the "Success at a Glance" box for some suggestions.

SUCCESS AT A GLANCE

Abbreviation Examples

&	and
b/c	because
/	the
=	means, definitions, is equal to
w/i	within
+	in addition to, positives
−	negatives
$	money, wealth
<	less than
>	greater than
↑	increased
↓	decreased
∴	therefore
*	very important

It is becoming more common for professors to put their notes on the Web or to have students purchase copies of their notes to follow during the lecture. These alternatives are useful as long as you continue to take a good set of notes yourself. We know that simply using someone else's notes, even if they are the professor's, rather than taking your own does not maximize your learning. Many students find that they tune out when they don't take their own notes—and often miss important points. The better approach is to take notes yourself and then compare them with the Web notes. (We discuss strategies for using Web notes later in the chapter.)

Taking Good Lecture Notes

Taking good notes involves active listening, attentiveness, concentration, and the ability to synthesize and condense a considerable amount of information on the spot. Effective note takers know that a lot of thinking goes on during note taking. Most students probably enter the lecture situation with every intention of staying alert, paying attention, and taking good notes. But for a variety of reasons, many students do not prevail.

From our observations, it seems that several factors enter into students' abilities to take good notes:

1. **Class Size.** The larger the class size, the easier it is to become unconnected with what the professor is saying. In addition, the further back or to the side that students sit in a classroom, the worse the problem tends to become. That's why it's important to stay in the professor's line of vision, sitting either close to the front or in the middle section of the room.

2. **Professor's Lecture Style.** When professors are not entertaining, or if they tend to speak in a monotone, it is hard to stay focused and actively involved in listening. Professors who are difficult to follow or who speak rapidly can cause students' minds to wander. We have also found that when the professor has put notes on the Web or reads directly from overheads, students tend to pay less attention.

3. **Time of Day.** Interestingly, students are most likely to fall asleep in an early morning class, presumably after they have had several hours of uninterrupted sleep. Granted, many students would consider themselves night people whose body clocks resist going to bed before the wee hours of the morning and also resist getting up prior to noon. If you count yourself in these numbers, try to avoid scheduling an early morning class. Some students also seem to have trouble paying attention right after lunch (because they are full and sluggish) or during the late afternoon hours (when they feel hungry and tired). If you have a class immediately after lunch, try to eat a light meal; if a late afternoon class is on your schedule, try eating a snack before class to keep up your energy.

4. **Health (Both Emotional and Physical).** Breaking up with your boyfriend or girlfriend, family problems, sick children, illness, or taking medications all can

influence your attentiveness in class. Everyone experiences problems at one time or another and no one can expect to be perfectly attentive all the time. But when emotional or physical problems become constant barriers to learning, it's time to think about a course of action to get back to health.

TIMELY TIPS

The Importance of Sleep

It is worth mentioning the importance of getting an adequate amount of sleep. Lack of sleep causes impaired concentration and the inability to focus and stay on task. If you go to bed at a decent hour, you should be able to get up at a decent hour to make the most of your day. Additionally, when you don't get enough sleep, you tend to get sick more often, which can cause you to fall behind in your classes.

General Note-Taking Guidelines

Let's begin our discussion of how to take good lecture notes with some general guidelines. These guidelines tend to work for every type of lecture, regardless of class size:

- **Sit Front and Center.** As we mentioned, students who sit in the front of the classroom or in the professor's line of vision tend to be more attentive and listen more actively than those who sit in the back. This holds true in both larger and smaller classes. In small classes, students who sit in the front tend to ask more questions and get to know their professors better. Also, research indicates a significant relationship between students' grades and seat location. That is, the closer they sit to the front, the higher their grade tends to be.

- **Adjust Your Note Taking to the Professor.** Every professor lectures a bit differently. Some are well organized and taking notes from them is a breeze. Others are unorganized, provide few transitional cues, and get off the topic very easily. Whatever your professor's lecturing habits seem to be, you need to figure them out early in the term and make the appropriate adjustments in your note taking.

- **Listen, Think, and Write.** Students who try to copy down everything the professor says tend to miss many key points because they can't keep up. Rather than trying to write down every word, listen first, think about what the professor is saying, and then write that thought, as much as possible, in your own words. Because professors tend to repeat information or say it a few different ways, it's important to listen and think before you write. Your intent should be to understand the concepts rather than get down every word.

- **Paraphrase.** Sometimes professors speak so quickly and try to cram so much material into a lecture that it is virtually impossible to get down all of the key points. If you find yourself getting more half thoughts than complete thoughts in your notes, or if you read over your notes and find that you can't piece together the important parts of the lecture, then you probably need to begin to do some serious paraphrasing. Paraphrasing, in this case, means getting down key concepts in your words and then filling in the details after class with information from the text. The following example shows the notes a professor might use for a lecture on the Tonkin Gulf incident and how a student's paraphrased notes might look.

Example of a Professor's Notes and a Student's Paraphrased Notes

Professor's Lecture Notes	Student's Paraphrased Notes
In 1964, President Lyndon Johnson took several steps to show the United States' commitment to defend South Vietnam. In February, Johnson ordered the Pentagon to prepare for airstrikes against the North. In May, his advisers drafted a resolution that authorized the military to escalate action. In June, General Maxwell Taylor, who was a strong proponent of more U.S. involvement in the war, was appointed ambassador to Saigon. And, in early August, patrol boats from the North supposedly clashed with two U.S. destroyers in the Gulf of Tonkin. Evidence of a real attack was skimpy at best. Johnson stated, "For all I know, our navy was shooting at whales out there." Nonetheless, Johnson announced on national television that Americans had been victims of "open aggression on the high seas." Withholding the fact that the U.S. ships had been assisting the South Vietnamese commando raids	<u>Tonkin Gulf Incident</u> <u>Steps leading to</u>: • Feb. 1964—LBJ ordered Pentagon to prepare for airstrikes against N. VN • May 1964—LBJ's advisors draft resolution to increase military action • June 1964—Taylor a strong supporter of ↑ involvement in VN becomes ambassador to Saigon • Aug.—Tonkin Gulf incident occurs—"assault" on U.S. ships in Gulf; little evidence that it happened; LBJ says US was a victim of aggressive acts that were unprovoked.

(continued)

Professor's Lecture Notes	**Student's Paraphrased Notes**

against two North Vietnamese islands in a secret operation planned by American advisors, the president condemned the attacks as unprovoked. He ordered retaliatory air strikes against the North for the first time and called on Congress to pass the previously drafted resolution giving him the authority to "take all necessary measures to repel any armed attack against the forces of the United States and to prevent further aggression." Assured by the president that this meant "no extension of the present conflict," the Senate passed the so-called Gulf of Tonkin Resolution 88 to 2; the House vote was 416 to 0. Johnson had not only signaled America's determination to stand by its allies, but also stymied Goldwater's effort to make Vietnam a campaign issue. He also now had a resolution that he likened to "grandma's nightshirt—it covered everything." His attorney general would soon describe the resolution as "the functional equivalent of a declaration of war" and the president would consider it a mandate to commit U.S. forces to Vietnam as he saw fit.

Results:

1. Retaliatory air strikes against N. VN

2. Congress passes the Tonkin Gulf Resolution=give LBJ authority to use "all necessary measures to prevent further aggressions"; passed Senate 88-2 and House 416-0

3. Stymied Goldwater's attempt to make VN a campaign issue.

4. LBJ could, in effect, do anything he wanted to escalate U.S. involvement

■   ■   ■

Learning how to take good lecture notes is an integral part of being a successful college student and an active learner. Like approaching textbook reading, taking good notes and using them as a successful study aid involves preparing to take notes, being an active listener during the lecture, and then rehearsing and self-testing after the lecture.

Getting Ready to Take Notes

Doing some preparation before you begin to take notes can make the difference between being an active and a passive listener. In order to get ready to take notes, you should:

- **Do the Assigned Reading.** Most professors expect you to read the appropriate text chapters before you come to class. Reading before the lecture gives you the advantage of making connections between the text and lecture. You will also be able to follow the "listen, think, write" rule better, because being familiar with the lecture topic will allow you to take down the key points in a more organized fashion. If you run out of time and can't read the text in its entirety, at least skim the chapter(s) using the techniques described in Chapter 10 to give you some idea of the key points that will be covered in the lecture.

- **Review Your Notes from the Previous Lecture.** Spend five or ten minutes before class to read through your notes from the previous lecture. By reviewing, you are refreshing your memory and getting your mind ready to become actively involved in learning. In addition, when you review, you can be sure that you understand the information that has been presented. Because many professors begin each class by answering student questions, you can get unclear information explained.

- **Have the Extra Edge.** Try to get to class with plenty of time to spare. Plan to use that time to review. Get out your notebook, get your paper ready (we'll talk more about this later), and of course, sit in the front.

Staying Active During Note Taking

In this section we will discuss not only the format and organization of good notes, but also the kinds of information that you should include in your notes. By following these suggestions, you will be able to remain alert and active throughout the class.

Format and Organization

If you were to examine the notes of five different college students, you would probably see five different formats. Perhaps none of the formats would match up with the method we recommend, the split-page method. We will concentrate on this particular method because it allows for self-testing, which we believe is crucial for active learning. Look again at the first note-taking example on page 179. You can see that a line has been drawn down the left-hand side of the paper, creating a two- to three-inch margin. You take your notes on the wider right-hand side of the paper and then after class use the left-hand margin to pull out the key points. You should have your lines drawn on several sheets of paper, your paper dated, and several pages numbered before your professor begins to lecture.

As you take notes, use the following guidelines:

- **Use a three-ring binder** rather than spiral-bound notebooks. A binder allows you to include class handouts and easily remove and insert notes.

- **Take notes in simple paragraph form,** rather than as a tightly structured outline. Outlines cause many students to get hung up on the outline format rather than the content of the lecture.

- **Leave spaces between ideas and underline key points** to enable you to see where one idea stops and another begins. This also helps to distinguish between the key points and the details.

- **Try to make your notes inviting to review.** Neatness and organization count because you will not want to spend much time with your notes if they are difficult to read and review.

- **Indent and mark details and examples.** Indenting helps you know what information is related. If your notes all run together, it's difficult to tell what is a key point and what is supporting information.

- **Make numbered lists**—reasons, characteristics, types, and so forth. Numbered lists enable you to know at a glance how many factors on the list you need to remember.

- **Use abbreviations whenever possible.** Abbreviating saves time and can distinguish certain kinds of information, such as indicating an example by "ex.," a definition by "def.," important information with an asterisk "*", and so forth.

Active Listening

It's not only important to know how you should take and organize your notes, but it is also important to be aware of the kinds of information you should include. Of course, the kinds of information you should put in your notes vary from class to class. For example, although you may include names, dates, and events in your history notes, your psychology notes will probably be more focused on research and theories than on key events. Listen for the following cues that your professor may give as a way of figuring out what is important to note:

- **Lists.** Lists of things begin with cues such as, "There were three major reasons why President Johnson committed more troops to Vietnam." "Short-term memory has five characteristics." "Mitosis progresses through eight stages." Any time you hear a number followed by several factors, stages, or characteristics, make sure you write the number of things along with the explanation. In other words, just don't write the stages of mitosis in your notes. Write down what happens in each stage as well.

- **Cause/Effect.** When you hear your professor discuss causes and effects, be sure to write them down. Cause/effect cues are common in history and political science. For example, there might be an event that caused a president to make a certain decision and this decision, in turn, had numerous effects on other events and decisions. In science, cause/effect can deal with concepts such as diseases or the food chain.

- **Definitions.** Perhaps the most frequent type of information your professor will give in a lecture will be definitions. Your professor might cue you by saying something as basic as, "*Intelligence* can be defined as . . ." It's a good idea to get definitions written in your notes precisely. If you only get down a portion of a definition or aren't sure that you have it exactly right, check your text or with your professor as soon after class as possible.

- **Examples.** Definitions are quite frequently followed by examples, yet often, students will see "example time" as an occasion to tune out. But examples discussed in class make for prime test questions. If you have to choose, we believe that it's more important to get examples than definitions in your notes (you can get the definitions from your textbook).

- **Extended Comments.** When the professor spends a lot of time explaining something, you can be sure that it is important information. Try to stay connected with the lecturer during extended comments and take down as much of the information as possible. Essay, short-answer, and higher-level multiple-choice items often come from these extended comments.

- **Superlatives.** Any time a professor uses words such as "most important," "best explanation," or "least influential," be sure to write it down. For example, there may be several explanations as to what constitutes intelligence, but your psychology professor might believe that one explanation is the best. These are the kinds of things professors love to ask about on exams.

- **Voice or Volume Change.** When professors think something is important or they want to stress it, they generally speak louder and slower. A change in voice can be a clear indication that something important is being said.

- **Process Notes.** Process notes consist of information the professor gives about tests, how to study, when study or review sessions are held, how to think about the information, or how he wants an essay structured. They can also include clues about what information might be on the exam and other hints related to task. Process notes often come right at the beginning of class, before some students are ready to take notes, or at the end of class, when some students are packed up and ready to leave. Sometimes professors will even comment after a particular lecture something to the effect, "Hmmm . . . Wouldn't this make an interesting essay question?" This is all vital information that should be written down in your notes.

Becoming an active listener takes time, especially for classes in which you have little interest. It's not too difficult to stay connected with the lecturer in classes that you like or in classes where you have a professor who is dynamic. It's much more difficult in those courses that are, in some

Studying Smarter

Some professors are putting their lecture notes on the Web daily. If any of your professors do this, check out their Web site. There are advantages and disadvantages to Web notes, however. Students who simply print out the notes and study them right before the exam tend to score lower than students who use the Web notes as a supplement to their own notes. If your professor supplies the notes for you, take them to class and follow along during the lecture. You'll be able to add more details during class.

way, less appealing. But try to think about the bigger picture. If you are an active listener and take organized notes for the entire class period, studying and learning the course material will be a much easier task.

Annotating and Self-Testing After Note Taking

You prepared to take notes before the lecture and you remained active and took notes in an organized way during the lecture, but you still aren't finished! Going over your notes after the lecture is perhaps the most important phase of note taking. As soon as possible after the lecture, it's important to read your notes to be sure that you understand all the major concepts presented. This is when you use the two- to three-inch margin on the left-hand side of your paper. As shown in the first example at the beginning of the chapter (page 179), this margin can be used to write in the key points or pose questions. (This is very similar to annotation that we discussed in detail in Chapter 11.) The annotations or questions are used to self-test as you study the course material.

Good annotations or questions have several features. They:

- focus on the major points or broad topics;
- get at higher level thinking by asking "how," "why," or "for example," not just "what" questions;
- are brief.

Annotating your lecture notes as soon as possible after the lecture helps get the information into your memory. In addition, when you go through your notes, you can determine if you have questions about what was presented in class. Writing questions or annotating gives you immediate feedback about what you understand and what you need to have clarified.

When it comes time to prepare for the exam, follow these steps to use your annotations or questions to self-test:

1. Read your notes, either to yourself or out loud, trying to get the information fixed in your memory.
2. Fold your paper back, exposing only what you have written in the left-hand column.
3. Ask yourself the question or explain the concept.
4. Flip your notes over to see how much of the material you have remembered.
5. If you knew it *accurately and precisely*, go on to the next concept. If you had problems, read your notes another time or two and try again.
6. As you learn the concepts, check them off in the margin.
7. When you begin the next study session, review what you know, but concentrate your efforts on what you don't know.

Self-testing by using annotations or questions in the margin of your notes should give you confidence as you enter a testing situation. When you self-test, you are monitoring your understanding and therefore have a fairly accurate idea of the concepts you know and comprehend and those that may still be somewhat unclear. As with other rehearsal strategies, self-testing of lecture notes has a tremendous payoff.

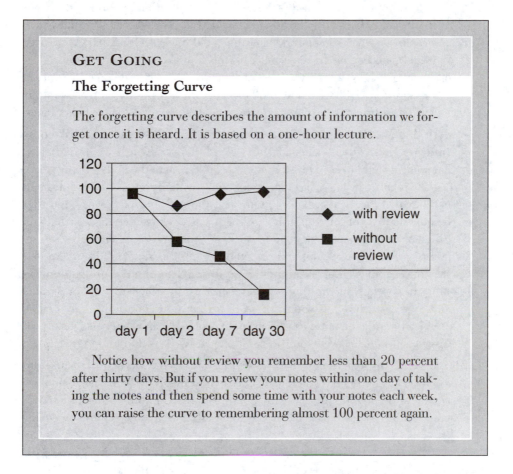

GET GOING

The Forgetting Curve

The forgetting curve describes the amount of information we forget once it is heard. It is based on a one-hour lecture.

Notice how without review you remember less than 20 percent after thirty days. But if you review your notes within one day of taking the notes and then spend some time with your notes each week, you can raise the curve to remembering almost 100 percent again.

Note-Taking Myths

We end this chapter by discussing some myths—information that students tend to believe about note taking that isn't necessarily true.

- **Myth 1: If You Can't Keep Up with the Professor, Tape Record the Lectures.** The truth is that when students tape lectures, they generally don't listen to the tapes. It's easy to understand why. If you are taking five classes, you hardly have time to do all your reading, studying, and other learning activities, let alone sit and listen to lectures for a second time. In addition, students who tape lectures find it much easier to tune out to what the professor is saying and will miss information written on the chalkboard or overhead. Our advice to you is to go to class, take the best notes you can, and supplement those notes with information from the text or by forming a study group that has as one of its goals to share notes with everyone. Unless you have a disability that necessitates recording class lectures, tape recording simply is not an efficient and active way to learn.

- **Myth 2: Copying a Classmate's Notes Is Better than Struggling with Them Yourself.** Think back to sometime in your distant past when you actually may have copied someone's homework. How much did you learn from that experience? We would guess not much. You won't learn much from copying someone else's lecture notes either, even if they are better than yours. A better plan is to compare your lecture notes with a classmate's. That can be a very positive and active strategy and you just might learn from your classmate some ways to take better notes.

- **Myth 3: If My Professor Provides Notes by Putting Them on the Web or Handing Them Out in Class, I Don't Have to Take Notes.** We have noticed that students tend to earn lower grades in classes where the notes are provided. This is probably because most students don't regularly review such notes and therefore don't learn the material until test time. If your professor hands out the notes in class or has you purchase them as a package, we suggest that you print out the notes and take them to class each day. As you listen to the lecture, fill in gaps by adding detail and providing examples. You can also make special note of topics emphasized by the professor. Then, to be sure you understand the concepts in your notes, after each class use the T-method or parallel notes (discussed next). If your professor puts her notes on the Web after class, attend class and take notes as you normally would. Then when you get the professor's notes off the Web you can compare the two sets and fill in any gaps.

- **Myth 4: It's Impossible to Take Notes in a Class That Involves Discussion.** When we have observed students in classes that involve a lot of discussion, we see very little note taking. Students seem to think that only information presented by the professor has merit and they fail to write down comments made

NETWORKING

Using Course Management Systems

Professors are using course management systems such as Web CT for many creative things. They may place their syllabi, quizzes, assignments, and other course information there. They may also post student grades or have virtual chats with the class. We know one professor who conducts exam reviews online. If your professor uses these systems, plan to visit the site often to keep up on new assignments or important information.

by their peers. However, if you think about the purpose of classes that involve discussion, you'll realize that the professor's role is generally just to initiate the discussion. It's the students who actually generate the ideas and those ideas often find their way to the exam.

We recommend that for a discussion class, you slightly modify the note-taking process. As shown in the accompanying example, rather than dividing your paper into a narrow and a wide margin, divide it into three equal columns. In the first column, write the question that is being posed or the theory that is being debated. In the second column, take notes on what the professor has to say about it. In the last column, take notes on what your classmates say. Then when you are studying, you can evaluate your classmate's comments and evaluate which are worth studying and which can be ignored. One of our graduate students modified this technique by adding possible test questions or paper topics and text page numbers to help her relate the discussion to her reading. The example shows her notes from a psychology of creativity class. Notice how she formatted the notes to follow the flow of conversation.

Sample Discussion Notes

Question Posed	Professor's Comments	Student Comments
Must creativity result in a product?		
		Depends on how you look @ it—whose perspective?
	So which is more important, process or product?	
Possible TQ? Process is more important than product. Defend or refute this statement		
		Artist—process Public—product
	Does an idea count as a product?	
p. 283 creativity outcomes		
		Product. Have to have tangible evidence of creativity
	Good point—anyone expand?	

Additional Note-Taking Strategies

Example of Parallel Notes

Professor's Notes

Impact on Voter Mobilization

- Mobilization matters.

- What the parties and the campaigns do has an impact on who and how many people turn out to vote.

- But you can only mobilize when there is a chance that you can win.

- Turnout is generally low in one-party dominant areas where the general election is noncompetitive.

Parallel Notes

When your professors use a range of technology—Web notes, PowerPoint presentations, graphs and visual aids, students tell us that their attention is often divided. One strategy that can help you concentrate is parallel notes. For this strategy, print out the notes the professor supplies before class and place them in a three-ring binder. As the professor lectures, take your own notes on the blank facing page, following along with the notes the professor supplied and filling in any gaps or added information. After the lecture, create your self-testing questions as in the other note-taking methods. The accompanying example shows notes from a political science class on voter mobilization.

Your Notes	Self-Testing
Much $ spent on getting out the vote	
Over several decades, turnout has declined. Presidential elections—turnout has fallen from nearly 65% in the 1960s to just over 50% in the 1990s.	Decline in voting—reasons
Efforts are often only in the states and congressional districts where elections are expected to be close, and are often partisan.	Partisan vs. non-partisan effort
But there are also less partisan efforts designed to boost turnout overall	
—voter participation in the United States is lower than most other well-established democracies.	
Questions to think about 1. Why is turnout lower in the United States than in other advanced democracies?	Would make good essay question!
2. How have turnout rates been changing for the electorate as a whole and for specific social groups? What are the implications of those trends for the two major political parties?	

The T-Method

This technique will help ensure that you understand what you've written in your notes. Use the T-method as soon as possible after class. It is shown in the accompanying example and explained in the following steps.

1. Draw a T at the bottom one-fourth of your last page of notes (you can use the back of the page if you need more room).
2. On the left side of the page, summarize the key points of the lecture.
3. On the right side of the page, predict some test questions about the material.

Example of the T-Method

Summary	Questions
Memory consists of 3 systems 1. encoding, 2. storage, 3. retrieval. Information first goes into short-term memory through rehearsal (maintenance or elaborative) where it is either encoded or forgotten quickly (less than 30 sec) Information that is encoded goes into long-term memory	1. What are the three memory systems? Define and describe characteristics. 2. Compare and contrast maintenance and elaborative rehearsal. 3. How does information move from STM to LTM?

☐ REAL COLLEGE
Chad's Challenge

DIRECTIONS: Read the following "Real College" scenario and respond to the question based on what you learned in this chapter.

"Why did I ever sign up for this eight o'clock class?" Chad wondered as he dragged himself out of bed around 7:30 A.M. Every day it was a real challenge—and he even liked Professor Wilson's anthropology class. He was, however, experiencing some trouble.

Chad never had problems taking notes in high school. His teachers spoke slowly and would repeat information when students asked. Plus, most of his high school teachers gave study guides to prepare for the tests, so all he had to do was to look up the answers that came mostly from the teacher's lectures. But Professor Wilson talked so fast and tried to get so much in one lecture that Chad usually only got a small portion of the key ideas that were presented. Then, because he was often late to class, he would walk in during the middle of an extended comment and would be unable to figure out what Professor Wilson was talking about. His notes were disorganized and full of doodles and more than once he almost fell out of his seat when he nodded off. Chad tried two different solutions prior to the first exam. First, he gave up taking notes altogether and brought a tape recorder to class. Second, he borrowed a classmate's notes and copied them. He made a very low D.

After this poor performance, he decided that he really didn't know how to take notes from Professor Wilson. He wanted to put in a concerted effort to take notes once again, but he was unsure of what to do.

What advice would you give to Chad so that he can improve? (You are not allowed to advise him to drop the class or take it later in the day during the next term.)

☐ THINKING CRITICALLY
Something to Think About and Discuss

We have offered some reasons why self-questioning works in practice here and in other chapters in this book. From what you have learned so far:

- What are the benefits of testing yourself on your notes?
- How important do you think it is to share and discuss your notes with a class-mate?
- What are the benefits and drawbacks to reviewing your notes each day?

☐ ADD TO YOUR PORTFOLIO

1. Try taking notes in all of your classes using the split-page, discussion, parallel note, or T-method for one week. Be sure to write questions or annotations. Evaluate what you like and don't like about these methods. How might you modify these methods to suit your own note-taking preferences?

2. For each of your current classes, try to determine how much overlap there is between the text and the lecture. Do your professors' test questions come primarily from the lectures or the text? How will this information affect your note taking?

CHAPTER 15

STRATEGIES ACROSS THE DISCIPLINES

Read this chapter to find answers to the following questions:

- How do my courses differ from each other?
- How do my textbooks differ from each other?
- How can I modify my strategies to suit different courses and texts?

SELF-ASSESSMENT

DIRECTIONS: Complete the following chart for each of your courses this term. Think about how you prepare for each class.

	Course 1	Course 2	Course 3	Course 4	Course 5
(course name)	————	————	————	————	————
I read the text before class.	Yes/No	Yes/No	Yes/No	Yes/No	Yes/No
I read the text after class.	Yes/No	Yes/No	Yes/No	Yes/No	Yes/No
My class lecture follows the text.	Yes/No	Yes/No	Yes/No	Yes/No	Yes/No
I am responsible for reading multiple texts for this course.	Yes/No	Yes/No	Yes/No	Yes/No	Yes/No
I try to study in the same way for each course.	Yes/No	Yes/No	Yes/No	Yes/No	Yes/No
I understand the professor's expectations for this course.	Yes/No	Yes/No	Yes/No	Yes/No	Yes/No

The way you have responded to these questions gives a good indication of how you approach reading and studying in your classes. Keep these answers in mind as you read the rest of the chapter.

Course Characteristics

All of your courses are not the same—obviously, the content in your history class is not the same as in your chemistry class. But have you noticed that the ways in which your classes are organized and structured also differ? Some of your classes may involve taking lots of lecture notes, others may involve class discussion, you may have a lab class in addition to a lecture class, or you may have lecture, lab, and discussion all in one course. In addition, the textbooks are often vastly different. In fact, you may have noticed that some of your textbooks are not even especially well written. Because class structure and text sources can be so wide-ranging, you will encounter different types of assessments depending on the course. You may have essay or multiple-choice exams, write journals or papers, give speeches or presentations, or be required to complete any number of different tasks. When you begin to study for your courses, you will base your decision of which strategies to choose on the type of class, type of text, and type of assessment. In order to prepare you for the variety of tasks you need to do, we will examine discipline-specific differences in college courses.

Studying Smarter
Choose your strategies for learning based on the type of course and type of tests you will experience.

SUCCESS AT A GLANCE

Questions to Think About

- How is the text arranged? Chronologically, topically, or otherwise?
- How much do the lecture and text overlap?
- Will I be able to read and understand the text before going to class?
- Will I be able to understand the lecture if I do not read before class?
- What kinds of strategies will work best for this discipline?

Textbook Characteristics

Saying that you can read each of your textbooks in the same way for each of your courses is like saying you can read *People* magazine in the same way as you read Shakespeare. Obviously, you have to adjust your reading to the type of course and the textbook you are using. As you encounter different college textbooks you will notice some basic differences depending on the content area. Textbooks in the humanities are different from textbooks in the social sciences or physical sciences.

Mathematics Textbooks

Reading a mathematics textbook is not like reading a novel or another textbook. Mathematics textbooks tend to use few words in order to keep ideas clearly outlined, so you must understand almost every sentence. You will be expected to comprehend abstract relationships and theories as you read about them. Mathematics texts tend to present new concepts, formulas, diagrams, and practice problems sequentially, which means that they build on one another. So mathematics learning is cumulative, which means that the concepts you are learning this week are based on the concepts already presented.

NETWORKING

Computer Testing

It is becoming more common for college students to take tests on the computer. On our campus, for example, students in all levels of mathematics take computerized exams and receive immediate feedback on how well they performed. In chemistry, students also take exams on the computer and once they get their score, they can work on the items they missed and submit those items a second time for partial credit. Although many students at first don't feel comfortable taking computerized exams, most quickly adjust. However, if practice computerized tests are available in your course, we suggest you take them to help you become more at ease with this method of testing.

You will find that mathematics textbooks are not very repetitive, making every concept count. With little chance of picking up missed information by reading further in the text, you must be sure you have mastered each concept before moving on to a new one.

Study Strategies for Mathematics Courses   In general, college mathematics courses are based on problem solving. In addition to what we generally think of as mathematics courses, computer science, engineering, statistics, chemistry, and physics are also math-based courses. Whether you are in a class of 10 or 300, you will be asked to apply math principles and formulas in a variety of situations. Sometimes mathematics courses are discussion-based, but most often they are lecture-based, with the instructor explaining new concepts and the students taking copious notes. Many times mathematics instructors focus lectures on working out problems on the board.

To approach reading in mathematics, it is a good idea to preview the text before class. If you find that you can read and understand the chapter before the lecture that is even better, but many students find that they comprehend mathematics texts better after listening to the lecture and seeing problems worked as examples in class. When you preview the text, note the concepts and formulas that are covered as well as any new terminology so that you will have some background information before listening in class. When you are in class, take good notes and ask questions. The more information and examples you have in your notes, the better it will be as you read the text.

· After class, read the text. It is best to read the chapter as soon after class as possible so that you will remember all of the key points and ideas discussed in class. Take your time as you read. Be sure that you understand each concept before moving forward. Annotate key words, formulas, definitions, and symbols in the margins to help you remember them. Note the symbols used in your text, because they have very specific meanings and must be used correctly when working math problems. For example, to understand $ab :: cd$, you must first understand that $::$ is the symbol for "is proportional to."

Because the information is cumulative, you cannot neglect math work. Plan to spend some time each night reading or working problems. As you read, work out the problems in your text. After reading examples, cover up the answer to the sample problem to work it out. It is also important to write down questions about concepts you need to have clarified so you can ask them during class, before the class moves on to a new concept. Try to create your own problems and solve them for additional practice. If you find that you are experiencing difficulty understanding your textbook, you may find it helpful to use another math book (you can probably find one in the library) as a reference book to help clarify confusing points. In addition, try verbalizing the problems. Talking the information through by putting symbols into words, for example, can let you know where your understanding is breaking down.

After you work the problems in each section of the chapter, it is essential that you pull the concepts together. Most professors will expect you to be able to respond to problems that combine several concepts—*even if they do not explicitly go over it that way in class.* Thus, it is a good idea to try to create and solve problems that require you to use several concepts presented in your chapters.

Science Textbooks

Science courses can be divided into two categories—math-based science courses and text-based science courses. Each category will have vastly different texts. Textbooks for math-based science courses, such as chemistry or physics, will contain formulas like your mathematics texts, but they will also contain important diagrams explaining scientific processes.

Text-based science courses, such as biology, agriculture, forestry, botany, astronomy, and geology, are often more similar to social science courses than mathematics courses. There is little mathematics involved; instead, you will be required to read, understand, and apply scientific processes discussed in the text. These courses usually include a lab in which you experience hands-on application of scientific principles.

You will find many new terms and definitions in science textbooks. Often, those new terms will be used later in the text to define other terms, so if you don't understand the term when it is introduced, you will have trouble understanding future reading. Science textbooks also discuss proven principles and theories in terms of their relationships to each other. Therefore, it is important to be aware of and understand how the theories connect and how they explain the science concepts you are learning.

Strategies for Science Courses   Because of the amount of new terminology involved in learning science, it is important for you to read your science textbooks before class. In this way, you will be familiar with the terms and concepts discussed in the text and you will be able to build your understanding of the concept as you listen in class. It is also a good idea to connect the concepts discussed in class with the concepts described in your text by comparing your lecture notes to your text annotations each night.

As with your math courses, science concepts are usually presented sequentially, which means they build on each other so if you do not understand the concepts presented early on, you will have difficulty later. Your best defense is to test yourself as you read to make sure you fully understand each concept. Adopt a scientific approach and ask yourself questions, such as:

- Is this concept or phenomenon a theory or has it been proven?
- What other theories is this concept related to?
- How does this phenomenon work? What is the scientific process involved?
- Why does this phenomenon occur?
- What does it show us?

You will need to go beyond memorizing bold-faced terms. So making a concept map of key terms and concepts to see how the ideas relate is another helpful strategy. When you preview each chapter, begin a concept map for the ideas contained in the chapter. As you read, fill in your concept map with the important scientific processes. You may want to make CARDS over the concepts and new terminology, but you must do more than just memorize the terms. Spread out your CARDS to show the hierarchy of terms or the order of the scientific process. This way you will be connecting the ideas together.

Science texts often contain diagrams or charts to explain concepts. Because science exams usually contain questions about the concepts described in diagrams or charts, you must be able to read and understand each one. As you read your text, annotate the diagrams and take the time to learn what they are depicting. A good self-testing strategy to make

Studying Smarter

In your science courses be sure that you can explain important diagrams in your text. Try to look only at the diagram (not the description in the text) and talk through the important information. This will help you prepare for almost any question the professor can ask on that topic.

sure you fully understand the concept is to cover up the words in the diagram and try to talk through the information. If you can explain how the concept works, you've shown you understand it. In addition, although exams in your science classes may consist of multiple choice, essay, or short-answer questions, many of your test questions will require you to apply science concepts to new situations. To answer these questions you must understand and be able to describe each concept. If you find that you cannot, reread your annotations and your lecture notes to be sure you understand the key points.

Humanities Textbooks

Humanities courses focus on all areas of human endeavor—invention, relationships, creation. Just about any area you can think of is represented in the humanities. Initially, many students think that humanities texts are easier to read than the texts in more fact-based courses like math or science, but humanities courses can be challenging because they require students to interpret, analyze, and evaluate the text. In general, humanities textbooks do not introduce much new content vocabulary, but you may encounter unfamiliar use of words or dialects. Topics in humanities textbooks are often presented chronologically, as in a literature textbook that is arranged by the year each story, poem, and play was written. However, sometimes they are organized topically, as in a philosophy textbook organized by themes. Humanities textbooks are usually not sequential nor do the concepts build on one another, so you should be able to read any chapter in your humanities texts and understand it without reading the previous chapters. Unlike science courses where you look to find how concepts are related, in humanities courses you will look for similarities and differences between themes, metaphors, ideology, and philosophy. Therefore, you will need strategies to help you think critically about what you are reading.

Strategies for Humanities Courses   Humanities courses include literature, philosophy, drama, music, art, and many more. In humanities courses, you are often asked to read from a variety of sources including novels, plays, and poetry, as well as from a traditional textbook. You also may be required to attend plays or musical events or other cultural activities in addition to class lectures.

Because many humanities courses are discussion-based, it is important to read the text before attending class. As you read, you should focus on analyzing and interpreting the information. Ask yourself questions such as:

- Why did the author choose to write this?
- What is the significance of what I am reading?
- What themes or metaphors are being used?
- How does this piece compare to other readings in this course?

In class it is usually important to take notes about what your classmates are discussing, because professors often create exam questions based on the class discussion. Using the three-column method of note taking discussed in Chapter 14 will be helpful in these courses. In addition to reading before class and taking good notes during class, you should connect the reading to the class discussion during your review after class. This review may entail annotating your text about themes, metaphors, symbolism, or issues discussed in class, marking important passages or quotations, or connecting themes across readings. Because humanities courses often involve writing papers or taking essay exams, it is always a good idea to keep track of ideas for possible paper topics as you are reading and to try to predict essay questions after listening to the class discussion.

TIMELY TIPS

Choosing Paper Topics

In many humanities courses, the professor outlines assignments for papers early in the semester. In that situation, choose your topic early and keep it in mind each time you read for the class. In this way you can pull out key quotes, major arguments, and other information that you will be able to use in your paper. You will find that choosing your topic early can be a huge timesaver.

Social Science Textbooks

Social science textbooks are usually concerned with what happens in a society. The social sciences involve the study of people in terms of political, economic, social, interpersonal, and cultural aspects of society. These texts are often filled with terms that may seem familiar, but have a specialized meaning. For example, the word "class" would have very different meanings in a sociology course than it would in an education course. Social science texts usually present ideas in either chronological order or topical form. For example, a history textbook usually discusses events in the order they occured in time (chronologically) but sociology texts often discuss ideas by topic.

Sections of social science texts are often highlighted in a text box or in some other manner. In high school, you probably used the same tactic whenever you saw a text box—you skipped it. However, in college texts these boxes often contain important information that is not contained elsewhere in the text. Sometimes they are supporting articles, or examples of a principle outlined in the text, or copies of original documents discussed in the chapter. But no matter what they contain, follow this general rule: *Read the text boxes.*

Many of your exam questions may come from text box information. Professors are aware that students tend to skip text boxes and they want to make sure students pay attention to the important information contained in the boxes, so they base test items on them.

Strategies for Social Science Courses   You will be asked to read and understand many new concepts in social science courses, so you will need strategies to help you organize large amounts of information. Social sciences courses include psychology, sociology, education, anthropology, history, political science, economics, and more. (We should note that history is viewed by some as a humanities course.) Students sometimes experience difficulty in social science courses because they try to memorize facts, forgetting that because the social sciences predominantly are based on theories, there are few facts. Also, social science texts often deal with large time spans, making it hard to simply memorize facts—a history class, for instance, could cover several thousand years in one semester.

As with your humanities courses, you should use the strategy of reading your social science textbooks before you attend class so that you are ready for class discussion or lecture. As you read, annotate the text and any diagrams or other typographical aids. Identify comparisons and contrasts between ideas, because they often make their way into social science exams. In addition, note possible test questions.

GET GOING

Being Prepared

Once you are out in the workplace, you wouldn't think about going to a meeting unprepared, but many students go to class each day without preparing. If you had to make a presentation to a new client you would want to be on top of things. To find your motivation for getting things done now, consider your work in college as a practice run for the work world. If you get into the habit of being prepared for your classes when you are in college, you will likely carry these habits over into the rest of your life.

Because you will need to be able to identify trends, trace their influence on historical events, and draw parallels with current events, you will need to use strategies that help you identify relationships between ideas. Charting is a good way to keep track of these relationships. Often students lose track of the big picture in their social science courses and get bogged down in the details. By charting the information, you will be able to see how ideas fit together into a larger concept. You will also be able to track trends or discover principles about the information. Another good strategy is to create a time line to help you remember the sequence of important events. But remember that most social science courses will involve more than just memorizing names and dates, so use your time line to help you see the big picture as well.

Using Technology to Study

Some students find that using a computer can greatly aid in learning and studying for courses. Here are some of the ways that students are using technology in learning:

- **Organizing Lecture Notes.** Some students like to retype their lecture notes because typing them on the computer helps them reorganize the information. We know of one student in an art history course who cut and pasted slides of paintings from her professor's Web site (and some from museum Web sites) right into her own notes. That way she could see the paintings as she studied her notes about them. Some students like to take notes on their personal digital assistant (PDA, such as a Palm Pilot) in class as another way to help organize all of the course information.

- **Creating Maps and Charts.** There are several software programs that can help you create concept maps and charts in a snap. These maps and charts help you organize and synthesize ideas (as discussed in Chapter 13).

- **Meeting with Virtual Study Groups.** Students can set up online study groups to meet at designated times before exams. This is a great way to study with others because the group tends to stay more on task than in a face-to-face study group.

- **Researching Information for Papers and Presentations.** The Internet can be a wonderful source of information when researching information for class presentations or papers. Of course, you need to be careful about the quality of the information you get. You also need to be careful that you do not plagiarize information from the Web.

This list is certainly not exhaustive. And, with new technologies coming out every day, we are sure you will find other ways to incorporate technology into your learning and studying.

☐ REAL COLLEGE
Caroline's Courses

DIRECTIONS: Read the following "Real College" scenario and respond to the question based on what you learned in this chapter.

Caroline is taking five courses this term: biology, political science, American literature, statistics, and music appreciation. So far she has approached learning in each course in the same way. She goes to class, listens to the lecture, and then reads the assigned chapters in the textbook. She tries to read the text the night before the lecture, but many times she does not get to the reading until right before the exam.

She is doing well in her music appreciation course, but is having trouble in all of the other classes. In American literature, the professor expects the class to discuss the novels and does not hold a lecture at all. Because she would rather listen to the professor before reading, Caroline usually doesn't have much to contribute to the discussion. Caroline does not take any notes in this class and feels that she doesn't really understand what she is supposed to be getting out of the reading. She has failed her first essay exam because the professor said that she was not reading critically enough.

In her biology class, the professor seems to lecture at 100 miles per hour. It seems as if he introduces twenty new concepts in every class. Caroline finds that she has trouble taking good notes because she never knows what the professor is talking about. She knows that something needs to change, but she isn't sure what she needs to do.

Statistics is a nightmare for her. She didn't understand what was going on from the first day of lecture. Now that they are about five chapters into the textbook, she is completely lost and doesn't know what to do. They only have two exams in statistics, a midterm and a final. Caroline is nervous about taking the midterm, which is in two weeks.

In political science, Caroline has so many reading assignments that she has trouble keeping track of them all. The class has reading assignments from the textbook, the newspaper, two full-length biographies, and sometimes the professor brings additional readings to class. They are also required to watch the national news each night because they are supposed to be connecting everything they read to current political events. Caroline is not sure how to go about connecting all of the different readings to current events.

Using what you know about text and course characteristics, how would you suggest Caroline approach learning in the courses that are presenting difficulties for her this term?

☐ THINKING CRITICALLY
Something to Think About and Discuss

Think about the courses you are taking this semester and carefully examine each of the texts for these courses. Then discuss the following questions with your classmates:

- How do the textbooks differ from each other?
- For each different category of courses, which of the following components are contained in your textbooks?
  - New terminology (vocabulary words specific to the content)

- New principles or theories described
- Chronological format (concepts organized by date)
- Sequential format (concepts built on one another)
- Topical format (concepts organized by topic)
- What kind of background knowledge, if any, does each text assume you have?

☐ ADD TO YOUR PORTFOLIO

Create a chart for each of your courses this semester to help you determine how to approach studying in that course. Consider the following questions in your chart:

1. What type of course is this? (mathematics, humanities, etc.)
2. How is the course structured? (topically, sequentially, chronologically, etc.)
3. What are the tasks in this course? (exams, essays, papers, etc.)
4. Which learning strategies do I currently use?
5. Which learning strategies would be most effective?

CHAPTER 16

BECOMING FLEXIBLE

Varying Your Reading Rate

Read this chapter to answer the following questions:

- What does it mean to be a flexible reader?
- How can I increase my reading speed?
- What are some habits that may slow my reading?

DIRECTIONS: Read the following article to assess your current reading speed. Use a stopwatch or a watch with a second hand to keep track of your time. When you have completed the reading, record your time and answer the comprehension questions. Use the formula following the passage to determine your reading rate. Time yourself only for reading the passage but not for answering the comprehension questions.

Students Are Dying; Colleges Can Do More

Drunk driving isn't a new problem, but it continues to ravage our campuses. I know we can change that.

—By Rob Waldron

Unfortunately, I am an expert on drinking and driving. As a high-school freshman in Wayland, Mass., I suffered through the death of a classmate on my hockey team who was killed in an alcohol-related crash. Two years later I attended the funeral of another classmate who died while driving under the influence. Twelve months after that, a wrestling teammate returning to Wayland from a college break totaled his car in a drunk-driving accident, partially paralyzing himself and causing permanent brain damage. His father, a town firefighter responding to a 911 call, was the one to find him on the roadside near death.

After all that, I thought I knew the worst about drunk driving. I was wrong. Three years ago my brother, Ryan, a Middlebury College senior, drove 70–100 miles an hour on a rainy rural road into a tree, ending his life. His blood-alcohol level was nearly three times the legal limit. Witnesses later recounted that he was swerving and speeding on a nearby road.

It was one of the worst accidents that officers at the crash site had ever seen. The two policemen assigned to wipe Ryan's blood and tissue off the car's broken windshield found it impossible even to talk to us about the details of what they found. According to the police report, before officers could transport Ryan to the funeral home, they had to remove a small branch that pierced his permanently flattened lips.

Ryan was last seen drinking on campus at a fraternity house that was serving vodka punch. He left the party intending to drive to his off-campus apartment three miles away to pick up a toga for yet another event. He never made it home. After his death, we found out that Ryan had developed a drinking problem while away at college. But even though he drank to excess at nearly every social function, usually three to four times a week, many of his friends never realized he was on his way to becoming an alcoholic.

It turns out that one of the staff members in the student activities office where Ryan often came to register his fraternity's parties had suspected that he had a drinking problem. And Ryan isn't the only Middlebury student to be involved in a dangerous alcohol-related incident: In the year before his death, one of Ryan's fellow students nearly died in a binge-drinking incident, saved only because the hospital pumped her stomach as she lay unconscious. Her blood-alcohol level was .425 percent.

What should we do about the Ryans of the world? I know that my brother was ultimately responsible for his own death, but in my view, college administrators can work harder to keep kids like Ryan from getting behind the wheel. But many schools have been reluctant to address the problem. Why? Perhaps because taking responsibility for drinking and driving will make trustees and college presidents legally liable for college students' drunk-driving behavior. If administrators accepted this responsibility, they might ask themselves the following questions: Should we expel students who receive a D.U.I.? Has the president of our university met with the mayor to create a unified policy toward drunk driving within our town? Have we contacted organizations like M.A.D.D. and S.A.D.D. to help us implement alcohol- and driving-education programs?

On campuses like Middlebury's, where many students own cars, administrators can use more aggressive methods to combat drinking and driving. Yet after Ryan's death his university ignored my family's request to fund a Middlebury town officer to patrol the main entry into campus for out-of-control drivers on weekend evenings. This, despite the fact that the Middlebury College director of health services informed me and my family that approximately 15 percent of the school's freshmen were so intoxicated at some point during the last year that a classmate had to bring them to the infirmary.

Why does the problem of drunk driving persist? It's not easy to solve. College students are young and irresponsible, and drinking is part of their culture. Administrators have not wanted to abolish social houses and fraternities for fear that ending such beloved college traditions would lower alumni donations.

To college presidents, trustees and all college officials, I ask that you go home tonight and consider your love for your own son or daughter, your own brother or sister. Imagine the knock on your door at 3 A.M. when a uniformed police officer announces that your loved one has died. Then go to a mirror and look deep into your own eyes. Ask yourself the question: Have I done enough to help solve this problem?

The choice is simple. You can choose to be a leader and an agent of change on a controversial issue. Or you can continue the annual practice of authoring one of your student's eulogies. My family, in its grief, begs you to do the former.

Newsweek, Oct. 30, 2000.

COMPREHENSION CHECK: Answer the following questions without looking back at the passage.

1. The author discusses:
   a. Why college students drink.
   b. How drunk driving accidents occur.
   c. Why drinking issues are difficult for colleges to address.
   d. Why colleges are not doing anything to help students learn to drink responsibly.

2. The author makes mention of _____ college.
   a. Middlesworth
   b. Middlebury
   c. Old Miss
   d. Michigan

3. The author believes that
   a. the college was responsible for his brother's death.
   b. his brother should not have gone to college.
   c. colleges can do more to prevent students from driving drunk.
   d. liability issues get in the way of teaching students about drinking and driving.

4. Which of the following questions were *not* presented as issues college administrators should ask?
   a. Should we expel students who receive DUIs?
   b. Has the university and the town worked toward creating a unified policy toward drunk driving?
   c. Have we contacted national organizations to help the college implement alcohol education programs?
   d. Should we ban drinking on campus?

5. The author's brother
   a. had developed a drinking problem in college.
   b. had developed a drinking problem in high school.
   c. considered himself a nondrinker.
   d. was an AA member.

RESULTS
Number of words: 840
Time: _____
(Use decimals for fractions of a minute. That is, if it took you 3 minutes and 45 seconds, record your time as 3.75 minutes.)
Rate of Speed (number of words ÷ time): _____
Comprehension Score: _____%
(Comprehension answers: 1. C, 2. B, 3. C, 4. D, 5. A)

Flexible Reading

What does the word flexible mean to you? You might think of a gymnast able to perform amazing physical feats. Or you might think about a choice, for example,

Studying Smarter

Push yourself to increase your reading speed to save yourself some valuable time.

"Which movie would you like to see?" "Whatever, I'm flexible." No matter the context, being flexible means that you can adapt to the situation. You don't often hear the word flexible used in learning situations, but you should begin to think about being a flexible learner. Flexible learners adapt their approach to learning based on the four factors that impact learning discussed in this text: their characteristics as a learner, the task, the study strategies they select, and the materials they must use. Flexible readers modify their approaches to text reading and adjust their reading speed to suit their purpose.

A flexible reader knows that it is unrealistic to attempt to read everything at the same speed. In other words, you cannot expect to read your chemistry textbook at the same speed at which you read the local newspaper. Your reading rate will vary depending on several factors:

- **The Difficulty of the Material to Be Read.** The easier the material, the faster you will be able to read.

- **Your Background Knowledge About the Topic.** The more you know about a topic, the faster you can read it.

- **Your Interest in the Topic.** The more interest you have in the material, the faster your rate.

The average adult reads about 200 words per minute; the average college student reads about 250 words per minute. Given the amount of reading that is required in college, it is to your advantage to increase your reading rate without sacrificing comprehension.

When you were learning to read difficult material in elementary school, your teacher probably advised you to slow down. Many college students follow the same advice to this very day when they read something difficult. However, if you are already reading at a slow rate and you slow yourself down even further, you actually might be making it harder to comprehend the text.

If a student is attempting to read the sentence, "The boy went to the store to get a loaf of bread and a gallon of milk," and is reading too slowly, he would read the sentence as individual words instead of phrases:

The/ boy/ went/ to/ the/ store/ to/ get/ a/ loaf/ of/ bread/ and/ a/ gallon/ of/ milk.

This student will have a more difficult time with comprehension because he must first recognize each of the individual words, then he must put the words together into meaningful phrases, and then he must put those phrases together into a sentence. By then, a good deal of time has passed (in reading terms) and a lot of the comprehension is lost. In this case, reading slower is *decreasing* the ability to comprehend the information.

Should you ever slow down when reading difficult material? Well, yes and no. You should slow down to the point of comprehension, but you should not read so slowly that you weaken comprehension.

Habits That Slow Reading

Many students may have at least one of several habits that slow their rate of reading speed. They developed many of these habits when they were children and, therefore, may not even be aware of them. As you read the following sections, think about your own reading habits.

Backtracking

A person who reads the same words over and over is backtracking. Think about the example sentence used earlier about the boy going to the store. A person who backtracks would read the sentence as:

The boy went to the store/ went to the store/ store/ to get a loaf of bread/ loaf of bread/ and a gallon of milk.

This habit can dramatically slow both reading and comprehension. Students backtrack when they are not confident that they have understood the reading or when they are not concentrating on what they are reading. If backtracking becomes a habit, students tend to do it no matter what they read, which is why it is one of the toughest habits to break.

To stop backtracking, you must convince yourself that you understand the information as you read. Backtracking differs from being conscious that you do not understand a particular sentence and need to go back and reread it. Most people who backtrack do not even realize they are doing it and will backtrack even when they understand the sentence perfectly.

One good way to stop the backtracking habit is to follow along with a pen or your finger as you read. You won't be able to backtrack unconsciously if you are following your finger, and it will help keep your eyes moving steadily forward. You might also find it helpful to cover up the text with a blank sheet of paper as you read so that you cannot look back without intentionally moving the paper away. Another solution if you backtrack is to be sure to take time to preread. Having an idea about where the chapter is headed will help your concentration and may also help stop your tendency to backtrack.

Subvocalization

If you say the words to yourself as you read, you are subvocalizing. Subvocalizers may move their lips, or they may say the words under their breath. When you were learning to read, you probably learned to sound out the words and the teacher asked you to read aloud. Later, when you began to read silently, you were still saying the words in your head. If you have never stopped "saying" the words you are probably subvocalizing. This habit slows reading rates because you can only speak about 200 words per minute, but most everyone has the ability to read and comprehend at much faster rates.

Luckily, this is a fairly easy habit to break. If you find that you move your lips as you read, put your finger over your lips and when you feel that they are moving, will yourself to stop. If you are saying the words under your breath, put your hand on your throat as you read. You will feel a vibration if you are subvocalizing and again you can will yourself to stop.

Fixations

Each time your eye focuses on a word or phrase it is called a fixation. Everyone fixates, but some people fixate too often or too long, which can slow reading down. Fixating on every word is also a habit left over from when you first learned to read. In elementary school you learned to recognize letters and then words, one at a time, which made you fixate often. In fact, you probably stopped at every word. However, effective readers do not fixate on every word. Instead, they read groups of words in a single fixation. A person who fixates too often would read the sentence as:

The/ boy/went/ to/ the/ store/ to/ get/ a/ loaf/ of/ bread/ and/ a/ gallon/ of/ milk.

This person is stopping on each word. To break the habit of fixating too often, a student needs to learn how to include more information in each fixation.

One way to break the habit of too many fixations is to use the **key word** method. In this strategy, you don't waste your time reading words like "the" or "and." Instead, you focus on the more meaningful words. As you fixate on the key words your eyes tend to include words like "the" without having to fixate on them. A person using the key word strategy often would read the sentence as:

*The **boy went** to the **store** / to get a **loaf** of **bread** / and a **gallon/** of **milk.***

Experiment with this method to see how many times you must fixate in order to get the main idea of a sentence and to prove to yourself that you can comprehend without focusing on every word.

Another strategy to reduce fixation is **phrase word** reading. In this strategy, you go through the passage and stop in the middle of each phrase. When you stop, your eye takes in the entire phrase. It is different from the key word strategy because you are not looking for specific words; rather, you are taking in larger chunks of information at a time. A person using the phrase word strategy would read the sentence as:

*The **boy went/** to the **store** / to get a **loaf of bread** / and a **gallon of milk.***

Some students learn best using the key word strategy; others say that they comprehend better using the phrase word strategy. Try out both strategies to see which one works best for you.

TIMELY TIPS

Double Your Reading Rate

What if we told you that with just a little time and effort you might be able to finish your textbook reading in half the time it usually takes? Many students can benefit from increasing their speed of reading. By using the tips discussed in this chapter for several months, most students can double their reading rate.

Increasing Your Reading Speed

Many companies advertise speed reading programs that cost several hundred dollars. However, you can increase your reading speed, and sometimes even double it, without spending big bucks. All you need is something interesting to read and some time each day to push yourself to read faster.

The purpose of pushed reading is to increase your overall reading speed. When you practice reading faster you should *not* use your textbooks or even novels assigned for class. Repeat: Do not use texts or materials that you will be tested over in your courses. You cannot expect to be able to speed read a difficult textbook filled with new concepts and comprehend all of the information. Likewise, if you speed read a novel in your literature class, you will miss the language that makes the novel a great work. You may grasp the basic plot, but little else. When you are practicing reading faster, use a piece of text that you find enjoyable—the campus newspaper or a novel you are reading for pleasure.

NETWORKING

Increasing Your Rate

Many sites on the Internet publish short stories or magazine articles. Find some stories that interest you on the Web and use them for your reading rate practice. You might want to check out *Rolling Stone*, *Newsweek*, or your favorite newspaper as a starting point. Then find some articles that will hold your attention for ten to fifteen minutes for your pushed reading. If you find that you read more slowly on the computer, as many people do, print out the stories before using them to increase your reading speed.

How to Read Faster

The techniques that follow can help you increase your reading speed.

- **Choose High-Interest Material.** It is best to push yourself to read faster with material that you are familiar with and enjoy. For example, if you like to read mystery novels, choose one to use for pushed reading.

- **Practice Every Day.** To increase your reading rate, you will need to push yourself to read faster every day for at least ten to fifteen minutes. Use your local or school newspaper or anything that will sustain your interest for that amount of time. You might want to choose three or four brief articles and take a short break after each one.

- **Read at Slightly-Faster-than-Comfortable Speeds.** As you read, push yourself to read slightly faster than you usually do. You should feel a little uncomfortable reading at this speed and feel that you would prefer to slow down, but you should also sense that you understand what you are reading.

- **Check Your Comprehension.** Increasing your reading rate while losing comprehension provides no benefit. Therefore, you need to check your comprehension of the material you are reading. However, because you are changing a habit, it is okay to have comprehension of only 70 to 80 percent of what you read during pushed reading. In fact, if you are having 100 percent comprehension you can probably push yourself to read faster. To check your comprehension, try to summarize the information. Did you identify all of the key ideas? What about important details and examples? If you find that you are not comprehending the information, slow down a bit.

- **Try to Read at the Same Time Each Day.** Finding fifteen minutes to read every day should not be much of a problem, but in order to keep an accurate record of your improvement you should try to find the time when you are most alert and try to read at that same time every day.

SUCCESS AT A GLANCE

Keys to Reading Faster

- Choose high-interest material.
- Practice every day.
- Read at slightly-faster-than-comfortable speeds.
- Check your comprehension.
- Try to read at the same time each day.
- Don't give up.

- **Don't Give Up.** Improving your reading rate is a slow but steady process. You may make some great improvements one week and then see little change the next. Don't worry about the fluctuations in your rate, as long as you are seeing an overall increase. However, if you find that you have gone several weeks without any improvement, make a conscious effort to push yourself even faster when you read.

How Fast Should You Read?

Students often ask how quickly they should read. This is not an easy question to answer because the rate at which you read depends on your purpose for reading and the type of material you are reading. Your goal is to be flexible in your reading and to choose a rate based on your purpose. In other words, you should be able to read a magazine or novel faster than a textbook.

Studying Smarter

Although students start out at different reading speeds, we suggest that you aim to reach a reading speed of at least 350–400 words per minute. At this rate you can be sure that you are reading fast enough to avoid hurting your comprehension. Be aware that this is a goal to shoot for and that for many people it will take some time to achieve.

In general, you should always strive to read faster than 200 words per minute because lower speeds can inhibit your comprehension. Otherwise, we are hesitant to give exact numbers because the rate at which you "should" read depends on several factors:

1. **How Quickly Do You Currently Read?** It would make no sense to tell a student to read at 400 words per minute if she is currently reading at 225 words per minute with 70 percent comprehension. Instead, we would tell her to use the pushed reading strategy described in this chapter to help increase her overall reading rate without sacrificing comprehension.

2. **What Is Your Purpose for Reading?**

   - **Slowest Speeds:** If you are reading to write a paper about a topic or to prepare for an exam you will read at fairly slow speeds. This includes reading difficult texts, poetry, technical manuals, textbooks, or literature with which you must take the time to notice and savor the language.

   - **Moderate Speeds:** If your purpose is to read for pleasure or for general information, you will be able to read more quickly. This type of reading includes novels, newspapers, magazines, and other reading for enjoyment.

   - **Quickest Speeds:** If you are scanning material for specific information, you will be able to read at very fast rates. This type of reading includes dictionaries, catalogs, phone books, and other reference books. Keep in mind, however, that this is not really reading in the true sense of the word.

3. **What Is Your Task?** If you will be tested over the material, take more time to really understand it. It makes no sense to rush through your history text if you are not getting all of the information. If you are reading for pleasure there may be times when you want to read slowly to enjoy your book, and times when you want to use pushed reading to increase your rate. Be sure to leave yourself some time for both.

GET GOING

Pushed Reading

For the next week, practice pushing yourself to read faster each day using the strategies you have learned in this chapter. Remember to read at a slightly-faster-than-comfortable pace. Use a stopwatch or a watch with a second hand to keep track of your time. When you have completed the reading, record your time. Then, as a comprehension check, think about what you have read. How much can you recall? As you increase your overall reading speed you will be able to finish your assignments more quickly and have more time to do other things.

☐ REAL COLLEGE
Rudy's Reading Rate

DIRECTIONS: Read the following "Real College" scenario and respond to the question based on what you learned in this chapter.

Rudy is first-year student at a small college. His goal is to finish his degree in computer science in four years, so he is taking fifteen to eighteen credit hours each term. However, he is overwhelmed by the amount of reading he has to do for each of his classes. He has to read technical reports and manuals for his computer science courses; novels, poetry, and plays in his English class; a very difficult textbook in his physics class; and a textbook and newspaper in his political science course. He knows that his problem is that he reads too slowly. Ever since grade school, he has always been the last one to finish his reading and the last one to turn in an exam. Rudy is sure that if he could just learn to read faster, he would do better in school. He has signed up for a speed reading course where he spends a lot of time using computer eye-movement programs, but he does not feel comfortable reading with that equipment and does not think it is helping. He generally tries to read everything as fast as he can, but he finds that he gets tired quickly and can't keep it up. He also finds that he really doesn't understand what he is reading in some of his courses.

Using what you know about increasing reading rate and the habits that slow down reading, what advice would you give Rudy about how to go about increasing his reading speed?

☐ THINKING CRITICALLY
Something to Think About and Discuss

How often do you fixate? Try this experiment with a partner to determine the number of fixations you make per line.

1. Punch a small hole in a sheet of paper with typed paragraphs on it.
2. Hold the blank side of the paper close to your eye so you can see through it.
3. Have your partner read the paragraphs contained on the sheet of paper and watch her eyes.
4. Count the number of fixations (times she stops) per line.
5. Change places with your partner and repeat to have your partner count your fixations.

Discuss the habits that may be slowing you and your partner's reading.

☐ ADD TO YOUR PORTFOLIO

For the next week, practice pushing yourself to read faster each day using the strategies you have learned in this chapter. Remember to read at a slightly-faster-than-comfortable pace. Choose something that is of interest to you, but is *not* one of your textbooks. Plan to do pushed reading for at least twenty minutes each day.

1. Use a stopwatch or a watch with a second hand to keep track of your time.
2. When you have completed the reading, record your time.
3. Then, as a comprehension check, think about what you have read. How much can you recall?
4. Think about the factors that influenced your speed. Were you tired, hungry, bored? Was there too much noise or other distractions? Were the conditions just right for pushed reading?

Use the following chart to record your progress.

Source	Number of Words	Time (minutes and seconds)	Speed in WPM (number of words ÷ time)	Comments

PREPARING FOR YOUR COLLEGE EXAMS

In Part Four we discuss strategies for exam preparation. In Chapter 17, you learn strategies in preparing for and taking objective exams. You are also introduced to some general test-taking strategies.

Chapter 18 presents strategies in preparing for and taking essay exams. You also learn about taking specialized exams such as open-book and take-home exams.

CHAPTER 17

PREPARING FOR OBJECTIVE EXAMS

Read this chapter to answer the following questions:

- What exam preparation strategies work in almost all situations?

- How should I prepare for objective exams?

DIRECTIONS: Think about the following questions and answer them honestly. Once you have finished reading this chapter, think about how you can change how you currently prepare for objective exams.

1. Taking a multiple-choice test is easy because all I have to do is recognize the correct answer.   T   F

2. To study for an objective test, I just memorize all the key terms.   T   F

3. It is best to spread out studying time over several days.   T   F

4. When I study, I choose one strategy that works and stick with it.   T   F

5. Cramming works because I can only get motivated under pressure.   T   F

6. Multiple-choice tests can ask application and synthesis questions.   T   F

7. To study for exams, I reread the text chapters.   T   F

8. When I study, I start with the first concept and work through all of the assigned reading in order.   T   F

You are on the right track in preparing for objective exams if you answered "false" to items 1, 2, 4, 5, 7, and 8 and "true" for items 3 and 6. Read the rest of the chapter to find the most efficient and effective ways to prepare for exams.

General Test-Preparation Strategies

Because we believe that preparing to take an exam begins on the day you begin to read about and listen to topics on which you will be tested, we almost feel as though having a special chapter on exam preparation goes against the philosophy of this book. That is, active learners are in a constant state of getting ready to take an exam—they don't distinguish when prereading, reading, and taking lecture notes turns into the rehearsal and review

Studying Smarter
Don't run out of time before you run out of test. When you go into a testing situation, have a plan to complete all of the items in the allotted time.

that goes into test preparation. That said, we also know that many activities that occur as test time gets closer might be more appropriately labeled as test-preparation strategies.

This chapter focuses on specific strategies that you can use to prepare for objective exams and Chapter 18 covers essay and specialty exams. Still, there are some general test-preparation guidelines that apply to almost any type of exam. We address these general strategies first because they are "quick starters" that can get you moving in the right direction.

In general, you should:

- **Start Early.** Be sure that you have completed your assigned reading at least several days before the test. Remember that reading and studying are not the same thing. All of your reading should be completed *before* you begin studying.

- **Get Organized.** Organize all of your studying tools and strategies—notes, annotations, study strategies—so that you can dig right in.

- **Distribute Your Time.** Rather than trying to cram all of your studying into one or two days, distribute your time over several days. Spending a total of six hours studying spread over four days is much more effective than spending six hours studying the day before, or even three hours a day for two days before the test.

- **Break Up the Work.** If you begin studying several days in advance, you will be able to break up the information you have to study into chunks of major concepts. In other words, don't sit down to study with the idea in mind that you will study every chapter and every page of notes. Study groups of information that seem to fit together, or at least identify which concepts you want to learn in a particular study session. This helps you stay more focused on the task at hand.

- **Stay Healthy.** Eat properly and get enough sleep. Try to remain in a studying routine rather than staying up all night cramming. Eat regular meals and exercise if that is part of your normal routine. In addition, adequate sleep is crucial to being at the top of your game, especially on days that you take exams. As part of staying healthy, it's also important to monitor your emotional health by evaluating your stress level. When you get too stressed out, it influences other aspects of your performance and becomes a vicious cycle.

- **Self-Test.** It's important to have a firm understanding of what you know and what you don't know. Remember that self-testing involves asking yourself

NETWORKING

Online Exams

Many professors now have sample exams online. Check out your professor's Web page or the department Web page to see what is available. In addition, visit the Web site of your textbook publisher. There are often quizzes, sample exams, links to additional information, and chat rooms where you can discuss the text with other students nationwide.

questions about the material, saying the information to yourself or to someone else, and then checking to see whether you are correct.

- **Study with a Classmate.** Studying with another serious-minded student has great benefits regardless of what kind of test you will take. One of the most successful models for studying with another is for both individuals to study on their own and then to get together to ask each other questions a day or two before the exam. Both parties can then find out which concepts they know very well and which ones they need to spend more time on.

- **Look at Old Exams.** Talk to others who have previously taken the class. Finding out as much information about the test as possible, whether it's from looking at old exams or by talking to others, is simply a smart thing to do. It's not cheating; it's being an informed consumer, so to speak. If professors permit students to keep their exams, you can be fairly certain that they will not be giving that same test again. But it's probably also a safe bet that the kinds of questions asked will be similar. When talking with students who have already taken the class with the professor, it's a good rule to find out specifics about the level of questions and grading.

Studying Smarter
Many campuses have test banks, which are places on campus where professors can put copies of retired tests on file for students to examine. If your campus has a test bank, use it to find out the types of questions your professor asks. As long as the professor knows that his test is part of a legitimate test bank, it is not academically dishonest to use these old tests.

Many of these general tips are common sense. But they are tips that students often overlook as they get caught up in exam preparation. In the next section, we will focus more specifically on preparation for and taking objective exams.

Objective Exams

Preparing for Objective Exams

Objective exams can consist of several different kinds of questions. The most common types are multiple-choice and true/false questions, but matching and fill-in-the-blanks are also objective questions. Another name for these types of questions is *recognition items* because all of the information is there; your task is to recognize it. For example, for multiple-choice questions, you have to recognize which answer out of the four or five choices is correct. For a true/false question, you have to recognize whether the statement is true or false. These items are considered objective because there is (or should be) only one correct answer, if the test is well written. In other words, in a multiple-choice question, only one of the answers should be correct. Moreover, if you studied and really know the information, the correct answer should be obvious to you.

Success at a Glance

Studying for Objective Tests

- Make a jot list of key points
- Organize this information around broad concepts
- Begin each study session with a review
- Rehearse and self-test
- Concentrate on areas of weakness

Because of the precise knowledge required to answer objective items, it is extremely important that two key factors guide your preparation: (1) organization of information; and (2) thinking about the information the way in which your professor expects.

Organization   Let's start with an example. Suppose you are in an introductory psychology course and every two to three weeks you have a fifty-item objective test—always all multiple-choice items. In any given testing period, you have about thirty pages of lecture notes and three or four chapters of information to study. Where do you begin? We have found that the best place to start when you know you will have an objective test is to make a jot list of all of the key concepts from the text and lectures. The accompanying example shows what a jot list might look like for the history chapter, "The Nation Divides: The Vietnam War and Social Conflict, 1964–1971," that begins on page 275. Notice that the jot list is not particularly formal. Rather, it simply serves to force you to think about the concepts before you begin to study. One way to come up with your jot list is to use the chapter headings and subheadings as a guide. Unless you make a conscious effort to jot down these concepts, you may leave out important information or simply gloss over concepts that you should spend a significant amount of time on.

Timely Tips

Organizing Information

In order to use your time effectively and efficiently when you are preparing for an objective test, organize the information as you go along. As you are annotating and creating your rehearsal strategies, keep an organized jot list of the key concepts that you will have to learn for the test. Then when it comes time to create a talk-through card, you will already have it completed.

Example of a Jot List

Chapter 25, "The Nation Divides"

LBJ presidency
   Great Society
   Liberal Supreme Court
War in Vietnam
   U.S. involvement
   Importance of 1968
Civil rights/Black power movement
New left (SDS movement)
Rebellion
   Women's lib
   Other rebellion
Conservative response
Nixon presidency
   Vietnam under Nixon

■   ■   ■

Once you have made your jot list, then you can organize the information to study. You will need to:

1. **Group together your rehearsal strategies** that relate to the overriding concept. (Let's use the history topic of "the LBJ presidency" as an example.) You should also know which sections of lecture notes go with this concept.

2. **Look for overlap** between the text and lecture and focus your studying on the big picture of the Johnson years rather than just concentrating on the text information one time and the lecture notes at another.

3. **Focus each study session** around a couple of broad concepts, such as "progression of the civil rights movement" or "or the presidency of LBJ" rather than simply trying to read through everything you have to learn for the entire test. In other words, one night you might study all the material related to the LBJ presidency, the next night concentrate on Nixon, and the third night learn issues concerning civil rights or the cold war, concepts that spanned both the Johnson and Nixon presidencies. Following this procedure encourages you to think actively and critically. Use your jot list as a guide. Then rehearse and self-test the material from the next broad concept. Your study schedule might look something like the example study schedule shown on the next page. Note that each study session begins with a review and that after you have covered all the material, you end with a self-testing session where you identify specific areas of weakness.

4. **Concentrate on any weakness** as you and your study partner question each other in one final study session before the exam.

5. **Talk though** the couple of ideas that were still giving you difficulty on the morning of the exam.

GET GOING

Maintaining Motivation During Studying

Staying motivated when you are preparing for a big test can sometimes be difficult because it is easy to feel overwhelmed. Studying specific concepts at planned times rather than trying to study everything in one session is one way to help you maintain motivation. When you end your study session by self-testing and realize how much you have learned it motivates you to continue the process until you have covered all the concepts.

Example of a Study Schedule

Session 1—Monday

Focus: 1964–1971 presidencies of Johnson and Nixon

4:30–5:00	Organize all information
5:00–6:00	Study: LBJ — Great Society, liberalism, early Vietnam (to 1968)
6:00–6:45	Eat dinner
7:00–8:00	Review: Great Society, liberalism, and early Vietnam Study: Vietnam after 1968, Civil rights/Black power, liberal movements, early Nixon years
8:30–9:00	Self-test

Session 2—Tuesday

Focus: Later Nixon years

10:00–10:30	Review 1964–1971 -All concepts from LBJ and early Nixon years
10:30–11:30	Study: Later Nixon years
11:30–12:00	Lunch
12:30–1:50	Class
2:00–3:00	Continue study of later Nixon years
3:00–3:30	Self-test

■   ■   ■

Thinking Organizing, both in terms of how you will group the concepts to be learned and how you will structure your study sessions, is crucial to performing well on objective tests. However, organizing won't help you much if you aren't sure about the level of thinking required. On essay tests, you can pretty much count on having to think critically and to analyze and synthesize information. But on objective exams, many students make the mistake of believing that the test questions are designed solely to see if they have memorized the material. That is, they think the questions don't go beyond asking for facts. Students who fall into this trap can experience grave difficulty and often don't do well. That's why it's important to know the kind of thinking that your professor expects. If she expects you to memorize the facts and most of the questions are factual in nature, you would study one way. If, however, she asks application, synthesis, examples, and other types of higher-level questions, you would study another way.

To clarify this point, let's look at several questions. Each of these questions is based on the history or psychology chapter included in the appendixes of this book (pages 251–294). The first example in each set of questions is a memory-level task. The second is a higher-level question. (The * indicates the correct answer.)

Set A (based on the history chapter)

1. (memory-level) The Civil Rights Act of 1964
   a. gave blacks the right to vote.

   b. outlawed discrimination in public facilities.*

   c. provided employment training for minorities.

   d. described the War on Poverty.

2. (higher-level) Overall, the goal of the Great Society programs was to
   a. assist blacks in breaking free of poverty.

   b. expand individual rights.

   c. institute and regulate the Medicare system.

   d. improve the quality of life for all Americans.*

Set B (based on the psychology chapter)

1. (memory-level) The Raven Progressive Matrices intelligence test would be considered
   a. a culture-fair test.*

   b. an environmental deprivation test.

   c. a multiple intelligences test.

   d. all of the above.

2. (higher-level) According to the influence of heredity theory, which relationship would have the lowest correlation with intelligence?
   a. brother/sister

   b. identical twins regardless of gender

   c. cousins from the same side of the family*

   d. father/daughter

It is fairly easy to see the differences in these questions. The first question in each set is very straightforward and requires little interpretation or thinking beyond the memory level. Studying for an objective test that asked this type of question would be a relatively easy task: You simply identify the key terms and ideas and memorize definitions, component parts, or the like. But think about the problem you might have if you simply memorized information and then had an exam that asked questions like the second one in each set. You would have a much more difficult time because you had thought about the information in an incorrect way. Even if you studied quite a bit, if you only memorized when the task was to go beyond memorization, taking the test would be a struggle.

The point is that you need to be clear about the professor's expectations and the way he tests, what we have called "task" throughout this book. As mentioned earlier, look at old exams, talk to students who have taken a class with the professor, or ask the professor. Whatever you do, have an accurate picture of the kind of test you will have. Then, as you are doing your rehearsal, review, and self-testing, you can frame your studying accordingly.

Taking Objective Exams

You have studied, you feel good about what you know, and you are absolutely ready to take your exam. Well, you're almost ready. The next (or final) thing you need to think about is a game plan. A sports analogy fits here: The basketball team has studied the playbook, looked at films of themselves and the opponent, and is mentally ready to play the game. They are pumped and psyched. But if they don't have a game plan, all their work may not result in a win. Any athletic team going into a game needs a game plan to follow—some sort of strategy for winning the game.

A testing situation for you is just like game day for the basketball team. You have prepared, you are mentally ready to take the test, and you want to do well. Now you have to follow through with your game plan for taking the test. To plan your strategy, it helps to ask yourself some questions before you get into the testing situation:

- How will I work through the test? Will I simply start with the first item and answer the questions in consecutive order?

- What will I do when I come across an item I'm not sure of? Will I skip it and come back to it later, or will I mark something before going on to the next item?

- How will I choose an answer when I absolutely can't even make an educated guess?

- How will I approach answering true/false questions?

- What will I do if I am running out of time and still have several questions to answer?

It's important to think about how you approach an exam before you are actually in a testing situation. We suggest the following guidelines.

- **Get to Class on Time.** Leave home early enough so that you don't have to rush. When you rush, you tend to get anxious, especially on an exam day. Once you get to class, get out your pen and anything else you might need. Relax and take a couple of deep breaths. Give yourself some positive reinforcement by saying such things as "I studied," "I know this stuff," and "I know I should do well on this exam."

- **When You Get Your Exam, Take a Minute or Two to Look Through It.** See how many items there are so that you know how to divide up your time. Also, remember something that is very important and often overlooked: *Read the directions* so you know what you are required to do.

- **Read the First Item.** If you don't know the answer, leave it blank and go to the next item. Do this with each item until you find one of which you are certain. We believe it is good advice to do the items you know first and then come back and spend more time on those of which you are unsure. The only problem this seems to create is that students sometimes make mistakes by putting an answer in the wrong place on their answer sheet. Therefore, if you are going to skip around on the test, you need to make sure that your answer goes in the corresponding place on your answer sheet.

- **Eliminate Answers Whenever Possible.** On a multiple-choice question, you might be able to eliminate two answer choices immediately, but the other two alternatives might both be plausible. If this occurs, you at least have a fifty-fifty chance of choosing correctly.

- **Use Information from Other Items on the Exam to Help You with Items You Don't Know.** Once you have gone through the entire test, you can often pick up information from one question that will help you answer another. That's why it's a good idea to go through and answer the items you know first.

- **Use All of the Allotted Time.** Many students fail to use all of the class period to take their exam and then end up making careless mistakes such as leaving items blank when they could have guessed. Even when you have answered every question, it's best to go through the test one more time just to be sure. Remember, it's easy to mark a wrong answer when you actually know the correct answer.

- **When Faced with a Situation in Which You Have to Guess, Make a Selection and Move On.** Go with your gut selection and don't change your mind unless you have found information later in the test that helps you remember an idea related to the question. On a multiple-choice exam, for example, some students will select the same answer choice for every question they don't know. For true/false questions you might answer all true or all false for items on which you guess. Whatever you do, however, never leave objective test items blank unless you are penalized for guessing.

Taking exams does not have to be extremely stressful. If you have studied well and have a game plan for taking exams, you'll find that you are usually more relaxed going in and will tend to do better.

☐ REAL COLLEGE
Teddy's Tactics

DIRECTIONS: Read the following "Real College" scenario and respond to the questions based on what you learned in this chapter.

In high school, Teddy was always a model student. He wasn't one of those kids who waited until the morning of a test to try to cram as much information as possible into his brain. Teddy usually started a day or two before his scheduled exams and reviewed the study guides that most of his teachers gave him. An hour or so of reading over this information typically resulted in a good test grade for him.

Now, early in his first semester of college, Teddy finds that these tactics aren't working so well for him. He earned a D on his first anthropology exam and things don't look all that promising for the multiple-choice test that he has in a few days in psychology. It's not that he doesn't have the time; he just doesn't know what to do.

His professors don't seem to be of much help at all. Gone are the study guides that once made studying easy. Gone are the kind of tests he had in high school that simply asked him to memorize facts from class lectures. And gone are the frequent tests that were so common in high school. In anthropology he only has two more tests and a short paper. Teddy knows that he has to do something to get back on track.

For the impending psychology test, at least he has kept up with his reading—well, almost. And he does know what the task is: He is responsible for five text chapters, all of his lecture notes, and two outside readings that focus on psychological research. The test will contain fifty multiple-choice questions, most of which the professor said would be example and application questions. There are another ten matching items where he will have to match researchers with important research they carried out.

What advice would you give Teddy about how he should get back on track?

What general advice would you give Teddy for studying for objective exams? How might he have to change his studying from anthropology to psychology?

☐ THINKING CRITICALLY
Something to Think About and Discuss

One way to get a feel for the difference between thinking about the information in a factual way and in a more conceptual, higher-level way is to rewrite questions. Using the Set A and Set B example questions that appear earlier in the chapter as a guide, use either the history or psychology chapter in the appendixes (pages 251–294) to write a factual question. Then write another question that draws from the same information yet taps higher-level thinking. Discuss these questions with a classmate.

☐ ADD TO YOUR PORTFOLIO

1. Create a study plan for your next objective test. What concepts will you concentrate on for each study session? How will you know when you understand and can remember all the information? How will you review?

2. Create a game plan for once you enter class to take the exam.

CHAPTER 18

PREPARING FOR AND TAKING ESSAY AND SPECIALTY EXAMS

Read this chapter to answer the following questions:

- How should you prepare for essay exams?
- What kind of a study plan should you have for preparing for essay exams?
- How should you study for special types of exams such as take-home and open-book exams?

SELF-ASSESSMENT

DIRECTIONS: The following questions are predictions for a history course. For each of the questions, decide whether the question is too broad (B), too narrow (N), or would make a good (G) essay question.

1. _____ From 1914 to the 1990s there have been obvious demographic shifts. Discuss the factors contributing to these shifts and the effects they have had technologically.

2. _____ How has life changed as a result of twentieth-century technology?

3. _____ Compare and contrast the weapons used in World War I with those used in World War II.

4. _____ What effect did the Great Depression during the 1930s have on politics?

5. _____ What influences did technological advances have on the progression and expansion of World War II?

Of course, your ability to respond to these essay questions will depend on the content covered in class. Nonetheless, 1 and 5 would be considered good essay questions, 2 and 4 would be too broad, and 3 would be two narrow. Keep this in mind when predicting essay questions for your own classes.

Essay Exams

Preparing for essay exams involves different strategies than preparing for objective exams. This often comes as a shock, especially to first-year college students who may have had little experience with essay exams in high school or, if they have had essay exams, they prepared for them in the same way they prepared for objective exams. As a general rule, essay preparation requires a different type of approach, a different way of thinking, and a different way of organizing.

Studying Smarter
Prepare for essay exams by predicting questions and then practicing your answers.

When we use the term *essay exam*, we are referring to any type of question that requires you to write an extended response. In this instance, essay tests would include:

- Traditional multi-paragraph responses to questions
- Short-answer questions that require you to write a paragraph or two in response to a more narrowly focused question
- Identification items, which require you to define a term, explain the significance of something, or write several sentences describing a person, place, event, etc.

Sometimes these types of exams are referred to as *recall* tests, because you are asked to recall all of the pertinent information from your memory. Unlike recognition questions (e.g., multiple-choice, true/false) that ask you to recognize the correct information, recall questions require you to remember the information on your own.

PORPE

SUCCESS AT A GLANCE

PORPE Time Line

P	O	R	P	E
Predict ➜	Organize ➜	Rehearse ➜	Practice ➜	Evaluate
Several days before	3–4 days before	3–4 days before	2 days before	After test

---

PORPE, is an acronym for *P*redict, *O*rganize, *R*ehearse, *P*ractice, and *E*valuate, a structured, organized strategy specifically designed to help you prepare for essay or short-answer exams.* You begin the PORPE studying process after you have completed your reading, constructed useful study strategies, and organized your lecture notes. As we explain the steps of PORPE, we have included examples based on a predicted essay question from the psychology chapter excerpt.

Step 1: Predict. (Predict several days before the test.) The first thing you need to do is to predict broad questions that your professor might include on the exam. Simply put, the better predictor you are, the better you will do on the exam. But predicting questions can be a tricky business. It has been our experience that when students begin to use this strategy, they either predict questions that are far too broad or way too narrow. For example, predicting an essay question such as, "Discuss the presidency of Lyndon Baines Johnson" would be too broad; a question such as, "Why was the Head Start Program started?" would be too specific. Generally, the fewer the number of questions you are required to answer on an exam, the broader your prediction questions should be.

Keep in mind when predicting that rarely will your specific question be precisely what the professor asks. But once you become a good predictor, there will be considerable overlap between what you predict and the actual questions on the test. The following is an example of a good essay prediction for a psychology course in which you were studying *Cognition and Intelligence*.

---

*Source for PORPE: M. L. Simpson, "PORPE: A writing strategy for studying and learning in the content areas," *Journal of Reading* (1986).

***Step 1: Predict:* Predict a question that you think might be asked on the exam.**

Question: For decades there has been a controversy over the reasons for individuals' differing levels of intelligence. Discuss the two factors that contribute to this controversy. Then discuss the research that exists about the relative contribution made by each factor.

■   ■   ■

Step 2: Organize. (Organize three or four days before the test.) After you have predicted several questions, you need to organize the information. Most students like to use an outline to organize so that they can see the key points they want to make and the support they want to provide for each key point. Other organizing strategies such as concept maps or charts also work well (see Chapter 12). When you organize the material, think about both key generalizations and information to support those generalizations. Spend some time organizing your thoughts so that you will study worthwhile material.

As you become more focused and predict specific questions, your outline should be more comprehensive and detailed. To fill in your outline, use the pertinent information that you included in your text annotations (Chapter 11), rehearsal strategies (Chapter 12), and what you have annotated in your lecture notes (Chapter 14). Be sure that you draw from both the text and lectures as well as any other sources for which you are responsible. And be sure to do a detailed outline for each of the questions you predict. The following example shows what an outline would look like for the essay question we predicted in Step 1 of PORPE.

***Step 2: Organize:* In an organized fashion, write down the ideas you want to include in your essay.**

Two explanations for differing levels of intelligence

1. Heredity

    a. Family relationships & IQ—the closer the family rel. the stronger the relationship (twins > brother/sister > cousins)

    b. Studies involving adopted children—adopt. children's IQ's more closely related to biological than adoptive parents

    c. Quantitative trait loci—certain genes associated with high IQ

    d. Research on identical twins separated as infants

Conclusions:
Heritibility of IQ = ~ 35% in childhood to 75% in adulthood

Increases in age shaped by environmental factors
Genetic factors play a role

2. Environment

   a. Flynn Effect—IQ has increased worldwide (~ 3 pts. but more in some areas) b/c of environmental factors which include

- Nutrition

- Urbanization

- TV

- More and better education

- Computers

   Still lack of sufficient evidence

   b. Studies of environmental deprivation/enrichment

- IQ reduced by lack of environmental stimulation

- Ramey & Ramey study—conditions for increase in IQ include: early intervention, broad in scope, intensive, good schools, etc.

   c. Biological factors encountered by children

- EX., malnutrition, pollution, drug and alcohol

Summary: Both factors play a role but there is some disagreement about the contribution of each

Step 3: Rehearse. (Rehearse several times for each question, beginning three or four days before the test.) This is the time to commit the information in your outline to memory. Read one of the questions you predicted. Then read through your outline slowly and deliberately. "Listen" to what you are saying. Does it make sense? Do you have enough support? Do the ideas flow? After you have read through the outline several times, ask yourself the question again. This time, try answering it without looking at the outline. Be sure that you are rehearsing the concepts accurately. If you are not sure of something, immediately return to your outline and read that part through again, or if you are really experiencing problems, check your text or lecture notes to clarify or add support. Then try to restate the answer to that portion of the question. Always keep in mind that when you rehearse, it's important to also engage in self-testing.

Step 4: Practice. (Practice two days before the test.) This is the time to practice writing out answers to some of your questions. Write under the same conditions that you will have in class. For example, if you will be required to answer two essay questions in a fifty-minute class period, take only twenty minutes to practice one of your questions. That would leave twenty minutes to practice on a second question and ten minutes to go back and proof your work.

You should also construct each answer so that it is organized the same way that you will organize it in class. Write in complete sentences, include appropriate examples, and be sure to have an introduction and a conclusion. The following practice essay example shows an answer for the question we predicted in Step 1 concerning reasons for individuals' differing levels of intelligence (page 239).

Example of a Practice Essay

There are two theories that attempt to explain why individuals have differing levels of intelligence. The first theory focuses on the role that heredity or genetics play in intelligence and the second focuses on the role that environment plays. Although neither theory totally explains intelligence, evidence exists that each makes contributions and that the two factors are linked.

There are four lines of research that support the influence of heredity. First, if heredity plays a role, the closer the family members, the larger the correlation between the family members. This prediction has been confirmed. Twins' intelligence is correlated at around .90, siblings' at .50, and cousins' at .15. Second, studies of adopted children show that their IQs are more closely related to their biological parents than their adoptive parents. Third, research in genetics has shown evidence that certain genes are associated with high intelligence. Finally, research on identical twins separated at birth and raised in different homes indicates that their IQs correlate almost as highly as those twins who are raised together.

But there is also evidence that environment plays a role in intelligence. First there is the Flynn Effect, which finds that in recent decades IQs have risen worldwide and at every age level. It seems unlikely that heredity could explain this rise. Rather, environmental factors such as nutrition, education, computers, and even television have been suggested as likely factors. In addition, studies of both environmental deprivation and environmental enrichment suggest that lack of stimulation early in life can lead to lower IQs. Moreover, if children are moved from nonstimulating environments (such as orphanages, for example) their IQ increases, sometimes dramatically. For these interventions to be successful, however, they must be early, intense, and broad in scope. Finally, there is considerable evidence that environmental factors such as malnutrition, pollution, and drugs and alcohol can affect intelligence.

Most psychologists would agree that both heredity and environment influence an individual's intelligence. What they do not always agree upon is the contribution of each. What we do know is that IQ is not related 100 percent to either factor.

Step 5: Evaluate. (Immediately after practicing.) Now comes the most difficult part—evaluating your own writing. After you have finished practicing, read what you have written. When you finish reading, get out your outline and any other study strategy materials you have been using and check for accuracy and completeness. Ask yourself the following questions:

- Is my introduction clear and focused?
- Are my generalizations complete and precise?
- Are my examples and supporting information accurate and complete?
- Do I have a conclusion that relates back to my introduction and overall thesis?

NETWORKING

Critiquing Essays over E-mail

If you have been working with a classmate in a course that requires you to write essay exams, you might try sending your study partner a copy of a practice essay over e-mail. Have your study partner critique your essay by evaluating its strengths and weaknesses. You can do the same for your study partner.

Once you have honestly answered these questions you can go back and do some rethinking and reorganizing, if necessary. You may even want to show your essay to your professor so that he can provide you with feedback. Or if your campus has a writing center, you may be able to get help with organizing your response.

TIMELY TIPS

Writing Done Right

We believe that one of the most useful skills you can learn in college is the ability to write. Using components of the PORPE strategy can help you prepare for essays, but can also help you to organize a paper, a group project, or just about any other writing task you may encounter in college or beyond. Most careers require you to be able to express yourself clearly in writing and you just may find yourself using some of the elements of PORPE every time you write.

Taking Essay Exams

When you are in the actual test-taking situation, remember these three important factors: (1) the amount of time you have to write each answer; (2) how you will structure each answer; and (3) the guidelines your professor provides about how she will evaluate or grade your essay. Each of these factors has a bearing on how you will spend your in-class, essay-writing time.

Time Allotted for Writing

Time is usually your biggest enemy when answering essay or short-answer questions. When you are deciding on your approach for taking the exam, think carefully about how you will divide up your time. For example, if you have one essay question and five fairly comprehensive identification items to answer, would it be best to spend half of your time on the essay and the other half on the identification? Or would it be better to spend more time on the essay and less time on the identification items? It's all give-and-take, but a good rule of thumb is to begin with what you know best and feel most comfortable with. If you know the answers to all the identification and feel a bit shaky on how best to approach the essay, start with the IDs and then use the remaining time to do the best job you can on the essay. In addition, consider the point value of each question. If the essay is worth forty points and each ID is worth three points, you will want to spend more time on the essay.

Structuring Your Essay

Few professors provide students with guidance on how they want essay or short-answer questions structured. As a result, many students will write a paragraph to answer an essay question and a sentence or two to answer a short-answer item. Usually when professors ask you to write an essay, they want extended comment. That is, they want you to write considerably more than a paragraph. When you think of an essay, you should plan on writing at least an introductory paragraph, several paragraphs that discuss specific points you think are important to answering the question, and then end with a concluding paragraph. Short-answer questions, as a general rule, are a paragraph or two long and tend to be somewhat less structured than an essay.

If your professor tells you exactly how she wants you to structure your essay, *follow exactly what she says*. However, if your professor does not provide any guidance, the following structure is generally accepted in most disciplines. We recommend that as you read each of the suggestions below that you refer to the example of a practice essay provided earlier in the chapter (page 241).

- Write an introductory paragraph that outlines your thesis and indicates that you understand what the question is asking. By thesis, we mean the overall focus of your essay or the argument you will be making. If the question has multiple parts, be sure that your introduction pulls in all the parts. The first paragraph should not be long and involved, but it should be clear and concise and give the reader a picture of your overall points.

- Each of your next several paragraphs should begin with a generalization about one of the key points you want to make. Don't worry about following the five-paragraph essay format you learned in high school. Instead, use as many paragraphs as necessary to answer the question fully. For example, if your question in political science asks you to discuss political, economic, international policy, and social issues, you would write four paragraphs, one dealing with each of the four issues. For each generalization, you should provide support in the form of events, names, dates, people, examples, and so forth—specific information that supports your point. Each paragraph should deal with only one key idea. Be careful about including several broad generalizations in the same paragraph. However, also be careful about writing a litany of facts without tying them together with generalizations. Whenever possible, have smooth transitions from one idea to the next by using words such as first, second, third; furthermore; in addition to; moreover; and so forth.

- Unlike objective tests where we encourage you to guess if you have to, for essay exams follow the "When in doubt, leave it out" plan. If you are not completely sure of something, do not put it in your essay. If you have included wrong information in your essay, your professor has no alternative but to take points off. But if your essay is sound and you have made numerous good points, you might get few or no points taken off if you leave out a bit of information.

- End your essay with a concluding paragraph that joins together the points you wanted to make. The conclusion doesn't have to be lengthy, but should return to your thesis and pull together the most important ideas related to that thesis.

Few professors would oppose this structure; if your professor does not provide guidance about format, this one will rarely, if ever, get you into trouble. But, if your professor spends a lot of class time explaining the essay format he expects, be sure to get down as much information as you can about what he wants, and then use his model when you practice your essay.

Studying Smarter

Remember that a human being will be reading your essay. Although professors rarely take off points for neatness, your grade will suffer if they can't read what you have written. Try to make their job easier by writing as neatly as you can. It is also a good idea to underline key words or phrases that you want to be sure that your professor reads.

Evaluation Guidelines

It's a tall order to write essays within the allotted time, have an acceptable structure, and manage to keep the mechanics and grammar errors down to a minimum. That's why it becomes important to know your professor's expectations before you go into the exam situation. For example, how strict will your professor be concerning mechanics, grammar, and usage? If your professor doesn't say anything in class about his expectations, be sure to ask. Most professors do not expect perfection, but they will probably deduct points on a paper that has so many errors that it is difficult to read and understand the essay. The bottom line is to know what your professor expects and then do your best to balance time, structure/content, and grammar/spelling issues.

A Word About Identification Items

Identification items ask you to write what you know about specific events, people, laws, dates, and so forth. They differ from essay/short-answer questions in that they are more focused and usually require only a few sentences of explanation. Sometimes you can even write in phrases rather than in full sentences when answering identification questions. There are two ideas to keep in mind when preparing for identification items:

1. There are usually many options for the professor to choose from. In history, for example, where identification questions are common, every chapter and lecture is filled with material that could be included on a test. So how do you decide which terms are the most important to study? A good place to begin is with your text. If your text provides a listing of key terms or if there is a chapter summary, making sure that you can identify what is in either of those sources usually is your best starting point. Match up those terms with what your professor has spent time on during lectures. Look for overlap, because identification items usually focus on material that has been addressed in a lecture or has been pointed out in the text.

GET GOING

Preparing to Answer Identification Items

When responding to identification items, few professors want you to just define the term. Rather, you also will be expected to give an example or explain the item's significance. This expectation should encourage you to think about and note examples or significant points in your annotations and your rehearsal strategies. If you do this as you go along rather than waiting until right before the exam, you will be much further ahead.

2. You have to know the kind of information your professor expects you to include. Most of the time, professors will want you to include more than just definitional information. They may want you to discuss the significance, provide an example, or explain how the item relates to some other issue or idea. Whatever the expectations, be sure that you know what they are. Many students receive only

partial credit on short-answer items simply because they failed to include all the information requested by their professor.

Specialized Exams

We conclude this chapter by briefly discussing how to prepare for specialized exams. Specialized exams may not be given as frequently in your college career, but you need to know how to prepare for them when they do come along. We discuss three types of specialized exams: (1) problem-solving exams, the most common of the specialized exams; (2) open-book exams; and (3) take-home exams.

Problem-Solving Exams

Several types of courses including mathematics, science, engineering, and business courses require you to solve problems. Because many students attempt to study for exams of this nature by doing the same problems over and over again, we think it is important to provide some additional strategies for studying for these types of exams.

Working the problems as a way of studying for this type of test is certainly a good idea and should be part of your studying routine. Note that we said "part of," because if all you do is work the same set of problems over and over again, you probably will not do very well. The important thing to remember is that you have to think about and conceptualize what you are doing. You won't get those exact same problems on the exam, so you have to think about the concepts underlying the problems. That's why we suggest that you talk through your problems. Put words to them. As you do a problem, think about and verbalize what you are doing. Annotate formulas into words that indicate you understand the problem. If you can't talk through problems as you solve them, you probably don't understand the concept.

Let's look at an example and talk through some of the thinking that would make it easier to solve this problem. Thinking about math problems in this manner, especially word problems, also lets you know if you understand the reasoning behind your method of solving the problem.

> **The Problem:** Susan begins a 20-mile race at 7:00 A.M., running at an average speed of 10 miles per hour. One hour later, her brother leaves the starting line on a motorbike and follows her route at the rate of 40 miles per hour. At what time does he catch up to her?
>
> **The Question:** What is the problem asking for? You are supposed to solve this problem to find out what time he catches up with her, so you will need to make sure that the answer you come up with is reflected as time.
>
> **The Solution:**
>
> 1. **Visualize the Problem.** This diagram shows that when Susan's brother overtakes her, they have both traveled the same distance.
>
>   Susan >>>>>>>>>>>>>>>>>>>>>>>
>   Her brother >>>>>>>>>>>>>

2. **What Is the Basic Idea Behind the Problem?** Both are traveling at a constant rate of speed so we would think about the basic equation as:

Distance = (Rate)(Time)
d = rt

3. **Explain the Variables.**

Let t = # of hours Susan runs until her brother catches her.
Then t – 1 = # of hours Susan's brother rides until he catches up (he leaves 1 hour later so he travels 1 hour less).

4. **Write and Solve the Equation.**

$$10t = 40(t - 1)$$
$$10t = 40t - 40$$
$$-30t = -40$$
$$t = \frac{-40}{-30} = \frac{4}{3} = 1\ 1/3 \text{ hours} = 1 \text{ hour and } 20 \text{ minutes}$$

5. **The Solution.** Remember that the question asked for time. Susan's brother caught her 1 hour and 20 minutes after she began the race at 7 A.M. Therefore, he would catch up with her at 8:20 A.M. If you wrote 1 hour and 20 minutes as your answer, you would not receive credit because you did not answer the question that was asked.

Strategies for Problem-Solving Exams   The following will help you prepare for problem-solving exams.

- **Make Up a Test for Yourself with the Types of Problems You Will Be Tested On.** Put some problems on note cards and then use them as a way of seeing whether you understand the concepts. After you have worked through the problems, shuffle the note cards and work on them again in a different order, concentrating on those that gave you problems.

- **Get Help Early.** Courses such as mathematics, physics, and chemistry tend to be arranged sequentially. That is, the ideas build on one another. If you miss or don't understand something presented in week two of the term, chances are you are going to have trouble with what is presented after that. If you think you are "mathematically challenged," you should arrange to be part of a study group, get a tutor, or make regular appointments to meet with your professor right at the beginning of the term.

Open-Book Exams

Open-book exams allow you access to your text, and sometimes even your notes, during the examination period. Open-book exams are generally given in the usual class period, which means you take them under timed conditions. This type of exam is often given in literature courses so that students can have access to specific pieces of text that they have been asked to read.

When students are told that they will have an open-book exam, they often breathe a sigh of relief. We have even heard students say that they didn't have to study because they were having an open-book test. But it takes just as much effort to adequately prepare for this type of test as it does to prepare for a more traditional objective or essay test.

Organization is the key in preparing for open-book exams. You first have to go through the usual preparation steps of predicting, organizing, rehearsing, practicing, and evaluating. But you have to put extra time into organizing. You should mark information that you might use to support points you expect to have to make or pull specific examples from the readings. You will need to have the information you deem important flagged in some way so that it is easy to find. For example, you can tab important passages or pages in your text with self-stick notes. Because you are in a timed situation, you must know where things are and have the information organized so that you can find it quickly.

Take-Home Exams

Take-home exams allow you to have access to your text and notes and put no time restrictions on the amount of time you can spend taking the test. The professor gives you the test questions, along with some basic instructions, usually to remind you that you can't get outside assistance to answer the questions. Some professors may even have you sign an academic honesty pledge. When professors give take-home exams, they generally expect a very high level of proficiency and thinking. For example, if they give you a take-home essay exam, they would expect your writing to display synthesis, analysis, and critical thought. They would expect a tremendous amount of support, and a paper virtually free of grammatical and spelling errors. Therefore, you usually have to spend a considerable amount of time working on take-home exams.

Even if you know you will have take-home exams in a course, it is extremely important for you to keep up. Do your reading, attend class, construct rehearsal strategies, and continue to review. Then, when you get your take-home exam from your instructor, you will be ready to organize all the information and spend less actual time on taking the test.

☐ REAL COLLEGE
Iris's Intentions (Gone Awry!)

DIRECTIONS: Read the following "Real College" scenario and respond to the questions based on what you learned in this chapter.

Iris had good intentions. And her semester was going quite well—up until this point, that is. Iris had some academic difficulties during her first semester in college, but she had learned from her mistakes, and so far so good. But now it was time for the real test. She knew that an exam was rapidly approaching in Dr. Jameson's history course and she was scared. Today was Thursday and the test was the following Tuesday. She had done a decent job of keeping up in her courses this semester, except for Dr. Jameson's, even though she had intended to stay on top of things in history. But somehow, she fell a little behind. Okay, a lot behind. Now it was time for the first of only two exams in the course and Dr. Jameson's exams had the reputation of being lethal. The most difficult thing was that half of the exam consisted of thirty multiple-choice questions and the other half was one essay question. That meant that she had to study in two different ways for the same test and she hadn't even completed the reading assignments yet. And to make things even worse she knew that most questions would come from the text and that she would have to pull in text-related information into her essay. Professor Jameson had already been very explicit about that in class.

Given the amount of time she has left to study and the kind of exam that she will have, what recommendations would you give to Iris? How should she prepare for and go about taking her history exam so that she can maximize her grade? If Iris had followed her intentions, what should she have done to prevent her problems?

☐ THINKING CRITICALLY
Something to Think About and Discuss

Think about the most difficult test you have had so far in your college career. What made this test difficult? How did you study for the test? Do you feel that you could have done better if you had studied differently? Looking back on the exam, how might you have prepared differently?

☐ ADD TO YOUR PORTFOLIO

For your next essay exam, try using the PORPE strategy. Remember you need to predict, organize, rehearse, practice, and evaluate its effectiveness. Which parts of the strategy seemed most beneficial to you? What modifications will you make for the next exam?

APPENDIX A

COGNITION AND INTELLIGENCE

from *Essentials of Psychology,* *Third Edition*

Robert A. Baron
Rensselaer Polytechnic Institute

Excerpt from Chapter 7, pp. 264–286. Copyright © 2002 Allyn and Bacon. This chapter has been excerpted for inclusion in *College Success Strategies* and does not include many figures and tables mentioned in the text.

Intelligence: Contrasting Views of Its Nature

Intelligence, like love, is one of those concepts that is easier to recognize than to define. We often refer to others' intelligence, describing people as *bright, sharp,* or *quick* on the one hand, or as *slow, dull,* or even *stupid* on the other. And slurs on one's intelligence are often fighting words where children—and even adults—are concerned. But again, what, precisely, *is* intelligence? Psychologists don't entirely agree, but as a working definition we can adopt the wording offered by a distinguished panel of experts (Neisser et al., 1996): The term **intelligence** refers to *individuals' abilities to understand complex ideas, to adapt effectively to the environment, to learn from experience, to engage in various forms of reasoning, to overcome obstacles by careful thought.*

Why do we place so much importance on evaluating others' (and our own) intelligence? Partly because we believe that intelligence is related to many important outcomes: how quickly individuals can master new tasks and adapt to new situations, how successful they will be in school and in various kinds of jobs, and even how well they can get along with others (e.g., Goleman, 1998). To some extent, our common sense ideas in this respect are correct. For instance, the person shown in Figure 7.12 is not acting in a way most of us would describe as intelligent—he is insulting the interviewer! The result? He probably won't get the job. But although intelligence *is* related to important life outcomes, this relationship is far from perfect. Many other factors, too, play a role, so predictions based on intelligence alone can be wrong.

Intelligence: Unitary or Multifaceted?

Is intelligence a single characteristic, or does it involve several different components? In the past, psychologists who studied intelligence often disagreed sharply on this issue. In one camp were scientists who viewed intelligence as a single characteristic or dimension along which people vary. One early supporter of this view was Spearman (1927), who believed that performance on any cognitive task depended on a primary *general* factor (which he termed *g*) and one or more *specific* factors relating to particular tasks. Spearman based this view on the following finding: Although tests of intelligence often contain different kinds of items designed to measure different aspects of intelligence, scores on these items often correlate highly with one another. This fact suggested to him that no matter how intelligence was measured, it was related to a single, primary factor.

In contrast, other researchers believed that intelligence is composed of many separate abilities that operate more or less independently. According to this *multifactor* view, a given person can be high on some components of intelligence but low on others and vice versa. One early supporter of this position was Thurstone (1938), who suggested that intelligence is composed of seven distinct primary mental abilities. Included in his list were *verbal meaning*—understanding of ideas and word meanings; *number*—speed and accuracy in dealing with numbers; and *space*—the ability to visualize objects in three dimensions.

Which of these views of intelligence has prevailed? Most modern theories of intelligence adopt a position somewhere in between these extremes. They recognize that intelligence may involve a general ability to handle a wide range of cognitive tasks and problems, as Spearman suggested, but also that intelligence *is* expressed in many different ways, and that persons can be high on some aspects of intelligence but low on others. As examples of this modern approach, let's briefly consider three influential views of intelligence.

Gardner's Theory of Multiple Intelligences

In formulating their views of intelligence, most researchers have focused primarily on what might be described as "normal" children and adults: persons who neither greatly exceed nor fall far below what most of us would view as "average" levels of intelligence. Howard Gardner (1983) argued that this approach was limiting psychology's view of intelligence. A better tactic, he suggested, would be to study not only persons in the middle of the intelligence dimension, but also ones at the extremes—acclaimed geniuses and those whose cognitive functioning is impaired, as well as experts in various domains and those who might be described as possessing special mental "gifts." For instance, consider the young athletes who compete in the Olympics. Watching these young people, I am often truly amazed by the feats they can perform. Is their ability to execute complex maneuvers like those shown in Figure 7.13 simply the result of extensive training? Or does their performance also show a special kind of intelligence—something very different from the verbal fluency we usually associate with the term *intelligence*, but perhaps just as important?

Gardner would argue strongly for the latter view. In fact, to aspects of intelligence most of us readily recognize, such as the verbal, mathematical, and spatial abilities studied by Thurstone, Gardner added such components as *musical intelligence*—the kind of intelligence shown by one of my friends who, without any formal training, can play virtually any tune on the piano; *bodily–kinesthetic intelligence*—the kind shown by the Olympic athletes shown in Figure 7.13; and *personal intelligence*—for instance, the ability to get along well with others. (I'll return to this latter topic in detail in the discussion of *emotional intelligence*.)

In sum, as its name suggests, Gardner's theory of multiple intelligences proposes that there are several important types of intelligence, and that we must understand each in order to get the big picture where this important human characteristic is concerned.

Sternberg's Triarchic Theory: The Value of Practical Intelligence

Another important modern theory of intelligence is one proposed by Robert Sternberg (Sternberg, 1985; Sternberg et al., 1995). According to this theory, known as the **triarchic theory** of intelligence, there are actually three basic types of human intelligence. The first, called *componential* or *analytic* intelligence, involves the

254 • Appendix A

abilities to think critically and analytically. Persons high on this dimension usually excel on standard tests of academic potential and make excellent students. It's a good bet that your professors are high on this aspect of intelligence. The second type of intelligence, *experiential* or *creative* intelligence, emphasizes insight and the ability to formulate new ideas. Persons who rate high on this dimension excel at zeroing in on what information is crucial in a given situation, and at combining seemingly unrelated facts. This is the kind of intelligence shown by many scientific geniuses and inventors, such as Einstein, Newton, and—some would say—Freud. For example, Johannes Gutenberg, inventor of the printing press, combined the mechanisms for producing playing cards, making wine, and minting coins in his invention; thus, he showed a high level of creative intelligence.

Sternberg terms the third type of intelligence *contextual* or **practical intelligence,** and in some ways, it is the most interesting of all. Persons high on this dimension are intelligent in a practical, adaptive sense—they have what many would term "street smarts" and are adept at solving the problems of everyday life (see Figure 7.14). In sum, Sternberg's theory suggests that there is more to intelligence than the verbal, mathematical, and reasoning abilities that are often associated with academic success. Practical intelligence, too, is important and contributes to success in many areas of life.

Cattell's Theory of Fluid and Crystallized Intelligence

In their efforts to determine whether intelligence consists of one or several different components, psychologists in past decades often made use of a statistical technique known as *factor analysis.* This technique identifies clusters of items on a test that seem to be related to one another and so can be viewed as measuring a common underlying *factor*—a specific aspect of intelligence. This technique was used by many researchers; Spearman, for instance, employed it as basis for his conclusion that there is a general or *g* factor that underlies all the others. Somewhat different conclusions were reached by Cattell (1963), who concluded that two major clusters of mental abilities exist: what he termed *fluid* and *crystallized intelligence. Fluid intelligence* refers to our largely inherited abilities to think and reason—in a sense, the hardware of our brains that determines the limits of our information-processing capabilities. In contrast, *crystallized intelligence* refers to accumulated knowledge—information we store over a lifetime of experience, plus the application of skills and knowledge to solving specific problems. In a sense, then, crystallized intelligence is the outcome of experience acting on our fluid intelligence. The speed with which one can analyze information is an example of fluid intelligence, while the breadth of one's vocabulary—how many words one can put to use—illustrates crystallized intelligence.

As I will suggest in Chapter 8, fluid intelligence seems to decrease slowly with age, but crystallized intelligence stays level or even increases (e.g., Baltes, 1987). This is why older, more experienced individuals can sometimes outperform younger ones on cognitive tasks ranging from scientific research to chess: Declines in older persons' fluid intelligence are more than offset by the vast store of knowledge in their crystallized intelligence.

☐ REVIEW QUESTIONS

- What is intelligence?
- What is Gardner's theory of multiple intelligences?
- What is Sternberg's triarchic theory of intelligence?
- What is fluid intelligence? Crystallized intelligence?

Measuring Intelligence

In 1904, when psychology was just emerging as an independent field, members of the Paris school board approached Alfred Binet with an interesting request: Could he develop an objective method for identifying the children who, in the language of that era, were described as being mentally retarded, so that they could be given special education? Binet was already at work on related topics, so he agreed, enlisting the aid of his colleague, Theodore Simon.

In designing this test Binet and Simon were guided by the belief that the items used should be ones children could answer without special training or study. They felt that this was important because the test should measure the ability to handle intellectual tasks—*not* specific knowledge acquired in school. To attain this goal, Binet and Simon decided to use items of two basic types: ones so new or unusual that none of the children would have prior exposure to them, and ones so familiar that almost all youngsters would have encountered them in the past. Children were asked to perform the following tasks: Follow simple commands or imitate simple gestures; name objects shown in pictures; repeat a sentence of fifteen words; tell how two common objects are different; complete sentences begun by the examiner.

The first version of Binet and Simon's test was published in 1905 and contained thirty items. Much to the two authors' pleasure, it was quite effective: With it, schools could readily identify children in need of special help. Encouraged by this success, Binet and Simon broadened the scope of their test to measure variations in intelligence among all children. The revised version, published in 1908, grouped items by age, with six items at each level from three to thirteen years. Items were placed at a particular age level if about 75 percent of children of that age could pass them correctly.

Binet's tests were soon revised and adapted for use in many countries. In the United States, Lewis Terman, a psychologist at Stanford University, developed the **Stanford–Binet test**—a test that was soon put to use in many different settings. Over the years the Stanford–Binet has been revised several times. One of the features of the Stanford–Binet that contributed to its popularity was the fact that it yielded a single score assumed to reflect an individual's level of intelligence—the now famous (some would say *infamous*) IQ.

IQ: Its Meaning Then and Now

Originally, the letters **IQ** stood for *intelligence quotient*, and a "quotient" is precisely what the scores represented. To obtain an IQ score, an examiner divided a student's mental age by his or her chronological age, then multiplied this number by 100. For this computation, mental age was based on the number of items a person passed correctly on the test: Test takers received two months' credit of "mental age" for each item passed. If an individual's mental and chronological ages were equal, an IQ of 100 was obtained; this was considered to be an average score. IQs above 100 indicated that a person's intellectual age was greater than her or his chronological age—in other words, that the individual was more intelligent than typical students of the same age. In contrast, numbers below 100 indicated that the individual was less intelligent than her or his peers.

Perhaps you can already see one obvious problem with this type of IQ score: At some point, mental growth levels off or stops, while chronological age continues to grow. As a result, IQ scores begin to decline after the early teen years! Partly because of this problem, IQ scores now have a different definition. They simply reflect an individual's performance relative to that of persons of the same age who have taken the same test. Thus, an IQ above 100 indicates that the person has scored higher than the average person in her or his age group, while a score below 100 indicates that the person has scored lower than average.

The Wechsler Scales

As noted earlier, the tests developed by Binet and later adapted by Terman and others remained popular for many years. They do, however, suffer from one major drawback: All are mainly verbal in content. As a result, they pay little attention to the fact that intelligence can be revealed in nonverbal activities as well. For example, an architect who visualizes a majestic design for a new building is demonstrating a high level of intelligence; yet no means for assessing such abilities was included in early versions of the Stanford–Binet test.

To overcome this and other problems, David Wechsler devised a set of tests for both children and adults that include nonverbal, or *performance*, items as well as verbal ones, and that yield separate scores for these two components of intelligence. Thus, Wechsler began with the view that intelligence is *not* a unitary characteristic, shown only through verbal and mathematical reasoning. However, he developed these tests at a time when the multifaceted nature of intelligence was not yet well understood, and it is not clear that Wechsler's various subtests actually do measure different aspects of intelligence. Despite such problems, the Wechsler tests are currently among the most frequently used individual tests of intelligence. (An overview of the subtests that make up one of the Wechsler scales, the *Wechsler Adult Intelligence Scale–Revised* (WAIS–3 for short) is presented in Table 7.4.)

Wechsler believed that differences between scores on the various subtests could be used to diagnose serious psychological disorders (see Chapter 12). However, research on this possibility has yielded mixed results at best.

A Wechsler test for children, the *Wechsler Intelligence Scale for Children* (WISC), has also been developed; it too is in widespread use. Patterns of scores on the subtests of the WISC are sometimes used to identify children suffering from various *learning disabilities.* Some findings indicate that children who score high on certain subtests, such as Picture Completion and Object Assembly, but lower on others, such as Arithmetic, Information, and Vocabulary, are more likely to suffer from learning disabilities than children with other patterns of scores (Aiken, 1991). Once again, however, not all findings point to such conclusions, so the value of the WISC (now in its third revision, WISC–3) for this kind of diagnosis remains somewhat uncertain.

One more point: Tests such as the WAIS are designed to measure the ability to acquire new information or skills, an ability implied by our definition of intelligence. Psychologists describe such tests as **aptitude tests,** and scores on these tests are often used to predict future performance. In contrast, **achievement tests** are designed to measure what you have already learned; for example, the tests you take in this class are designed to be achievement tests. The distinction between these two types of tests is not precise, however. For instance, many aptitude tests (including college entrance examinations) include measures of vocabulary, which, to a degree, reflect past learning. But in general it is useful to think of aptitude tests as ones designed to predict future performance and achievement tests as ones that reflect current performance and the results of past learning.

Group Tests of Intelligence

Both the Stanford–Binet and the Wechsler scales are *individual* tests of intelligence: They are designed for use with one person at a time. Obviously, it would be much more efficient if *group* tests could be administered to large numbers of people at once. The need for such tests was driven home at the start of World War I, when the armed forces in the United States suddenly faced the task of screening several million recruits. In response to this challenge, psychologists such as Arthur Otis developed two tests: *Army Alpha* for persons who could read (remember, this was back in 1917), and *Army Beta* for persons would could not read or who did not speak English. These early group tests proved highly useful. For example, the tests were used to select candidates for officer training school, and they did accurately predict success in such training.

In the succeeding decades many other group tests of intelligence were developed. Among the more popular of these are the *Otis tests,* such as the Otis–Lennon School Ability Test (Otis & Lennon, 1967); the *Henmon–Nelson Tests* (Nelson, Lamke, & French, 1973); and the *Cognitive Abilities Test* (CAT) (Thorndike & Hagen, 1982). All are available in versions that can be administered to large numbers of persons. The advantages offered by such tests soon made them very popular, and they were put to routine use in many school systems—especially in schools in large cities, such as the one I attended. During the 1960s, however, this practice was called into serious question and became the focus of harsh criticism. While there were many reasons for this controversy, the most serious was the charge that such tests were unfair to children from disadvantaged backgrounds—especially youngsters from certain minority groups. We'll return to these objections in a later section. Here, however, we'll pause briefly to address the following question: What are the basic requirements for a useful test of intelligence? For information on this crucial issue, please see the following **Research Methods** section.

The Cognitive Basis of Intelligence: Processing Speed

"Quick study," "quick-witted," "fast learner"—phrases such as these are often used to describe people who are high in intelligence, both academic and practical. They suggest that being intelligent involves being able to process information quickly. Is there any scientific evidence to support this idea? In fact, there is. Psychologists interested in studying intelligence have moved beyond tests such as the Stanford–Binet and Wechsler scales in an attempt to try to identify the basic cognitive mechanisms and processes that underlie intelligence—and that enable people to score high on intelligence tests (e.g., Deary, 1995). This work has led to two major developments. First, several tests have been constructed that are based on the findings of cognitive psychology and on our growing understanding of many aspects of cognition (Naglieri, 1997). Among these the most noteworthy are the *Kaufman Assessment Battery for Children* and the *Kaufman Adult Intelligence Test* (e.g., Kaufman & Kaufman, 1993), and the *Woodcock–Johnson Test of Cognitive Abilities* (Woodcock & Johnson, 1989). The Woodcock–Johnson Test, for instance, attempts to measure important aspects of both fluid and crystallized intelligence.

Second, a growing body of research has focused on the finding that the speed with which individuals perform simple perceptual and cognitive tasks (processing speed) is often correlated with scores on intelligence tests (Neisser et al., 1996; Vernon, 1987). For example, significant correlations (on the order of 2.30 to 2.40) have often been found between various measures of *reaction time* (one measure of processing speed) and scores on intelligence tests (see, e.g., Deary & Stough, 1996; Fry & Hale, 1996).

Another and even more promising cognitive measure of intelligence is a measure known as **inspection time.** This measure reflects the minimum amount of time a particular stimulus must be exposed for individuals to make a judgment about it that meets some preestablished criterion of accuracy. The shorter the duration time necessary for a given individual to attain a given level of accuracy, presumably, the faster the speed

Figure 7.17 Inspection Time: How It's Measured

To measure inspection time, psychologists ask research participants to indicate whether the long side of a stimulus (left) is on the left or the right. Immediately after a participant sees each stimulus, it is masked by another one in which both sides are long (*right*). Participants are not told to respond as quickly as possible; rather, they are instructed to take their time and be accurate. Inspection time is measured in terms of the time they require in order to make such decisions at some predetermined level of accuracy.

Stimulus   Mask

of important aspects of that person's cognitive (mental) operations. To measure inspection time, psychologists often use procedures in which individuals are shown simple drawings like the one in Figure 7.17 and are asked to indicate whether the longer side occurs on the left or right. Participants are *not* told to respond as quickly as possible. Rather, they are instructed to take their time and to be accurate. Inspection time is measured by the time they take to make such decisions at a prespecified level of accuracy—for example, 85 percent.

What does inspection time measure? Presumably, the amount of time individuals require for the intake of new visual information. Supporters of this measure argue that this task—perceiving new information—is basic to all higher-level mental operations in human thought (e.g., Deary, 1995; Deary & Stough, 1996). Further, they note that this measure is closely related to current theories of perception and decision making, theories emphasizing that new visual information is perceived in discrete samples and then combined into judgments such as "I see it" or "I don't see it." Growing evidence indicates that inspection time is indeed closely related to intelligence, as measured by standard tests. In fact, inspection time and scores on such tests correlate 2.50 or more (e.g., Kranzler & Jensen, 1989).

In sum, inspection time appears to be a very promising measure for probing the nature of human intelligence—for understanding the basic cognitive processes that underlie this important characteristic. And since understanding a process is often an essential first step to being able to change it in beneficial ways, this is valuable progress.

The Neural Basis of Intelligence: Intelligence and Neural Efficiency

In Chapter 2, and again in discussing memory in Chapter 6, I noted that everything we do, think, or feel rests, in an ultimate sense, on neurochemical events occurring in our brains. If that is indeed true—and virtually all psychologists believe that it is—then an intriguing possibility arises: Can we trace individual differences in intelligence to differences in neural functioning? The answer suggested by a growing body of evidence is *yes* (e.g., Matarazzo, 1992; Vernon, 1993). Such research suggests, first, that *nerve conduction velocity*—the speed with which nerve impulses are conducted in the visual system—correlates significantly with measures of intelligence (e.g., the Raven Progressive Matrices test) (Reed & Jensen, 1993).

Other, and related, research has examined metabolic activity in the brain during cognitive tasks (e.g., Haier, 1993). Presumably, if intelligence is related to efficient brain functioning, then the more intelligent people are, the less energy their brains should expend while working on various tasks. This prediction has generally been confirmed: The brains of persons scoring highest on written measures of intellectual ability do expend less energy when these individuals perform complex cognitive tasks. The data in these studies have been gathered by means of the PET technique of brain imaging described in Chapters 2 and 6. Using similar imaging technologies, scientists have recently identified an area in the lateral prefrontal cortex of each brain hemisphere that may play an important role in intelligence by providing a global work space for organizing and coordinating information and carrying it back to other parts of the brain as needed (Duncan et al., 2000). Apparently, the relative performance of this "work space" determines how adept a person is at solving cognitive problems—precisely the characteristic that intelligence tests attempt to measure.

Finally, some findings suggest that there is a link between brain structure and intelligence (Andreason et al., 1993). Specifically, scores on standard measures of intelligence such as the Wechsler Adult Intelligence Scale are related to the size of certain portions of the brain, including the left and right temporal lobes and the left and right hippocampus. Moreover, this is true even when corrections are made for individuals' overall physical size.

In sum, it appears that the improved methods now available for studying the brain and nervous system are beginning to establish the kind of links between intelligence and physical structures that psychologists have long suspected to exist. Such research is very recent, so it is still too soon to reach firm conclusions. It does appear, though, that we are on the verge of establishing much firmer links between intelligence—a crucial aspect of mind—and body than has ever been true before.

For a discussion of yet another technique used by psychologists to measure cognitive abilities—and to make important predictions about future success—please see the following **From Science to Practice** section.

FROM SCIENCE TO PRACTICE

Predicting Career Success: Competency Assessment

Earlier, I noted that standard intelligence tests are not very effective in predicting success outside academic circles. They are moderately related to achievement in fields that require skills similar to those needed for success in school (e.g., science, law, medicine) but are quite ineffective in predicting success in other contexts, including the one in which most people spend much of their adult lives: the business world (e.g., Whitla, 1975). Is there a better way to predict success in such settings? Fortunately, there is.

This approach is known as **competency assessment,** and it is based on the following reasoning: If we start with two groups—one known to be highly successful and the other known to be only average in terms of career success—and then search for differences between them, the differences we identify may be useful in predicting success in other groups of persons. But how do we go about identifying the key differences between highly successful and less successful persons? One useful procedure involves what are known as *behavioral-event interviews* (e.g., Spencer & Spencer, 1993). In these interviews persons rated by others who know

(continued)

them well as being outstanding at their jobs, and persons rated as being only average, describe what they said, thought, felt, and did in various work-related situations (e.g., how they reached decisions, how they dealt with sudden emergencies, and so on). Their answers are then carefully examined for patterns of differences. Such differences, when identified, are labeled *competencies:* Presumably, these are the key skills or abilities that distinguish outstanding performers from average ones. Using such interviews, researchers have identified several competencies that seem to play a key role in success in several fields, such as being a business executive. These include skill at several kinds of thinking, such as inductive reasoning and analytical thinking; a strong desire for success; flexibility; wanting to have an impact on others; willingness to take initiative; self-confidence; and good understanding of others (a cluster of skills psychologists often describe as *social skills*).

Are *all* these skills necessary for success? Not necessarily; further studies indicate that being highly successful seems to require only that individuals possess several of them—for instance, five of the competencies listed (e.g., Nygren & Ukeritis, 1993).

Now for the most important question: Does possession of these competencies do a good job of predicting career success? Research findings suggest that they do. For instance, in one major project, McClelland (1998) studied the executives in a large corporation. On the basis of behavioral-event interviews, the researchers classified the executives as being highly qualified or average in potential. They then followed the executives' performance for several years. As expected, those classified as being highly qualified were rated by their bosses as doing a better job, and received significantly higher bonuses, in two different years (see Figure 7.18). Another important finding was this: Although almost half of the executives hired in the usual way by the company quit within a year, none of those hired on the basis of competency assessment (having been rated as outstanding in potential) quit. Hiring and training each new executive cost the company more than $250,000, so by using competency assessment the organization saved more than $4 million in a single year!

In sum, competency assessment appears to provide a useful technique for predicting success in the world of work. So although standard intelligence tests don't seem to do a very good job in this respect, psychologists have used their understanding of human behavior and their knowledge of human cognition and intelligence to devise other, more effective procedures. Clearly, this represents an important contribution by the science of psychology to the solution of important practical problems.

☐ REVIEW QUESTIONS

- What was the first individual test of intelligence, and what did scores on it mean?
- What are the Wechsler scales?
- What are standardization, reliability, and validity?
- What is inspection time, and what does it measure?
- What findings suggest that intelligence is related to neural functioning or brain structure?
- What is competency assessment, and how is it used?

Human Intelligence: The Role of Heredity and the Role of Environment

That people differ in intelligence is obvious. *Why* such differences exist is quite another matter. Are they largely a matter of heredity—differences in the genetic materials and codes we inherit from our parents? Or are they primarily the result of environmental factors—conditions in the world around us that affect our intellectual development? I'm sure you know the answer: Both types of factors are involved. Human intelligence is clearly the result of the complex interplay between genetic factors and a wide range of environmental conditions (e.g., Plomin, 1997). Let's now consider some of the evidence pointing to this conclusion.

Evidence for the Influence of Heredity

Several lines of research offer support for the view that heredity plays an important role in human intelligence. First, consider findings with respect to family relationship and measured IQ. If intelligence is indeed determined by heredity, we would expect that the more closely two persons are related, the more similar their IQs will be. This prediction has generally been confirmed (e.g., McGue et al., 1993; Neisser et al., 1996). For example, the IQs of identical twins raised together correlate almost +.90, those of brothers and sisters about +.50, and those of cousins about +.15 (see Figure 7.19). (Remember: Higher correlations indicate stronger relationships between variables.)

Support for the impact of heredity on intelligence is also provided by studies involving adopted children. If intelligence is strongly affected by genetic factors, the IQs of adopted children should resemble those of their biological parents more closely than those of their adoptive parents. In short, the children should be more similar in IQ to the persons from whom they received their genes than to the persons who raised them. This prediction, too, has been confirmed (Jencks, 1972; Munsinger, 1978; Plomin et al., 1997).

Additional evidence for the role of genetic factors in intelligence is provided by recent studies focused on the task of identifying the specific genes that influence intelligence (e.g., Rutter & Plomin, 1997; Sherman et al., 1997). These studies have adopted as a working hypothesis the view that many genes, each exerting relatively small effects, probably play a role in general intelligence—that is, in what many aspects of mental abilities (e.g., verbal, spatial, speed-of-processing, and memory abilities) have in common (e.g., Plomin, 1997). In other words, such research has not attempted to identify *the* gene that influences intelligence, but rather has sought *quantitative trait loci* (QTLs): genes that have relatively small effects and that influence the likelihood of some characteristic in a population. The results of such studies suggest that certain genes are indeed associated with high intelligence (e.g., Chorney et al., 1998).

Finally, evidence for the role of genetic factors in intelligence has been provided by research on identical twins separated as infants (usually, within the first few weeks of life) who were then raised in different homes (e.g., Bouchard et al., 1990). Because such persons have identical genetic inheritance but have been exposed to different environmental conditions—in some cases, sharply contrasting conditions—studying their IQs provides a powerful means for comparing the roles of genetic and environmental factors in human intelligence. The results of such research are clear: The IQs of identical twins reared apart (often from the time they were only a few days old) correlate almost as highly as those of identical twins reared together. Moreover, such individuals are also amazingly similar in many other characteristics, such as physical appearance, preferences in dress, mannerisms, and even personality (see Figure 7.20). Clearly, these findings point to an important role for heredity in intelligence and in many other aspects of psychological functioning.

On the basis of these and other findings, some researchers have estimated that the **heritability** of intelligence—the proportion of the variance in intelligence within a given population that is attributable to genetic factors—ranges from about 35 percent in childhood to as much as 75 percent in adulthood (McGue et al., 1993), and may be about 50 percent overall (Plomin et al., 1997). Why does the contribution of genetic factors to intelligence increase with age? Perhaps because as individuals grow older, their interactions with their environment are shaped less and less by restraints imposed on them by their families or by their social origins and are shaped more and more by the characteristics they bring with them to these environments. In other words, as they grow older, individuals are increasingly able to choose or change their environments so that these permit expression of their genetically determined tendencies and preferences (Neisser et al., 1996). Whatever the precise origin of the increasing heritability of intelligence with age, there is little doubt that genetic factors do indeed play an important role in intelligence throughout life.

Evidence for the Influence of Environmental Factors

Genetic factors are definitely *not* the entire picture where human intelligence is concerned, however. Other findings point to the conclusion that environmental variables, too, are important. One such finding is that performance on IQ tests has risen substantially around the world at all age levels in recent decades. This phenomenon is known as the *Flynn effect* after the psychologist who first reported it (Flynn, 1987, 1996). Such increases have averaged about 3 IQ points per decade worldwide; but, as shown in Figure 7.21 on page 278, in some countries they have been even larger. As a result of these gains in performance, it has been necessary to restandardize widely used tests so that they continue to yield an average IQ of 100; what is termed "average" today is actually a higher level of performance than was true in the past.

What accounts for these increases? It seems unlikely that massive shifts in human heredity occur from one generation to the next. A more reasonable explanation, therefore, focuses on changes in environmental factors. What factors have changed in recent decades? The following variables have been suggested as possible contributors to the continuing rise in IQ (e.g., Flynn, 1999; Williams, 1998): better nutrition, increased urbanization, the advent of television, more and better education, more cognitively demanding jobs, and even exposure to computer games! Many of these changes are real and seem plausible as explanations for the rise in IQ; but, as noted recently by Flynn (1999), there is as yet not sufficient evidence to conclude that any or all of these factors have played a role. In any case, whatever the specific causes involved, the steady rise in performance on IQ tests points to the importance of environmental factors in human intelligence.

Additional evidence for the role of environmental factors in intelligence is provided by the findings of studies of *environmental deprivation* and *environmental enrichment.* With respect to deprivation, some findings suggest that intelligence can be reduced by the absence of key forms of environmental stimulation early in life (Gottfried, 1984). In terms of enrichment, removing children from sterile, restricted environments and placing them in more favorable settings seems to enhance their intellectual growth. For example, in one of the first demonstrations of the beneficial impact on IQ of an enriched environment, Skeels (1938, 1966) removed thirteen children, all about two years old, from an orphanage in which they received virtually no intellectual stimulation—and virtually no contact with adults—and placed them in the care of a group of retarded women living in an institution. After a few years, Skeels noted that the children's IQs had risen dramatically—29 points on average (although later corrections reduced this figure to about 10 to 13 points; Flynn, 1993). Interestingly, Skeels also obtained IQ measures of children who had remained in the orphanage and found that these had actually dropped by 26 points on average—presumably as a result of continued exposure to the impoverished environment at the orphanage. Twenty-five years later, the thirteen children who had experienced the enriched environment were all doing well; most had graduated from high school, found a job, and married. In contrast, those in the original control group either remained institutionalized or were functioning poorly in society.

While more recent—and more carefully controlled—efforts to increase intelligence through environmental interventions have not yielded gains as dramatic as those reported by Skeels (1966), some of these programs *have* produced beneficial results

(Bryant & Maxwell, 1997; Guralnick, 1997). However, as noted recently by Ramey and Ramey (1998), such changes are most likely to occur when the following conditions are met: (1) The interventions begin early and continue for a long time; (2) the programs are intense, involving home visits several times per week; (3) the children receive new learning experiences delivered directly to them by experts rather than indirectly though their parents; (4) the interventions are broad in scope, using many different procedures to enhance children's development; (5) the interventions are matched to the needs of individual children; and (6) environmental supports (e.g., excellent schools) are put in place to support and maintain the positive attitudes toward learning the children gain. Needless to say, programs that meet these criteria tend to be expensive. But they can also yield important financial benefits; for instance, one study cited by Ramey and Ramey (1998) suggests that appropriate early intervention programs might have prevented more than 300,000 children in the United States alone from developing IQs that placed them in the "mentally retarded" category (i.e., IQs below 70). Given that such children often require extensive corrective assistance and training, the potential savings to be realized through early enrichment might well be substantial. So there are strong economic arguments, as well as social and humanitarian ones, for instituting the best and most extensive early intervention programs a given society can afford.

Additional support for the role of environmental factors in intelligence is provided by the finding that many biological factors that children encounter while growing up can affect their intelligence. Prolonged malnutrition can adversely affect IQ (e.g., Sigman, 1995), as can exposure to lead—either in the air or in lead-based paint, which young children often eat because it tastes sweet (e.g., Baghurst et al., 1992). We have already examined the adverse effects on the health of developing fetuses of exposure to such factors as alcohol and drugs; here I simply want to add that research findings indicate that these factors can also adversely affect intelligence (e.g., Neisser et al., 1996). In sum, therefore, many forms of evidence support the view that intelligence is determined, at least in part, by environmental factors. Especially when these are extreme, they may slow—or accelerate—children's intellectual growth; and this effect, in turn, can have important implications for the societies in which those children will become adults.

Environment, Heredity, and Intelligence: Summing Up

There is considerable evidence that *both* environmental and genetic factors play a role in intelligence. This is the view accepted by almost all psychologists, and there is little controversy about it. Greater controversy continues to exist, however, concerning the *relative* contribution of each of these factors. Do environmental or genetic factors play a stronger role in shaping intelligence? As I noted earlier, existing evidence seems to favor the view that genetic factors may account for more of the variance in IQ scores within a given population than environmental factors (e.g., Plomin, 1997; Neisser et al., 1996). Many people, including psychologists, are made somewhat uneasy by this conclusion, in part because they assume that characteristics that are heritable—ones that are strongly influenced by genetic factors—cannot readily be changed. *It's important to recognize that this assumption is false.* For instance, consider height: This is a characteristic that is highly heritable—one that is influenced by genetic factors to a greater extent than by environment. Yet despite this fact, average heights have increased in many countries as nutrition has improved (and, perhaps, as young persons have been exposed to the growth hormones used to increase food production). So the fact that a trait is strongly influenced by genetic factors does *not* imply that it cannot also be affected by environmental factors.

The same thing is almost certainly true for intelligence. Yes, existing evidence suggests that it is affected by genetic factors. But this in no way implies that it cannot be influenced by environmental conditions, too—and, as we've seen, it certainly is. The recognition that genetic factors play an important role in intelligence in no way implies that intelligence is etched in stone—and definitely does *not* constitute an excuse for giving up on children who, because of poverty, prejudice, or neglect, are seriously at risk.

☐ REVIEW QUESTIONS

- What evidence suggests that intelligence is influenced by genetic factors?
- What evidence suggests that intelligence is influenced by environmental factors?
- Can characteristics that are highly heritable be influenced by environmental factors? Suppose several genes that influence intelligence are identified. Would it be ethical to alter these genes so as to produce higher levels of intelligence in many persons? What might be the effects on society of doing so?

Group Differences in Intelligence Test Scores: Why They Occur

Earlier, I noted that there are sizable differences among the average IQ scores of various ethnic groups. In the United States and elsewhere, members of some minority groups score lower, on average, than members of the majority group. Why do such differences occur? This has been a topic of considerable controversy in psychology for many years, and currently there is still no final, universally accepted conclusion. However, it seems fair to say that at present, most psychologists attribute such group differences in performance on standard intelligence tests largely to environmental variables. Let's take a closer look at the evidence that points to this conclusion. I'll then present some findings that argue *against* the view that group differences in intelligence derive from genetic factors. Finally, I'll turn to a different category of group differences in intelligence test scores—gender differences.

Group Differences in IQ Scores:
Evidence for the Role of Environmental Factors

I have already referred to one form of evidence suggesting that group differences in performance on intelligence tests stem primarily from environmental factors: the fact that the tests themselves may be biased against test takers from some minority groups. Why? In part because the tests were standardized largely on middle-class white persons; thus, interpreting the test scores of persons from minority groups in terms of these norms is not appropriate. Even worse, some critics have suggested that the tests themselves suffer from **cultural bias:** Items on the tests are ones that are familiar to middle-class white children and so give them an important edge in terms of test performance. Are such concerns valid? Careful examination of the items used on intelligence tests suggests that they may indeed be culturally biased, at least to a degree. Some items do seem to be ones that are less familiar—and therefore more difficult to answer—for minority test takers. To the extent that such cultural bias exists, it is indeed a serious flaw in IQ tests.

On the other hand, though, it's important to note that the tests are generally about as successful in predicting future school performance by children from all groups. So while the tests may be biased in terms of content, this in itself does not make them useless from the point of view of predicting future performance (e.g., Rowe, Vazsonyi, & Flannery, 1994). However, as noted by Steele and Aronson (1996), because minority children find at least some of the items on these tests unfamiliar, they may feel threatened by the tests; and this, in turn, may reduce their scores.

In an effort to eliminate cultural bias from intelligence tests, psychologists have attempted to design *culture-fair* tests. Such tests attempt to include only items to which all groups, regardless of ethnic or racial background, have been exposed. Because many minority children are exposed to languages other than standard English, these tests tend to be nonverbal in nature. One of these, the **Raven Progressive Matrices** (Raven, 1977), is illustrated in Figure 7.22. This test consists of sixty matrices of varying difficulty, each containing a logical pattern or design with a missing part. Individuals select the item that completes the pattern from several different choices. Because the Raven test and ones like it focus primarily on *fluid intelligence*—our basic abilities to form concepts, reason, and identify similarities—these tests seem less likely to be subject to cultural bias than other kinds of intelligence tests. However, it is not clear that these tests, or any others, totally eliminate the problem of subtle built-in bias.

Additional evidence for the role of environmental factors in group differences in test performance has been divided by Flynn (1999), one expert on this issue, into two categories: indirect and direct. *Indirect evidence* is evidence from research in which efforts are made to equate environmental factors for all test takers—for instance, by eliminating the effects of socioeconomic status through statistical techniques. The results of such studies are mixed; some suggest that the gap between minority groups and whites is reduced by such procedures (e.g., Flynn, 1993), but other studies indicate that between-group differences still remain (e.g., Loehlin, Lindzey, & Spuhle, 1975; Lynn, 1996). These findings suggest that while socio-economic factors contribute to group differences in IQ scores, other factors, as yet unknown, may also play some role.

Direct evidence for environmental factors, in contrast, involves actual life changes that take many minority persons out of the disadvantaged environment they often face and provide them with an environment equivalent to that of other groups. Obtaining such evidence is, of course, very difficult; many minority persons do grow up in environments quite distinct from those of other groups. According to Flynn (1999), however, one compelling piece of direct evidence for the role of environmental factors in group differences does exist. During World War II, African American soldiers fathered thousands of children in Germany (much of which was occupied by U.S. troops after the war). These children have been raised by white mothers in what is essentially a white environment. The result? Their IQs are virtually identical to those of white children matched to them in socioeconomic status (e.g., Flynn, 1980). Given that the fathers of these children scored very similarly to other African American soldiers, these findings suggest that environmental factors are in fact the key to group differences in IQ: When such factors are largely eliminated, differences between the groups, too, disappear.

Group Differences in IQ Scores: Is There Any Evidence for the Role of Genetic Factors?

Now for the other side of the story—the suggestion that group differences in intelligence stem largely from genetic factors. In 1994 this issue was brought into sharp focus by the publication of a highly controversial book entitled *The Bell Curve*. Because the book was written by two well-known psychologists, Richard Herrnstein and Charles Murray, it received immediate attention in the popular press and soon became a best-seller. The book focused on human intelligence and covered many aspects of this topic. The most controversial portions, however, dealt with what is known as the **genetic hypothesis**—the view that group differences in intelligence are due, at least in part, to genetic factors.

In *The Bell Curve* Herrnstein and Murray (1994) voiced strong support for the genetic hypothesis. They noted, for instance, that there are several converging sources of evidence for "a genetic factor in cognitive ethnic differences" (p. 270) between African American and other ethnic groups in the United States. Proceeding from this conclusion, they suggested that intelligence may not be readily modifiable through changes in environmental conditions. They proposed, therefore, that special programs aimed at raising the IQ scores of disadvantaged minorities were probably a waste of effort.

As you can imagine, these suggestions were challenged vigorously by many psychologists (e.g., Sternberg, 1995). These critics argued that much of the reasoning in *The Bell Curve* was flawed and that the book overlooked many important findings. Perhaps the harshest criticism of the book centered on its contention that because individual differences in intelligence are strongly influenced by genetic factors, group differences are, too. Several researchers took strong exception to this logic (e.g., Schultze, Kane, & Dickens, 1996; Sternberg, 1995). They contended that this reasoning would be accurate only if the environments of the various groups being compared were identical. Under those conditions, it could be argued that differences between the groups stemmed, at least in part, from genetic factors. In reality, however, the environments in which the members of various ethnic groups exist are *not* identical. As a result, it is false to assume that group differences with respect to IQ scores stem from genetic factors, even if we know that individual differences in such scores *are* strongly influenced by these factors. (And, as we saw earlier, when environmental differences are removed or minimized, group differences in intelligence, too, disappear.)

So where does all this leave us? With the conclusion that although individual differences in IQ scores are certainly influenced by genetic factors, there are no strong grounds for assuming that such factors also contribute to group differences. While some researchers continue to insist that sufficient evidence exists to conclude that genetic factors play a role (e.g., Rushton, 1997), most take strong exception to this view and contend that the evidence for this view is relatively weak (e.g., Neisser, 1997). As I like to put it, *The Bell Curve* has certainly "rung," at least in an economic sense—the book sold tens of thousands of copies and received a great deal of public attention—but from the standpoint of scientific knowledge, it definitely does *not* ring true.

☐ REVIEW QUESTIONS

- What evidence suggests that group differences in intelligence stem largely from environmental factors?
- Is there any evidence for the role of genetic factors in group differences in intelligence?

Emotional Intelligence: The Feeling Side of Intelligence

When I was in high school, one student stood out as the "superbrain" of our school: Paul Kronen. He was so smart it was scary. Unfortunately, Paul was not very good with people. Many things he did rubbed people the wrong way. First, he was arrogant. He was smart, he knew it, and he made sure that *you* knew it too. In addition, Paul was what I'd now describe as *emotionally unstable.* His moods swung widely and quickly from one extreme to another. Even more important, he seemed incapable of restraining his temper or his impulses: He would get into angry exchanges with teachers because he just didn't know when to quit—when to stop contradicting them and making them look bad in front of the class. Taking all this into account, I was not really surprised to learn that Paul didn't live up to his initial promise. He was brilliant, all right, but only in certain respects; in others, he was truly backward.

These memories of my childhood friend suggest that there is another kind of intelligence, quite distinct from that measured by IQ tests. In fact, one psychologist—Daniel Goleman (1995, 1998)—has argued strongly that this other kind of intelligence is more important for a happy, productive life than IQ. Goleman terms this kind of intelligence **emotional intelligence** (or **EQ** for short) and defines it as a cluster of traits or abilities relating to the emotional side of life. Let's take a closer look at the major components of emotional intelligence and then examine current evidence concerning its existence and effects.

Major Components of Emotional Intelligence

Goleman (1995) suggests that emotional intelligence consists of five major parts: (1) knowing our own emotions, (2) managing our emotions, (3) motivating ourselves, (4) recognizing the emotions of others, and (5) handling relationships. Each of these elements, he contends, plays an important role in shaping the outcomes we experience in life.

Knowing Our Own Emotions   As I noted in Chapter 9, emotions are often powerful reactions, so it would seem at first glance that everyone ought to be able to recognize their own feelings. In fact, however, this is not always the case. Some persons are highly aware of their own emotions and their thoughts about them, but others seem to be almost totally oblivious to these. What are the implications of such differences? First, to the extent individuals are not aware of their own feelings, they cannot make intelligent choices. How can they tell whom to date or marry, what job to take, which house or car to buy, or even what to order in a restaurant? Second, because such persons aren't aware of their own emotions, they are often low in *expressiveness*—they don't show their feelings clearly through facial expressions, body language, or other cues most of use to recognize others' feelings (Malandro, Barker, & Barker, 1994). This can have adverse effects on their interpersonal relationships, because other people find it hard to know how they are feeling or reacting. For these reasons, this first component of emotional intelligence seems to be quite important.

Managing Our Own Emotions   Have you ever lost your temper or cried when you didn't want to show such reactions? Have you ever done something to cheer yourself up when you felt anxious or depressed? If so, you are already aware of the fact that we often try to *manage* our emotions—to regulate their nature, intensity, and expression (e.g., Zillmann, 1996). Doing so is very important both for our own mental health and from the point of view of interacting effectively with others (see Figure 7.23). For instance, consider persons who simply cannot control their temper; are they bound for success and a happy life? No. They will probably be avoided by many people and will *not* get the jobs, promotions, or lovers they want.

Motivating Ourselves   Thomas Edison, the famous inventor, once remarked: "Success is two percent inspiration and ninety-eight percent perspiration." Do you agree? While inspiration or creativity is certainly important (see the next section of this chapter), I'm inclined to believe that Edison was right. By "perspiration," however, I mean more than simply hard work: I also include aspects of emotional intelligence, such as being able to motivate oneself to work long and hard on a task, remaining enthusiastic and optimistic about the final outcome, and being able to delay gratification—to put off receiving small rewards now in order to get larger ones later on (e.g., Shoda, Mischel, & Peake, 1990). Being high in such skills can indeed contribute to success in many different contexts.

Recognizing and Influencing Others' Emotions   Another aspect of emotional intelligence, as described by Goleman, is the ability to "read" others accurately—to recognize the mood they are in and what emotion they are experiencing. This skill is valuable in many practical settings. For instance, if you can accurately gauge another person's current mood, you can tell whether it's the right time to ask her or him for a favor. Similarly, persons who are skilled at generating strong emotions in others are often highly successful in such fields as sales and politics: They can get other people to feel what *they* want them to feel.

Handling Relationships   Some people seem to have a knack for getting along with others: most people who meet these people like them, and as a result they have many friends and often enjoy high levels of success in their careers. In contrast, others seem to make a mess of virtually all their personal relationships. According to Goleman (1995), such differences are another reflection of differences in emotional intelligence or, as some researchers would phrase it, differences in *interpersonal intelligence* (Hatch, 1990).

What does interpersonal intelligence involve? Such skills as being able to coordinate the efforts of several people and to negotiate solutions to complex interpersonal problems, being good at giving others feedback that doesn't make them angry or resentful (e.g., Baron, 1993a), and being a team player. Again, these skills are clearly distinct from the ones needed for getting good grades or scoring high on tests of intelligence, but they often play a key role in important life outcomes.

Emotional Intelligence: Evidence on Its Existence and Effects

Goleman's (1995, 1998) books on emotional intelligence have been best-sellers, so you may well have heard about the concept before taking this course. Unfortunately, though, most of the evidence Goleman offers concerning the existence and impact of emotional intelligence is anecdotal or indirect in nature. Psychologists, of course, strongly prefer more concrete kinds of evidence. Accordingly, researchers have put the concept of emotional intelligence to the test, trying to determine whether the distinct skills described by Goleman cluster together as a single (if multi-faceted) factor, and whether this factor influences important life outcomes.

With respect to the first of these issues, evidence is mixed. While some researchers (Mayer, Caruso, & Salovey, 1998; Salovey & Mayer, 1994) have reported findings consistent with Goleman's suggestions and with their own, similar definitions of emotional intelligence, others have obtained less encouraging results. For example, in a recent and carefully conducted study, Davies, Stankov, and Roberts (1998) focused on two important questions: (1) Are the methods currently used to measure emotional intelligence adequate—that is, are they reliable and valid? And (2) is emotional intelligence really different from other seemingly related concepts—for instance, social intelligence and several aspects of personality (e.g., empathy)? To answer these basic questions, they conducted several studies in which hundreds of participants varying in age, education, gender, and nationality completed measures designed to assess each aspect of emotional intelligence and several other variables as well. Results indicated that only one of the components emphasized by Goleman and other advocates of emotional intelligence emerged as clear and independent: *emotion perception*—the ability to accurately read others' emotions.

Does this mean that the theory of emotional intelligence is useless and that discussing it has been a waste of time—yours as well as mine? I don't believe so. Another interpretation of existing evidence concerning emotional intelligence is this: At present, we don't have adequate methods for measuring all aspects of emotional intelligence. Further, these components may, in fact, be somewhat independent of each other. Thus, we may not be able to assign individuals a single overall EQ score comparable to the single IQ score yielded by many intelligence tests. In a sense, though, this is not surprising. After all, the more psychologists study intelligence, the more they recognize that it probably consists of a number of distinct components—verbal, spatial, speed-of-processing, and perhaps many others. So the fact that we also possess distinct and perhaps largely independent abilities relating to the emotional side of life simply mirrors this pattern. One point *is* clear, however: At present, we do not possess fully adequate tests for measuring emotional intelligence. Until we do, we will not be able to fully determine its role in important aspects of our lives.

And yet, having said that, I should add that other research offers support for the view that some of the components included in emotional intelligence—especially emotion perception—can indeed have measurable effects. For instance, in recent studies, Gideon Markman and I (e.g., Baron, 2000; Baron & Markman, 2000) have focused on the following question: Why is it that some entrepreneurs are so successful in starting new businesses, while others fail? This is an important question, because in recent years it is the companies started by entrepreneurs that have created most new jobs around the world (e.g., Shane & Venkataraman, in press). We've used several different methods to study this issue, and what we've found, repeatedly, is this: Entrepreneurs who are adept at "reading" others accurately and who adapt easily to new social situations (what we describe as "social adaptability") are significantly more successful, financially, than entrepreneurs who score lower in these skills. To the extent that these two traits are related to emotional intelligence, our findings can be viewed as offering indirect support for the view that EQ influences the outcomes people experience in practical contexts. But stay tuned: The idea of emotional intelligence is an appealing one with important implications, so it is certain to be the topic of research by psychologists in the years ahead.

☐ REVIEW QUESTIONS

- What is emotional intelligence?
- What does evidence to date suggest about the existence of emotional intelligence? Its effects?

APPENDIX B

THE NATION DIVIDES: THE VIETNAM WAR AND SOCIAL CONFLICT, 1964–1971

from *Created Equal: A Social and Political History of the United States*

Jacqueline Jones
Brandeis University

Peter H. Wood
Duke University

Thomas Borstelmann
University of Nebraska

Elaine Tyler May
University of Minnesota

Vicky L. Ruiz
University of California at Irvine

Chapter Outline

The soft-spoken black man with the strange Northern accent first showed up in the small town of McComb, Mississippi, in the summer of 1961. Robert Parris Moses had come on a mission of democracy. An organizer for the new Student Nonviolent Coordinating Committee (SNCC), he was there to encourage impoverished African Americans to register to vote. Over the next four years in the Deep South, Bob Moses paid a price for his commitments. Local police imprisoned him, and white suprema- cists beat him severely and murdered dozens of his fellow activists in the black free- dom movement. But Moses remained committed to nonviolence and racial integration. His quiet courage became legendary in the movement. One summer night in 1962, he returned to a deserted SNCC office in Greenwood, Mississippi, that had just been ransacked by a white mob; three other SNCC workers had barely escaped with their lives. Moses looked around, made up a bed in the corner of the devastated main room, and went to sleep. He refused to be intimidated.

During the 1960s, an extraordinary number of idealistic young people became involved in public life in an effort to make real their nation's abstract promises of freedom and justice. The civil rights movement inspired the social movements that followed: for ending the war, for preserving the environment, and for liberating women, Latinos, Indians, and gay men and lesbians. But organizing for change inevitably brought activists up against fierce resistance from what they called "the establishment." Disillusionment and radicalization often followed. Public life became deeply contentious by 1968 as young radicals challenged more conserva- tive citizens on issues of race, war, and gender.

The escalating American war in Southeast Asia loomed over all. Lyndon John- son brought the nation to its apex of liberal reform with his extensive Great Soci- ety legislation. However, the high-flying hopes of Democratic liberals crashed to earth with the destructive war that the Johnson administration waged against sea- soned communist revolutionaries in far-off Vietnam. Out of the wreckage of 1968 emerged a Republican president, Richard Nixon, and a growing conservative back- lash against the social changes advocated by people of color, the counterculture, the antiwar movement, and the rising tide of women's liberation.

Lyndon Johnson and the Apex of Liberalism

Wealth provided the foundation on which the Great Society was built. American economic expansion since World War II had created history's richest nation by 1960. From 1961 to 1966, the economy accelerated at an annual growth rate of more than 5 percent with very low inflation, stimulated by large tax cuts and extensive military spending. The 41 percent increase in per capita income during the 1960s was not evenly distributed, however. Economist Paul Samuelson explained in 1970, "If we made an income pyramid out of a child's blocks, with each layer portraying $1000 of income, the peak would be far higher than the Eiffel Tower, but almost all of us would be within a yard of the ground." And the distribution of wealth (stocks and real estate) was far more skewed than that of income. U.S. policymakers believed that economic expansion would continue indefinitely and the nation could therefore afford government policies to improve the welfare of less affluent Americans.

The New President

Lyndon Baines Johnson was one of the most remarkable American characters of the twentieth century, both a giant among political leaders and a bully with those who worked for him. Johnson grew up in a family struggling to stay out of poverty in the Texas hill country west of Austin. He entered Democratic politics early as an avid supporter of Franklin Roosevelt and the New Deal, aided by the business savvy and loyalty of his wife, Lady Bird Johnson, who grew wealthy through ownership of TV and radio stations. As First Lady, she became widely known for her leadership in highway beautification. Lyndon Johnson rose like a rocket through Congress to become perhaps the most powerful Senate majority leader ever (1954–1960) and then vice president (1961–1963). Kennedy's assassination catapulted him into the Oval Office as the nation's first Texan president.

Johnson retained Kennedy's cabinet and advisers and used the memory of the fallen young president to rally support for his administration. Johnson turned out to be the more liberal of the two men in part because his early years in Texas had given him a visceral understanding of poverty and discrimination that his predecessor lacked. Johnson's focus was different, too. He retained Kennedy's anticommunist commitments abroad, but his heart remained at home, where he wanted to perfect American society.

Table 26.1 The Election of 1964

Candidate	Political Party	Popular Vote (%)	Electoral Vote
Lyndon B. Johnson	Democratic	61.1	486
Barry M. Goldwater	Republican	38.5	52

First he had to win reelection, because less than a year remained until voters went to the polls in 1964. The Republicans nominated right-wing Senator Barry Goldwater of Arizona, a sign of the party's sharp swing away from its moderate eastern elements toward its fiercely conservative western and southern constituencies. Goldwater believed in unrestricted markets and a minimal role for the federal government in every aspect of American life except the military. He spoke casually about using nuclear weapons against communists abroad. Goldwater declared that "extremism in the defense of liberty is no vice," but Johnson zeroed in on that extremism and swept to the largest electoral majority of any president (61 percent).

The Great Society: Fighting Poverty and Discrimination

In pursuit of what he called the Great Society, Johnson first declared a "War on Poverty." No citizen in the richest nation on earth should live in squalor, he believed. More than one out of five Americans still lived below the conservatively estimated official poverty line ($3,022 for a nonfarm family of four in 1960), and 70 percent of these were white.

The president and a large congressional majority passed several measures to alleviate poverty. They sharply increased the availability of money and food stamps through the Aid to Families with Dependent Children ("welfare") program, and they raised Social Security payments to older Americans. Several programs focused on improving educational opportunities as an avenue out of poverty: Head Start offered preschool education and meals for youngsters, the Elementary and Secondary Education Act sent federal funds to the least affluent school districts, and an expanded system of student loans facilitated access to college. The Job Corps provided employment training, and Volunteers in Service to America (VISTA) served as a domestic Peace Corps, funneling people with education and skills into poor communities to serve as teachers and providers of other social services.

No barrier to opportunity in the early 1960s was higher than the color bar. Both opportunist and idealist, Johnson as president shed his segregationist voting record (necessary for election in Texas before 1960) and became the most vocal proponent of racial equality ever to occupy the Oval Office. Two factors facilitated his change in position. Blatant inequalities for American citizens weakened the United States in its competition with the Soviets and Chinese for the loyalty of the nonwhite Third World majority. Moreover, the African American freedom struggle in the South had reached a boiling point. Black frustration was mounting over white brutality and the seeming indifference or even hostility of the national government.

The Civil Rights Act of 1964 fulfilled the implicit promise of the *Brown v. Board of Education* decision a decade earlier. The 1964 act made desegregation the law of the land as it outlawed discrimination in employment and in public facilities such as restaurants, theaters, and hotels. The Voting Rights Act of 1965 outlawed poll taxes and provided federal voting registrars in states that refused the ballot to

African Americans. The single most important legislation of the twentieth century for bringing political democracy to the South, the Voting Rights Act increased the percentage of blacks voting in Mississippi from 7 percent to 60 percent in two years.

The Great Society: Improving the Quality of Life

Johnson's vision of the Great Society extended to the broader quality of life in the United States. Health care was perhaps the most fundamental issue for citizens' sense of personal security. After 1965, the new Medicare system paid for the medical needs of Americans age sixty-five and older, and Medicaid underwrote health care services for the indigent. In 1964, when more than half of adults smoked tobacco, the surgeon-general issued the first government report linking smoking to cancer. Higher federal standards for automotive safety followed a year later. Public pressures also led to the establishment of new requirements for publishing the nutritional values of packaged food. The federally funded Public Broadcasting System (PBS) was established to provide television programs that were more educational than the fare tied to advertising on the three corporate networks (NBC, CBS, and ABC). In fact, most Great Society measures targeted all Americans rather than just the disadvantaged.

Nothing more directly threatened the quality of American life than the degradation of the natural environment. The costs of the unrestrained and much-heralded economic growth since World War II showed up in the nation's air, water, and land. The leaded gasoline that fueled products of the booming auto industry created smog, industrial effluents polluted lakes and rivers, and petrochemical wastes poisoned the ground. The products of science that had contributed so much to the production of wealth were turning out to have hidden costs, and a new wave of citizen action to protect the environment began to build.

Growing public awareness prompted the Clean Air Act (1963) and the Clean Waters Act (1966), which set federal guidelines for reducing smog and preserving public drinking sources from bacterial pollution. Even the long dam-building tradition in the American West faced new questions, with the Wild and Scenic Rivers Act enacted in 1968. Meanwhile, Congress passed the Wilderness Act in 1964, setting aside 9 million acres of undeveloped public lands as a place "where man is a visitor who does not remain."

The Liberal Warren Court

The Supreme Court under the leadership of Earl Warren steadily expanded the constitutional definition of individual rights. This shift reached even those deemed to have lost many of their rights: prisoners. *Gideon v. Wainwright* (1963) established the right of indigent prisoners to legal counsel, and *Escobedo v. Illinois* (1964) confirmed the right to counsel during interrogation, a critical hindrance to the use of torture. After *Miranda v. Arizona* (1966), police were required to inform people they arrested of their rights to remain silent and to speak to a lawyer.

The Warren Court bolstered other rights of individuals against potentially coercive community pressures. Decisions in 1962 and 1963 strictly limited the practice of requiring prayers in public schools. In 1963 the Court narrowed standards for the definition of "obscenity," allowing freer expression in the arts but also in pornography. *Griswold v. Connecticut* (1965) established the use of contraceptive devices as a matter of private choice protected by the Constitution. In 1967 the Court heard the case of Mildred Jeter, a black woman, and Richard Loving, a white man, Virginians who had evaded their state's ban on interracial marriage by traveling to Washington, D.C., for their wedding and then returned to Caroline County to live. In the aptly titled *Loving v. Virginia*, the Court declared marriage one of the "basic civil rights of men" and overturned the laws of the last sixteen states restricting interracial unions.

The Supreme Court's interpreting of the Constitution to expand individual rights disturbed many conservative Americans. They saw the Court as another arm of an intrusive national government that was extending its control over matters previously left to local communities. For them, the goal of integration did not justify the busing of school children. Rising crime rates troubled them more than police brutality. Many Roman Catholics were troubled by the legalization of contraceptives. Incensed by the ban on requiring school prayer, Protestant fundamentalists sought redress through political involvement, which they had previously shunned, initiating a grassroots religious conservative movement that helped bring Ronald Reagan to power in 1980.

Into War in Vietnam

The 1960s also marked the culmination of the U.S. government's efforts to control revolutionary political and social change abroad. The Truman Doctrine's logic of containing communism spanned the entire globe, but few imagined that the United States would overreach itself, tragically, in Vietnam. Johnson's accomplishments at home were forever overshadowed by the war he sent Americans to fight in the quiet rice paddies and beautiful highland forests of Southeast Asia. An aggressive U.S. anticommunist policy abroad collided with leftist revolutionaries throughout the Third World, and it was ill fortune for the Vietnamese that this collision struck them hardest of all.

The Vietnamese Revolution and the United States

The conflict in Vietnam began as one of many efforts to end European colonialism. Vietnamese nationalists, varying in ideologies but led by Ho Chi Minh and the Indochinese Communist party, sought since the 1930s to liberate their country from French colonial rule. Japanese advances during World War II put the Vietminh (Vietnamese nationalists) on the same side as the Americans, and Ho worked closely with the U.S. Office of Strategic Services (OSS), precursor to the Central Intelligence Agency (CIA).

After the defeat of Germany and Japan, however, the French wanted to regain control of their colonies in Africa and Asia, including Vietnam. The British provided troop transport ships for French soldiers, and the United States provided most of the funds to support France in its war against the Vietminh (1946–1954). Cold War priorities won out: a weakened France had to be bolstered as the linchpin of a reintegrated, anticommunist western Europe, while the Vietminh were led by Communist party members. The Vietnamese defeated the much more heavily armed French at the battle of Dien Bien Phu in May 1954. Two months later, the Geneva Accords divided the country temporarily at the seventeenth parallel until national elections could be held within two years to reunify Vietnam. Ho's forces solidified their control of the north, the French pulled out entirely, and the Eisenhower administration made a fateful decision to intervene directly to preserve the southern part of Vietnam from communism. The United States created a new government led by the Roman Catholic, anticommunist Ngo Dinh Diem in a new country called "South Vietnam."

The Vietnamese Revolution was only half over, however. The French colonialists withdrew, but the Saigon regime did not hold elections. In the North, the sometimes brutal internal revolution for the creation of a socialist society proceeded with an extensive program of land redistribution. In the South, Diem ruled for eight years with increasing repression of communists and other dissenters. U.S. funding kept him in power. Southern members of the old Vietminh began a sabotage campaign against the Saigon government and formed the National Liberation Front (NLF) in 1960, with the support of North Vietnam. Diem and his American supporters called them Viet Cong or VC, roughly equivalent to the derogatory American term *Commies*. As the struggle to overthrow Diem intensified, several of his own generals assassinated him in November 1963 with the tacit support of U.S. officials in South Vietnam and Washington.

Johnson's War

Lyndon Johnson inherited his predecessors' commitment to preserving a noncommunist South Vietnam. Bolstered by Kennedy's hawkish advisers, he believed that American credibility was at stake. But Johnson faced a swiftly deteriorating military situation. The NLF, which the administration portrayed as merely a tool of North Vietnam, was winning the political war for the South, taking control of the countryside from the demoralized Army of the Republic of Vietnam (ARVN). Faced with the choice of escalating U.S. involvement to prevent an NLF victory or withdrawing entirely from the country, Johnson escalated.

How he did so was crucially important. There was neither a national debate nor a congressional vote to declare war. Johnson did not want to distract Congress from his Great Society agenda, nor did he want to provoke the Soviet Union or China. But he believed he had to preserve a noncommunist South Vietnam or else face a debilitating backlash from Republicans, who would skewer him as McCarthy had done to Truman over the "loss" of China fifteen years earlier. So the president used deception, describing offensive American actions as defensive and opening up a credibility gap between a committed government and a skeptical public.

In August 1964, North Vietnamese ships in the Gulf of Tonkin fired on the U.S. destroyer *Maddox*, which was aiding South Vietnamese sabotage operations against the North. The president portrayed the incident as one of unprovoked communist aggression, and Congress expressed almost unanimous support through its Gulf of Tonkin Resolution. With this substitute for a declaration of war, Johnson ordered American planes to begin bombing North Vietnam, and the first American combat troops splashed ashore at Da Nang in South Vietnam on March 8, 1965. In July the administration made the key decision to add 100,000 more soldiers, with more to follow as necessary.

American strategy had two goals: to limit the war so as not to draw in neighboring China (to avoid a repeat of the Korean War) and to force the NLF and North Vietnam to give up their struggle to reunify the country under Hanoi's control. The problem was the political nature of the guerrilla war in the South: a contest for the loyalty of the population, in which NLF operatives mingled easily with the citizenry. This kind of war made the enemy difficult to find, as had often been true for the British in fighting the American revolutionaries in the 1770s. The "strategic hamlet" program uprooted rural peasants and concentrated them in fortified towns, creating "free fire zones" in their wake where anything that moved was a target. The U.S. Air Force pounded the South as well as the North, dropping more bombs on this ancient land (smaller than either Germany or Japan) than had been used in all theaters on all sides in World War II. These tactics destabilized and traumatized society in South Vietnam as one-fourth of the population became refugees.

Americans in Southeast Asia

Given America's wealth, size, and superior weaponry, most U.S. soldiers who went to Vietnam in 1965–1966 had no doubt they would win the war. They typically looked down on Asians. Very few knew anything about Vietnamese history or culture, and almost none spoke the Vietnamese language. Although a small number of Americans worked closely with their South Vietnamese allies, most GIs encountered Vietnamese in subservient roles as laundry workers, prostitutes, waitresses, and bartenders. Blinkered by anticommunism and far removed from their own revolutionary roots, Americans from the top brass to the lowest "grunts" marched into a country they did not understand but assumed they could control.

President Johnson spoke of the conflict in Vietnam as a case of one sovereign nation—the North—invading another one—the South. However, few Vietnamese saw the war in those terms. The United States, dismissing the failure of the French before them, had intervened not so much in an international war as in an ongoing revolution that aimed to reunify the country. Few Vietnamese, whatever their opinions of communism, viewed the corrupt Saigon regime as legitimate or democratic. After all, it was kept in place by foreigners, whereas the North was ruled by people who had expelled the French foreigners.

Initial U.S. optimism reflected a grave underestimation of the NLF and the North Vietnamese. Ho Chi Minh was an extremely popular leader, and intervention from the other side of the world only strengthened his position. As the war expanded, NLF recruiting in the South snowballed, and the people of North Vietnam remained loyal to their authoritarian government. Communist forces proved willing to endure fantastic hardship and sacrifices to prevail. Their morale was much higher than that of the ARVN.

Who were the 3 million Americans who went to Vietnam? The initial forces contained experienced soldiers, but as the war escalated, this professional army was diluted with hundreds of thousands of young draftees. Student deferments protected more comfortable Americans, so GIs were predominantly those who lacked money and education. Although 70 percent were white men, black, Hispanic, and Native American enlistees shipped out in disproportionate numbers. In sharp contrast to the motives of the NLF and the North Vietnamese army, these young men (along with 10,000 women who volunteered as nurses) were not in Vietnam to win the war regardless of the cost or duration. They had only to survive twelve months before returning home to the safety of a peacetime society.

North Vietnamese regular army units came South to match the growing number of U.S. forces, and they occasionally engaged the Americans in large set battles, as at Ia Drang Valley in the fall of 1965. U.S. troops fought well in such firefights, making devastating use of their superior weapons and air power. However, the bulk of the fighting consisted of smaller engagements with deceptive enemies on their home turf who faded in and out of the civilian population with ease. Ambushes and unexpected death haunted Americans on patrol, and relentless heat and humidity wore them down.

American soldiers felt mounting frustration and rage over the nature of the war that they were ordered to fight. Lacking a clear battlefront and an understandable strategy for winning the war, they were commanded simply to kill the often mysterious enemy. Yet distinguishing civilians from combatants in a popular guerrilla war was not always easy, especially when so many civilians evidently supported the NLF and so few Americans spoke Vietnamese. Realizing that few of the people they were supposed to be defending actually wanted them there but under orders to produce enemy bodies, U.S. troops on the ground began to slide toward a racial war against all Vietnamese.

Many GIs resisted this logic, sometimes showing real kindness to Vietnamese civilians. But atrocities on both sides inevitably followed from this kind of war. The worst came in the village of My Lai on March 16, 1968, where 105 soldiers from Charlie Company—enraged by the recent deaths of several comrades in ambushes—slaughtered, often after torturing or raping, more than 400 Vietnamese women, children, and old men. The army covered up the massacre for a year and a half, and eventually found only Lieutenant William Calley, the leader of Charlie Company's First Platoon, guilty of murdering Vietnamese civilians.

1968: The Turning Point

In late 1967, the public face of the war effort remained upbeat, as General Westmoreland declared that he could now see "some light at the end of the tunnel." But hopes of an imminent victory were crushed by the startling Tet Offensive (named for the Vietnamese New Year) that began on January 30, 1968. NLF insurgents and North Vietnamese troops attacked U.S. strongholds throughout South Vietnam. The blow to American public confidence in Johnson and his military commanders proved irreversible. Far from being on the verge of defeat, as the administration had been claiming, the communists had shown that they could mount simultaneous attacks around the country.

The Tet Offensive coincided with two other crises in early 1968 to convince American political and business elites that U.S. international commitments had become larger than the nation could afford. First, a week before Tet began, the North Korean navy seized the U.S. intelligence ship *Pueblo* in the Sea of Japan and temporarily imprisoned its crew. U.S. commanders were left scrambling to find enough forces to respond effectively without weakening American commitments in Europe and elsewhere. Second, a British financial collapse devalued the pound and

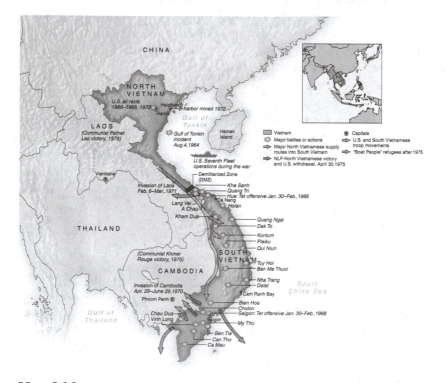

Map 26.2

The American War in Vietnam

Before U.S. combat troops entered Vietnam in 1965, few Americans knew where this Southeast Asian country was. Vietnam's geography and place names quickly became familiar in the United States as hundreds of thousands of young Americans served there and some 58,000 died there. Vietnam's elongated shape, its borders with Cambodia and Laos, and its proximity to China all affected the course of the fighting between 1965 and 1973.

caused the London government to announce its imminent withdrawal from its historic positions east of the Suez Canal, placing new military burdens on the United States in the Middle East. These events reduced international confidence in the U.S. economy, causing a currency crisis in March 1968 as holders of dollars traded them in for gold.

The political career of Lyndon Johnson was a final casualty of these events. His support on the left withered as the antiwar and black power movements expanded. Meanwhile, his more centrist supporters were joining the backlash against civil rights, urban violence, and antiwar protesters, peeling off to the Republican party. On March 12, antiwar challenger Senator Eugene McCarthy of Minnesota nearly defeated the incumbent president in the New Hampshire Democratic primary. Johnson's vulnerability was obvious. Senator Robert Kennedy of New York joined the race two weeks later. In a televised speech on March 31 that caught the divided nation by surprise, Johnson announced an end to U.S. escalations in the war, the start of negotiations in Paris with North Vietnam, and an end to his own political career. He would not seek reelection.

The Movement

While national leaders were defending what they called the "frontiers of freedom" abroad, young Americans in the mid- and late 1960s organized to expand what they considered the frontiers of freedom at home. Television for the first time tied the country together in a common culture whose shared images were transmitted simultaneously around the nation. The expanding war in Vietnam radicalized people who had initially been optimistic about reforming American society. Black power, the New Left, the counterculture, women's liberation, and other liberation movements often had quite divergent goals. But participants overlapped extensively and activists spoke of "the Movement" as if it were a unified phenomenon. At the heart of the youth movements of the decade lay a common quest for authenticity—a rejection of hypocrisy and a distrust of traditional authorities—that fused cultural and political protest.

From Civil Rights to Black Power

By 1966 the civil rights movement fractured as it confronted the limits of its success. It had achieved the goals of ending legal discrimination and putting southern African Americans in the voting booth, but it had not brought about a colorblind society. Racial prejudice among white conservatives remained virulent, and white liberals, such as those in the Kennedy and Johnson administrations, revealed themselves as not always trustworthy allies. Expecting only hostility from conservatives, civil rights workers were more disillusioned with what they saw as liberal betrayals.

The Justice Department and the Federal Bureau of Investigation (FBI) did little to restrain the violence of the Ku Klux Klan until the murders of white organizers Michael Schwerner and Andrew Goodman in the summer of 1964—along with black coworker James Chaney. Two months later, at the national Democratic party convention in Atlantic City, New Jersey, Johnson crushed the effort of the biracial Mississippi Freedom Democratic party to replace the state's regular, all-white Democratic delegates. The president was determined to avoid further alienating white southern voters as he pursued a huge victory margin in the November elections. Outraged at this betrayal, Fannie Lou Hamer—a courageous sharecropper who had been beaten by Mississippi police for her efforts to register black voters—declared in a televised appearance at Atlantic City, "I question America."

The black freedom struggle for centuries had woven together elements of racial separatism with elements of integration into the larger American culture. For many younger African Americans, the pendulum swung toward a need for greater independence from the white majority. They took inspiration from Malcolm X, the fiery and eloquent minister of the Nation of Islam (Black Muslims), who until his murder in 1965 captivated listeners with denunciations of white perfidy and demands for black self-respect. In 1966 SNCC members began to speak of the need for "black power" rather than for the integrated "beloved community" they had initially sought in 1960.

The Black Panther party formed in Oakland, California, in response to police brutality. The heavily armed Panthers engaged in several shootouts with police and were eventually decimated by an FBI campaign against them. White Americans were shocked by the uprisings and riots that swept through black urban communities during the summers of 1964–1968. Triggered by the actions of white police, the riots expressed the fierce frustrations of impoverished people whose lives remained largely untouched by the achievements of the civil rights struggle. The most destructive outbreaks occurred in the Watts district of Los Angeles in 1965 and in Detroit and Newark in 1967.

Black power thrived primarily as a cultural movement that promoted pride in African American and African history and life. The slogan "black is beautiful" captured this spirit: long degraded by their white compatriots as inferior, black Americans in the late 1960s and 1970s reversed this equation to celebrate their cultural heritage. This could be as basic as a hairstyle, the natural Afro replacing hair straightened to look like Caucasian hair. At universities, new departments of African American studies fostered the exploration of black history. Unlearning habits of public deference to whites, most African Americans began referring to themselves as "black" rather than "Negro."

Cultural black power mixed with a different kind of political black power by the late 1960s: the election of black officials. Although militant black power advocates garnered the most media attention, most African Americans supported Lyndon Johnson and used the Voting Rights Act to pursue their goals in the realm of electoral politics. In 1966 Carl Stokes of Cleveland was elected the first black mayor of a major American city, and African Americans won local offices across the South.

The New Left and the Struggle Against the War

In 1962 a group of liberal college activists founded the Students for a Democratic Society (SDS), calling for a rejuvenation of American politics and society to replace the complacency that they saw pervading the country. Racial bigotry and poverty particularly troubled these optimistic young reformers, along with the overarching threat of nuclear destruction (highlighted anew by the missile crisis in Cuba). They hoped to become a kind of "white SNCC," promoting participatory democracy to redeem the promise of Cold War America.

SDS served as the central organization of the New Left. Communism was simply not important to these activists, nor was conservatism, which was then at its lowest point. They focused instead on the behavior of the liberals who ran the U.S. government from 1961 to 1968. They developed a critique of "corporate liberalism" as promoting the interests of the wealthy and the business community far more than providing for the needs of the disadvantaged.

After 1965, SDS's initially broad reform agenda narrowed to stopping the Vietnam War. SDS members organized the first major antiwar protest outside the White House on April 17, 1965, bringing their organization into alliance with the small group of religious and secular pacifists already working against the war. Mainstream Democrats also began abandoning Johnson over the war as it grew. The president had alienated the powerful chair of the Senate Foreign Relations Committee, J. William Fulbright of Arkansas, with his misleading reports during the brief U.S. military intervention in the Dominican Republic in April 1965 to defeat a left-leaning but not communist coup attempt. Fulbright then held televised hearings on the American war in Southeast Asia in January 1966, raising grave doubts about its wisdom. Draft resistance increased: young men moved to Canada, as did SNCC's Bob Moses, or went to jail, as did champion boxer Muhammad Ali.

Antiwar protesters followed the same trajectory of radicalization as black power advocates. Their dismay turned to rage as the Johnson administration continued to expand a war that was destroying much of Vietnam while killing tens of thousands of American soldiers for no reason its opponents considered legitimate. In combination with or in support of black militants, white radicals took over buildings on university campuses in 1968–1969: Columbia, Cornell, Harvard, San Francisco State, and many others. SDS ultimately broke apart in the confusion and exhilaration of its growing demand for revolution against the larger systemic enemies, imperialism and capitalism, not just corporate liberalism. But radical rage could not be understood apart from the ongoing destruction of Vietnam by a government acting in the name of all Americans.

Cultural Rebellion and the Counterculture

While the New Left moved from wanting to reform American society to wanting to overthrow it, the counterculture sought to create an alternative society. Called "hippies" by those who disliked them, these young people were alienated by the materialism, competition, and conformity of American life in the Cold War. They tried to live out alternative values of gentleness, tolerance, and inclusivity. Sporting headbands, long hair, and beads, many identified with traditional Native Americans. In place of junk foods, they promoted health foods;

in place of profit-seeking businesses, they established co-ops. "Do your own thing" was a common slogan.

In reaction against the conformity of mainstream society, members of the counter-culture explored the limitations of consciousness to expand their self-knowledge. They went beyond the nicotine and alcohol that were the common stimulants of their parents' culture to experiment with such mind-altering drugs as marijuana, peyote, hashish, LSD, cocaine, and even heroin. Spirituality was an important path into consciousness for many in the counterculture. Religious traditions associated with Asia, particularly Buddhism, gained numerous adherents, as did the spiritual customs and traditional practices of Native Americans. Others rediscovered the "authentic" Jesus obscured by the institutional structures of the formal Christian church (earning themselves the nickname "Jesus freaks"); Campus Crusade for Christ, InterVarsity, and other evangelical college groups spread across the country. Music served as the most common coin of the countercultural realm, from the political folk sound of Joan Baez and Bob Dylan to the broadly popular Beatles and the more distinctly countercultural rock 'n' roll of the Grateful Dead and Jefferson Airplane.

Older Americans experienced the counterculture largely as spectacle. The mainstream media emphasized the alternative aspects of the hippie lifestyle in its coverage. Viewers were varyingly disgusted by, attracted to, and titillated by the hair, clothing, nudity, and blurred gender distinctions. Meanwhile, entrepreneurs realized that they could market the antimaterialist counterculture profitably. Young Americans eagerly bought up records, clothing, jewelry, and natural foods—a revealing demonstration of how consumer values pervaded American life.

One of the most visible changes of the 1960s was often called the sexual revolution. Changes in Americans' sexual behavior in the 1960s reflected in part the counterculture's goal of living an authentic, honest life in which words matched actions. The sexual revolution removed some of the penalties for the premarital and extramarital sex that had previously been fairly common but unacknowledged. The appearance of the birth control pill in 1960 underpinned the shift to more open sexual relationships by freeing women from the fear of pregnancy. Attitudes toward abortion also became more tolerant. New York passed the first state law legalizing some abortions in 1970, and three years later the Supreme Court established a woman's constitutional right to abortion in the landmark case of *Roe v. Wade*.

Women's Liberation

The movement for women's liberation built on developments earlier in the decade, including Betty Friedan's *The Feminine Mystique* (1963), a widely read book that captured the frustrations of many women who had accepted the role of suburban homemaker after World War II. Friedan and other liberal feminists founded the National Organization for Women (NOW) in 1966 to lobby against sexual discrimination in the public sphere in such areas as employment, wages, education, and jury duty. These challenges had radical implications for women's and men's earnings and thus for responsibilities within families, but NOW did not yet focus on issues inside the private sphere of the home.

The shift to the view that "the personal is political" came from younger, mostly white women who had been active in the civil rights and antiwar struggles. Inspired by the courage and successes of the protest movements in which they figured prominently, these female activists had also learned that traditional gender roles restricted them even in organizations dedicated to participatory democracy. Ironically, radical men could be as patronizing and disrespectful of women's abilities as mainstream men. Younger feminists in 1967 and 1968 agreed with NOW's challenge to discrimination in the public sphere, but they focused even more on the personal politics of women's daily lives, on critical issues such as parenting, child care, housework, and abortion.

The new wave of feminism that washed through American culture at the end of the 1960s triggered fierce debates about the nature of gender. Was there a uniquely feminine way of knowing, seeing, and acting, or were women in essence the same as men, distinguishable ultimately by their individuality? Was womanhood biologically or only culturally constructed? Feminists disagreed sharply in their answers.

However, diversity within the feminist movement did not hide a common commitment to expanding women's possibilities. The women's movement that emerged out of the 1960s permanently transformed women's lives and gender relations in American society, in areas ranging from job and educational opportunities, sexual harassment, and gender-neutral language to family roles, sexual relations, reproductive rights, and athletic facilities.

The Many Fronts of Liberation

Like the women's movement, the Chicano, pan-Indian, and gay liberation movements of the late 1960s were grounded in older organizing efforts within those communities. The struggles for "brown power," "red power," and "gay power" also reflected the newer influence of black power and its determination to take pride in what the dominant American society had denigrated for so long. Activists on college campuses successfully pressured administrations to establish interdisciplinary ethnic studies programs, such as the first Chicano studies program at California State University at Los Angeles in 1968. Ethnic cultural identity went hand in hand with the pursuit of political and economic integration into mainstream American life.

The most prominent push to organize Latinos was the effort led by Cesar Chávez to build a farm workers' union in California and the Southwest. These primarily Mexican American migrant workers harvested most of the hand-picked produce that Americans ate, but their hard work under severe conditions failed to lift them out of poverty. National consumer support for boycotts of table grapes and iceberg lettuce helped win recognition for the United Farm Workers (UFW) union and better pay by 1970. Younger Mexican Americans across the Southwest looked with pride on their Mexican heritage, even appropriating the formerly pejorative term *Chicano*.

Puerto Ricans, the largest Spanish-speaking ethnic group located primarily on the East Coast, experienced a similar growth in militancy and nationalist sentiment during the late 1960s. By the 1960s, more than a million islanders had moved to the East Coast, most to the New York City area. Despite being the only Latino immigrants already holding American citizenship when they arrived, Puerto Ricans experienced similar patterns of both discrimination and opportunity as Mexican Americans.

The most destitute of Americans, Indians also sought to reinvigorate their communities. On the Northwest Coast, they staged "fish-ins" in the mid-1960s to assert treaty rights, and in 1968 urban activists in Minneapolis formed the American Indian Movement (AIM). On November 20, 1969, just days after the largest antiwar march in Washington, seventy-eight Native Americans seized the island of Alcatraz in San Francisco Bay "in the name of all American Indians by right of discovery." For a year and a half, they used their occupation of the former federal prison site to publicize grievances about anti-Indian prejudice and to promote a new pan-Indian identity that reached across traditional tribal divisions. In 1973 armed members of AIM occupied buildings for two months at Wounded Knee, South Dakota, site of the infamous 1890 U.S. Army massacre of unarmed Sioux. Tribal governments sought "red power" in their own quieter way. They asserted greater tribal control of reservation schools across the country.

Although they lacked a unifying ethnic identity, gay men and lesbians also found opportunities to construct coalitions in the more open atmosphere of the late 1960s. Building on the earlier but quieter community organizing of older homosexuals in New York, San Francisco, and Los Angeles, more militant youth began to express openly their anger at the homophobic prejudice and violence prevalent in American society. This demand for tolerance and respect reached the headlines when gay patrons of the Stonewall Bar in New York fought back fiercely against a typically forceful police raid on June 27, 1969. Activists of the new Gay Liberation Front emphasized the importance of "coming out of the closet": proudly acknowledging one's sexual orientation as legitimate and decent.

The Conservative Response

The majority of Americans had mixed feelings about the protests that roiled the nation. They were impressed by the courage of many who stood up against discrimination, and by 1968 they wanted to find a way out of the war in Southeast Asia. But they were alienated by the style and values of others who loudly demanded change in American society. Moderate and conservative citizens and generations of recent European immigrants resented what they saw as a lack of appreciation for the nation's virtues and successes. The political and social upheavals of 1968 opened the door to a Republican return to the White House, and Richard Nixon slipped through.

Backlashes

A backlash developed in response to the increasing assertiveness of people of color. European Americans in every part of the United States had long been accustomed to deference from nonwhites and racial segregation, either by law in the South or by custom elsewhere. Conservatives resented what they considered blacks' ingratitude at the civil rights measures enacted by the federal government, including black power's condemnation of whites as "crackers" and "honkies." Urban riots and escalating rates of violent crime, along with the Supreme Court's expansion of the rights of the accused, deepened their anger. They associated crime with urban African Americans, for although whites were still the majority of criminals, blacks (like any other population with less money) were disproportionately represented in prisons. The rise of often angry nonwhite nationalism dismayed most European Americans. They were troubled by the militancy of Chicanos in the Southwest, Puerto Ricans in the Northeast, Indians on reservations and in cities, and African Americans almost everywhere.

Another backlash developed as a defense of traditional hierarchies against the cultural rebellions of the 1960s. Proud of their lives and values, conservatives rejected a whole array of challenges to American society. Raised to believe in respecting one's elders, they resented the disrespect of many youth, who warned, "Don't trust anyone over 30." A generation that had fought and sacrificed in the "good war" against the Nazis found the absence of patriotism among many protesters unfathomable. The United States remained one of the most religious of industrialized societies, and conservative churchgoers emphasized obedience to authorities. They feared the effects of illegal drugs on their children.

The backlash against the social changes of the 1960s contained elements of class antagonism as well. Working-class whites resented the often affluent campus rebels and the black and Latino poor targeted by some Great Society programs. They believed that their values of hard work, restraint, and respectability were increasingly unappreciated and even mocked. Republican leaders from Goldwater to Nixon to Reagan gave voice to these resentments and drew votes away from Democratic blue-collar strongholds. Democratic governor George Wallace of Alabama also became a spokesperson for the anger of many "forgotten" whites on both sides of the Mason-Dixon line.

The Turmoil of 1968 at Home

The traumas of 1968 brought the conservative backlash to the critical stage. First came the Tet Offensive in Vietnam, creating fears that the war might become an interminable quagmire. Then, on April 4, a gunman named James Earl Ray assassinated Martin Luther King Jr. in Memphis, where he had gone to support a strike by sanitation workers. King had become more openly radical in his final years, opposing the war and working on class-based organizing of poor people. But he remained the nation's leading apostle of nonviolence, and his murder evoked despair among millions of citizens, especially African Americans. Police battled rioters and arsonists in black neighborhoods of 130 cities across the nation, with forty-six people dying in the clashes.

Summer brought more shocking news. Charismatic senator Robert Kennedy's entry into the presidential campaign had inspired renewed hopes among Democratic liberals. But on the night of his victory in the June 5 California primary, Kennedy was killed by a deranged gunman. Vice President Hubert Humphrey seemed assured of the nomination at the Democratic convention in Chicago in August, despite his association with Johnson's war policies. Some 10,000 antiwar activists, including hundreds of FBI *agents provocateurs* (spies seeking to provoke violence), showed up to engage in protests outside the convention. Chicago's Democratic mayor Richard Daley unleashed thousands of police on protesters, bystanders, and photographers in an orgy of beatings that subsequent investigations called a police riot. Ninety million Americans watched on television as a deeply divided Democratic party appeared helpless before the violence.

Into the vacuum of public anger and alienation that accompanied the liberals' self-destruction in Chicago stepped two men. The spread of the conservative backlash from 1964 to 1968 gave George Wallace a wider constituency for his right-wing populist message of hostility to liberals, blacks, and federal officials. With the national Democratic party committed to racial integration, Wallace ran for president as an independent candidate and won 13.5 percent of the popular vote in November. Republican candidate Richard Nixon campaigned as the candidate of "law and order" and promised that he had a secret plan to end the war in Vietnam. Nixon won the popular vote by less than 1 percent.

The Nixon Administration

A lonely, aloof man of great tenacity and ambition, Richard Nixon had worked hard to remake his public image for 1968. Widely viewed as a somewhat unscrupulous partisan since his early career in Congress, he had refashioned himself as a statesman with a broad vision for reducing international tensions between the great powers. He sounded like a conservative in the campaign against Humphrey, but once in the White House he governed as the most liberal Republican since Theodore Roosevelt, pressed by a Congress still controlled by Democrats.

Table 26.2 The Election of 1968

Candidate	Political Party	Popular Vote (%)	Electoral Vote
Richard M. Nixon	Republican	43.4	301
Hubert H. Humphrey	Democratic	42.7	191
George Wallace	American Independent	13.5	46

Nowhere was this clearer than on issues related to natural resources. Much had happened to the environment since Republican Theodore Roosevelt's conservation efforts, little of it for the better. A powerful movement was building to protect natural resources and human health from the effects of air and water pollution. Biologist Paul Ehrlich's best-selling *The Population Bomb* (1968) warned of the dire consequences of the globe's runaway growth in human population. In 1969 the government banned the carcinogenic pesticide DDT. That same year, a huge oil spill off Santa Barbara fouled 200 miles of pristine California beaches, and the Cuyahoga River in Cleveland, its surface coated with waste and oil, caught fire and burned for days. Environmentalists around the country proclaimed April 22, 1970, as "Earth Day."

Congress responded with legislation that mandated the careful management of the nation's natural resources. The Environmental Protection Agency was established in 1970. Amendments to the Clean Air (1970) and Clean Water (1972) Acts tightened restrictions on harmful emissions from cars and factories. The Endangered Species Act (1973) created for the first time the legal right of nonhuman animals to survive, a major step toward viewing the quality of human life as inextricable from the earth's broader ecology.

What Nixon did care deeply about at home was politics, not policy. Antiwar demonstrations reached their height during Nixon's first two years in the White House (1969–1970). He and Vice President Spiro Agnew loathed the protesters, whom they saw as weakening the nation. The two men pursued what Agnew called "positive polarization": campaigning to further divide the respectable "silent majority," as the president labeled his supporters, from voluble liberal Democrats in Congress and radical activists on the streets, whom they associated with permissiveness and lawlessness. In this broad cultural battle for political supremacy, the president appealed to conservative white southern and northern ethnic Democrats.

Early in his administration, Nixon began wielding the power of the federal government to harass his political opponents. Johnson had used the FBI, the CIA, and military intelligence agencies to infiltrate and thin the ranks of antiwar demonstrators and nonwhite nationalists. Nixon continued those illegal operations, agreeing with his predecessor that radical activists constituted a threat to national security. Nixon went beyond other presidents in assembling an "Enemies List" that included prominent elements of the political mainstream, especially liberals, the press, and his Democratic opponents. The president was particularly concerned about controlling secret information. The Pentagon Papers were a classified Defense Department history of U.S. actions in Vietnam, revealing that the government had been deceiving the American public about the course of the war. When disillusioned former Pentagon official Daniel Ellsberg leaked the study to the *New York Times* for publication in 1971, Nixon was enraged. The White House created a team of covert operatives nicknamed the Plumbers to "plug leaks" by whatever means necessary.

Escalating and De-escalating in Vietnam

Nixon and his national security adviser, Henry Kissinger, had ambitious plans for shifting the relationships of the great powers to America's advantage. To deal with China and the Soviet Union, they first had to reduce the vast U.S. engagement in the small country of Vietnam, which had grown wildly out of proportion to actual U.S. interests there. Under the Nixon Doctrine, the United States would provide military hardware rather than U.S. soldiers to allied governments, which would have to do their own fighting against leftist insurgencies. In South Vietnam, this doctrine required "Vietnamization," or withdrawing American troops so ARVN could shoulder the bulk of the war.

The key to a successful withdrawal from Vietnam for Nixon was to preserve U.S. "credibility." The perception of power could be as important as its actual exercise, and the president wanted other nations, both friend and foe, to continue to respect and fear American military might. There was no immediate pullout but a gradual process that lasted for four years (1969–1973), during which almost half of the total U.S. casualties in Vietnam occurred. Nixon did his utmost to weaken the communist forces during the slow withdrawal. The president ordered the secret bombing and invasion of neighboring Cambodia and Laos, an intensified aerial assault on North Vietnam, and the mining of Haiphong Harbor near Hanoi. Enormous protests rocked the country after the announcement of the Cambodian invasion on April 30, 1970. National Guard troops killed four students at a demonstration at Kent State University in Ohio and two at Jackson State College in Mississippi, deepening the sense of national division.

A majority of Americans now opposed the nation's war effort, a level of dissent unprecedented in U.S. history. Most telling of all was the criticism of some veterans returning from Vietnam. The morale of American soldiers still in Vietnam plummeted as the steady withdrawal of their comrades made clear that they were no longer expected to win the war. Drug abuse and racial conflict increased sharply among GIs. Even "fragging" (killing one's own officers) escalated before the peace accords were signed in Paris and the United States evacuated its last combat troops in 1973.

Credits

From *Created Equal: A Social and Political History of the United States* by
Jacqueline Jones, Peter H. Wood, Thomas Borstelmann, Elaine Tyler May, and
Vicky L. Ruiz. Copyright © 2005 by Pearson Education, Inc.

From *Essentials of Psychology*, Third Edition, by Robert A. Baron. Copyright ©
2002 Allyn and Bacon.

Robert Waldron, "Students are Dying; Colleges Can Do More." From *Newsweek*,
October 30, 2000.

Index

Additional Titles of Interest

Note to Instructors: Any of these Penguin-Putnam, Inc., titles can be packaged with this book at a special discount. Contact your local Allyn & Bacon/Longman sales representative for details on how to create a Penguin-Putnam, Inc., Value Package.

Albee, *Three Tall Women*
Alger, *Ragged Dick & Struggling Up*
Allison, *Bastard Out Of Carolina*
Austen, *Pride & Prejudice*
Austen, *Sense & Sensibility*
Behn, *Oroonoko, The Rover & Others*
Bellow, *Adventures of Augie March*
C. Brontë, *Jane Eyre*
E. Brontë, *Wuthering Heights*
Cather, *My Ántonia*
Cather, *O Pioneers!*
Chesnutt, *The Marrow of Tradition*
Chopin, *The Awakening & Selected Stories*
Christe, *Death on the Nile*
Conrad, *Nostromo*
Delillo, *White Noise*
Dickens, *Great Expectations*
Dos Passos, *Three Soldiers*
Douglass, *Narrative of the Life of Frederick Douglass*
Golding, *Lord of the Flies*
Hansberry, *A Raisin in the Sun*
Hawthorne, *The Scarlet Letter*
Jen, *Typical American*
Karr, *The Liars Club*
Kerouac, *On the Road*
Kesey, *One Flew Over the Cuckoo's Nest*
King Jr., *Why We Can't Wait*
King, *Misery*
Lewis, *Babbitt*

McBride, *The Color of Water*
Morrison, *Beloved*
Naylor, *The Women of Brewster Place*
O'Brien, *The Things They Carried*
Orwell, *1984*
Paine, *Common Sense*
Postman, *Amusing Ourselves to Death*
Rose, *Lives on the Boundary*
Rose, *Possible Lives: The Promise of Public*
Shakespeare, *Four Great Comedies: The Taming of the Shrew, A Midsummer's Night Dream, Twelfth Night, The Tempest*
Shakespeare, *Four Great Tragedies: Hamlet, Macbeth, King Lear, Othello*
Shakespeare, *Hamlet*
Shakespeare, *King Lear*
Shelley, *Frankenstein*
Sinclair, *The Jungle*
Steinbeck, *Of Mice & Men*
Steinbeck, *The Pearl*
Stevenson, *The Strange Case of Dr. Jekyll & Mr. Hyde*
Stowe, *Uncle Tom's Cabin*
Truth, *The Narrative of Sojourner Truth*
Twain, *Adventures of Huckleberry Finn*
Wilson, *Fences*
Wilson, *Joe Turner's Come & Gone*